Corporate Creativity

Corporate Creativity

Developing an Innovative Organization

Edited by
Thomas Lockwood
and
Thomas Walton

ALLWORTH PRESS
NEW YORK

DESIGN MANAGEMENT INSTITUTE

12   11   10   09   08   5   4   3   2   1

Published by Allworth Press
An imprint of Allworth Communications, Inc.
10 East 23rd Street, New York, NY 10010

Cover design by Jon Craine and Alan Lee
Interior design by Susan Ramundo
Page composition/typography by Susan Ramundo

ISBN-13: 978-1-58115-656-0

Library of Congress Cataloging-in-Publication Data
    Corporate creativity : developing an innovative organization / edited by
    Thomas Lockwood and Thomas Walton.
        p.   cm.
    ISBN 978-1-58115-656-0
    1. Creative ability in business.   2. Technological innovations—Management.
3. Organizational learning.   I. Lockwood, Thomas.   II. Walton, Thomas.

HD53.C674 2009
658.4'063—dc22

2008050394

Printed in the United States of America

DEDICATION

*This book is dedicated to all of the DMI members and
stakeholders around the world that have supported
the Institute since its founding in 1975.*

Contents

Acknowledgments

We would like to express our gratitude to all of the authors whose work is included in this book. Your insights and professional input is greatly appreciated and makes editing this book a true pleasure. We would also like to acknowledge and thank all of the other authors who have contributed articles to DMI's *Design Management Journal* and *Design Management Review* publications over the years; they have made this body of knowledge the most extensive resource on design management in the world. We must also credit the outstanding work of the former president of DMI, Mr. Earl Powell, PhD (hon), who not only founded these publications and served as their publisher but was also responsible for the content from the beginning through 2005. His efforts have increased our understanding and advanced the role of design in business immensely.

Foreword

"Imagination is more important than knowledge."
—ALBERT EINSTEIN

WELCOME TO THE realm of corporate creativity—and no, I do not intend that phrase as an oxymoron. A key objective for nearly every organization is to innovate and, in doing so, create meaningful value for its stakeholders and its customers. To that end, the successful organizations of the future will be those that make the most of the creativity of their employees and their partners. As Marty Neumeier so simply observes in The Designful Company, "Creativity in its various forms has become the number-one engine of economic growth."

In the following chapters, we will take a closer look at the processes of discovery and invention with the aim of helping organizations create processes, artifacts, and experiences. We hope to provide a picture of the creative process in design and innovation, as well as in making meaning and value for customers. Today's open source systems—from Linux to the whole universe of wikis and social networking sites—make it all the more possible to arrive at new solutions and answers to problems, and to tap into collective creativity.

Creativity is a mental activity, but it can also be part of a systems model. In fact, because it challenges traditional management processes and styles, creativity requires adaptive systems, and is dynamic. The domains of creativity lie in action and experimentation. As Will Rogers once said, "Even if you're on the right track, you'll get run over if you just stand there."

CREATIVITY FOR THE PUBLIC AND PRIVATE SECTORS

This book is meant to help draw out the creativity that lies hidden in businesses as well as in society at large, in the public as well as in the private sector. There are many ways to help an organization spark creative breakthroughs, and it's never too late to start because creativity is a journey, not a destination. Developing your inner resources is part of the very fabric of creativity.

For most people, the idea of creativity is more associated with artists than with their daily work in business, but this could not be further from the truth. After all, the world is full of problems to be solved. Charles Eames once responded to the question, "What are the boundaries of design?" by asking, "What are the boundaries of problems?"

Learning to think creatively in one discipline opens the door to understanding creativity in other disciplines. That's why our approach to creativity is integrative and multidisciplinary. We want to help you solve small problems or even huge systems problems. I think everyone would like to learn how to tap more fully into their creative resources and see creativity applied to their daily business lives.

We're not trying to address the basic cognitive, physiological, and social issues of creativity in this book; rather, we're hoping to develop a creative workforce. In this age of innovation, business requires a creative spark. It's no longer the province of the "creatives" at the advertising agency. As Robert and Michele Root-Bernstein have said, building creativity is about "schooling the imagination." In the following pages you will find some polarity of ideas, and many examples of "creative abrasion," "informed play," and the blurring of disciplinary boundaries.

SECTIONS OF THIS BOOK

As Jeff Mauzy notes, although there is no one "correct" way to foster corporate creativity, we can study creativity as it occurs in individuals, coalitions and teams, and organizations. Mauzy also argues that creativity can be divided into three categories: creative thinking, climate, and action. With these two ideas in mind, we've organized this book into three sections: create, collaborate, and innovate. In the create section, we look into the topic of creative thinking and address the dynamics of personal and team creativity, how creativity works, and reinvigorating creativity in organizations. The collaborate section explores working in groups and climate and environment for innovation, including dynamics of the creative process. The third section, innovate, gives numerous examples of innovation and explores creative initiatives and business results.

A WEALTH OF OPINION

Twenty-six authors contributed to *Corporate Creativity*, myself included. Each article was originally published by DMI in the Design Management Journal or the Design Management Review, and they were chosen for their excellence and relevance to understanding creativity and innovation. By looking at ideas and stories, we hope to show how creativity can bring new products to market, transform businesses into brands, and help customers enjoy meaningful experiences.

The great thing about this approach is that we can present a range of ideas from across industries and disciplines. The results are not only diverse, opinionated, reflective, and thought-leading, but they also represent some of today's leading creative organizations.

This is the second book in our anthology series. Over the years, the Institute has published over 900 articles covering many aspects of design strategy, design leadership, design management, and of course, design as related to brand-building and innovation. I trust you will find the insights in this book beneficial to you, and I thank you for your interest in our work.

THOMAS LOCKWOOD, PhD
PRESIDENT, DMI

Corporate Creativity

CREATE

This first section looks into the basic notion of developing our personal creativity. This may sound like a daunting task to some, but it need not be so. To most of us, imagination, creativity, and an open mind come naturally; some of the most creative people in the world are still in preschool and early elementary school. The trick is to keep our creative faculties alive as we become adults and join the workforce.

We have organized this section to guide the reader along the path from developing his or her personal creativity to developing creative discipline, primarily based on design. The premise of Jeff Mauzy's seminal chapter is this: If you want a more creative organization—and who doesn't?—develop more creative employees. Mauzy offers a number of techniques and methods that can be applied to unleash and increase personal creativity. Where the workplace is concerned, fostering the kind of environment in which this can occur means putting key elements in place to foster creativity, including understanding the process of creative thinking, removing blocks, using specific methods to get fresh ideas, and allowing employees to exercise their natural creative abilities. This doesn't mean a major reorganization; what it does mean is allowing employees to take risks without fear of failure. Mauzy also discusses four critical dynamics of creativity: motivation, curiosity and fear, breaking and making connections, and evaluation. Stefik and Stefik remind us that those wonderful "Aha" moments emerge when creativity is permitted to run deeply and broadly, breaking through constraints and putting us in new mindsets. Robert Rasmussen discusses how creative individuals can work best by working in creative teams, which begins to set the stage for another key imperative in corporate creativity, and that is corporate culture.

Anne Archer and Doris Walczyk remind us that corporate culture is a complex mixture of beliefs, attitudes, values, rituals, and behaviors, all of which influence the playing field for corporate creativity. One of the main ways corporate creativity is demonstrated is by innovation, and one of the main ways innovation is demonstrated is by design. To that end, co-editor Thomas Lockwood shares insights about integrating design into corporate culture and identifies the key drivers, based in part on his PhD thesis about integrated design management. Lastly, Mark Barngrover explores some interesting processes about developing creative teams and making design champions at Procter & Gamble. The key ideas are to build a climate that supports constant creativity and to encourage employees to exercise creativity in all aspects of their work. This involves developing a foundation to transform ideas into innovations.

This section leads us to three important conclusions about individual creativity:

"Aha" moments: Catch them when you can. A core competency of the act of invention is transforming subconscious "eureka" moments of into actionable ideas. After all, the whole notion of creativity stems from developing ideas. Some ideas are better than others, and some are really good—the trick is to recognize which is which. Sometimes our own experiences can get in the way. We think, Oh, that won't work, or, We tried that already. But the real "Aha" moments come when we lay down our defenses and let our imaginations be free. Rasmussen refers to this as "tipping the sacred cows"—and allowing yourself to take risks with good intent. Sometimes the ideas just happen, but you have to be able to recognize them. Many people keep a blank journal handy as often as possible, jot ideas most anywhere and anytime, and are then amazed at how many good ideas emerge. As Albert Szent-Gyorgyi has written, "Discovery consists of looking at the same thing as everyone else and thinking something different." Ideation is a bit like sailing: you have to tack from side to side to catch the wind. So allow yourself this room to think, and be ready to catch those ideas when you can!

Creative processes are about finding the right degree of framework. Creative ideas can be encouraged by putting a framework in place. As mentioned, this can be as simple as keeping a journal handy to record your moments of brilliance. It can also include techniques such as changing your perspective, changing your activities, looking at opposites, breaking assumptions, and allowing yourself to fail—in fact, to fail quickly. (One of the core principles at Pixar Animation Studios is to fail often and fail quickly.) That way, you can sort out the not-so-hot ideas from the great ones and move to build on the best more quickly. It's also important to look at your problem from multiple perspectives and to involve other people in doing so. The goal is to build a climate that supports creativity and to develop a foundation to transform ideas into innovations. There are many frameworks presented in this section that do just that.

Tell stories, visualize broad ideas, and sketch concepts, in that order. It seems that all too often people are in a hurry to get to designing. After all, that is often seen as the end goal for many creative endeavors. Every business uses (or should be using) design to differentiate products, create meaningful experiences, and develop services that actually serve, but when creativity is applied at a broader level, we find more effective processes—or frameworks—by moving a bit differently through the process. These are the "thinking tools" of imagination and creativity. Communication begins with storytelling, and this is a great way to set the stage for any problem that needs a creative solution. Start with a story—a strategic conversation, not a project brief. Set the framework in conversational terms. This often requires an adaptive culture, and a work environment that allows people to feel vested in the projects. There is a great deal to be said about corporate culture and creativity, and it starts with simply allowing time to have strategic conversations, often supported by storytelling and visualizations of ideas. One of the challenges of business is having too many ideas and not knowing which of them might lead to success. Having strategic conversations, telling stories, and visualizing broad concepts help us to sort through those ideas.

Chapter 1

Managing Personal Creativity

by Jeffrey H. Mauzy, Innovation Consultant,
Strategy Planner, Synectics, Inc.

To improve corporate creativity, Jeffrey Mauzy advocates improving the creative abilities of individual employees. Elaborating on this theme, he probes the process of creative thinking and the factors that limit these opportunities, he details several interesting exercises for generating more and fresher ideas, and he outlines steps managers should take to leverage the creative output of their staffs.

WALK INTO ANY preschool, and you'll find some of the best creative thinking anywhere: finger paintings with purple people and polka-dot skies, fanciful tales of magical, far-away places. There are lessons for the corporate world in the day care center downstairs.

Young children are naturally creative. They must create ways to learn and construct a world view from a collection of initially disconnected events and colors and movement and sound. So what happens between the open, effortless experimentation of our childhood and the blocks in creative thinking experienced by many adults? Sociological, psychological, physical, and behavioral factors conspire to stifle our natural ability for original thought. And overcoming those barriers is one key to recapturing our creativity.

This is not news to corporations. Many organizations have responded to competitive and economic pressures with the conviction that creativity and innovation are the keys to success. In fact, a June 1995 study commissioned by the US Department of

Labor and conducted by Ernst & Young with the Harvard and Wharton business schools found that 85 percent of US companies are currently involved in workplace innovation programs. Such programs usually include training managers in effective group processes, as well as coaching teams on how to generate ideas and implement the most promising ones.

The success of such group-oriented programs varies widely. Many companies have been extraordinarily successful at bringing innovative products and services to market through the effective use of teamwork. Others flounder because of such factors as inadequate training or a lack of organizational commitment to the programs. But there is one approach that can help both successful and unsuccessful companies achieve their goals for innovation: developing the personal creativity skills of individual members of an organization. If you want a more creative organization, develop more creative employees.

Personal creativity, as defined here, means the ability of an individual to create new, relevant ideas and perspectives. Today, very little attention is given to developing the creative thinking skills of individuals within organizations. But in our work with clients in a wide array of industries—nearly half the Fortune 500 companies and thousands of individuals—my colleagues and I at Synectics have observed and tested techniques that can help people strengthen their innate creative abilities and problem-solving capacities and bring new ideas about products, processes, and policies back to the organization. The techniques and exercises presented in this article were identified and tested at Synectics on a variety of clients over many years. Many were used by creative people long before Synectics noticed them. Synectics's role was to isolate and experiment with the techniques, altering them as needed to produce reliable, quick results.

Developing creativity involves the following four elements:

1. Understanding the process of creative thinking

2. Identifying blocks to creative thinking and the skills individuals can use— and managers can foster—to increase creative responses

3. Using methods to get fresher ideas and solutions more often

4. Allowing a personal creative drive and lifelong creative vision that will help individuals, including managers, to achieve their personal and professional goals

We have assembled these elements in a flow that makes sense to most of our clients. Start with a model of the creative thinking process (as a mental guide for what and how we learn). Address the things that block creative thinking. Understand and exercise the underused mental functions that can encourage creative thought (because they will become invaluable in later techniques, as in life). Show ways to get new thoughts on demand (using our newly exercised creative capacities). And discuss the role of evaluation (because we all link evaluation to ideas, but often do a poor job of evaluating those ideas, in employees and even in ourselves).

Each step in the process of developing creativity can be viewed independently, and every exercise has been found to have some positive effect on a person's level of creative response. Used collectively, however, the steps and exercises produce better results. Space limitations dictate that we can display only a few exercises here.

A MODEL OF THE CREATIVE THINKING PROCESS

Synectics developed a model of the creative thinking process for the purposes of training clients (see Figure 1). It depicts the dynamics most critical to generating new thought: Where do thoughts come from? How does a person get new thoughts? What interferes with the process of getting new thoughts? What sort of thoughts should you be look-

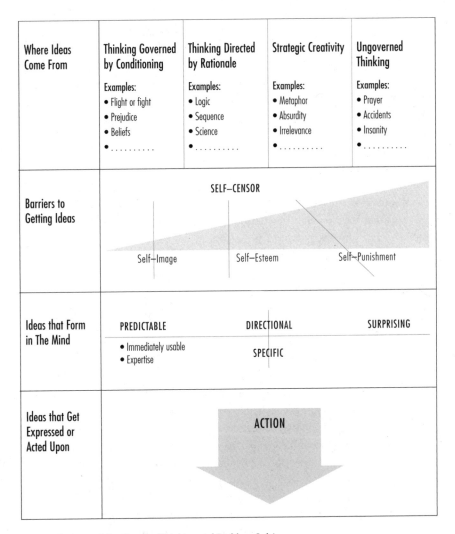

Figure 1. Framework for Creative Thinking and Problem-Solving

ing for? How do you work with these thoughts—in particular, how do you negotiate between interesting, new, but seemingly impossible, ideas and less original, but safe, ones that can be implemented easily?

Where ideas come from. Moving from left to right along the where-ideas-come-from spectrum, shown in the top row of the model, we progress from the sources of the most conventional types of thinking to the sources of the most original thought. The left half of the spectrum—thinking governed by conditioning and by rationale—represents the types of thinking practiced by most people most of the time. We depend on these kinds of thought patterns, and for good reason. They have given us cars that go and planes that stay in the air. But we depend on them so much that we don't question them when they no longer work for us (when we are confronted by a problem and just can't seem to find a new solution).

Beware of an automatic response toward safe ideas. Encourage risk among employees and respond in ways that reward that risk.

Creative people have conscious and unconscious strategies and ways of thinking that help them access fresh ideas. The right half of the spectrum—strategic creativity and ungoverned thinking—represents those ways in which people can more readily access original thought. In the strategically creative mode of thought, people let their minds wander. They walk away from the problem, sleep on it, turn it upside down, think in metaphors—all of these are patterns of thought that do not come naturally to those accustomed to working in results-oriented business environments. The ungoverned end of the spectrum works well for some, but only the boldest feel comfortable exploring this domain where chance and accident reign. Whether one explores the farthest reaches of the spectrum or not, the more the mind can range across the entire spectrum of thinking, the more fresh ideas will spring forth.

▲ Allow time for reflection.

▲ Don't overload employees.

▲ Teach methods for creative thought to teams and to individuals.

Blocks to creative thinking. What prevents the mind from ranging across the spectrum? From the time we are young, parents, peers, supervisors, school, and society all teach us that experimentation can be harmful to ourselves and to others: "Don't play in the street." "That's gross." "Do you have permission to do that?" "Better clear the idea with your boss first." Statements like these emerge from both external and internal blocks to creative thinking, depicted in the second row of the model.

Reliance on rational thinking. Certain forms of thought have historically proven to describe the way things are and to predict the results of events reliably. Teachers, scientists, and most bosses reward us for using these established thinking patterns, and they discourage us, sometimes in almost unnoticeable ways, from varying from those patterns. Eventually, this reward/punishment behavior becomes internalized.

Self-censoring. Our experience in the world affects our ideas and how we come up with them. Good behavior is expected and so goes unnoticed and unrewarded, whereas bad behavior is the exception and is punished. New ideas have a higher potential for danger, so we learn to be suspicious of them. Eventually, our self-censoring mechanisms become so internalized that many of our ideas and potential ideas become inaccessible to our conscious minds.

Internal climate. A punishing or hostile climate can kill creativity faster than any other factor. And such a climate is hard to patch back up. Leaders, as well as everyone, must pay attention to the climate and talk openly about how to improve it.

▲ Work to build a safe environment, where people can take risks without fear.

▲ Encourage, and reward, experimentation.

▲ Set aside money for experiments.

Self-punishment. Have you ever said to yourself, "That was a stupid idea," or "You dummy?" Have you ever hit yourself when you made a mistake? Imagine how few risks you would take if your boss or your friend upbraided you in this way every time they thought you were mistaken. Self-punishment can extinguish the risk-taking behavior that is critical to creativity. It sets up the same fear-avoidance patterns discussed in the self-censoring section earlier; these internal mechanisms can begin to act on ideas before we even have them.

Be aware of how you respond to ideas and proposals. Do you see it from the presenter's side? What are the benefits of the idea? If you don't care for the idea, do you let the presenter know you see the benefits? Are you clear about why you have problems with the idea? Does the presenter leave feeling good even if the idea is rejected? Is there room for push-back?

Ideas that form in the mind. The third row of the model, labeled "ideas that form in the mind," concerns thoughts that we still have not expressed but now recognize as ideas or possible solutions to the task at hand. Moving from left to right along the spectrum, we progress from predictable ideas to those that surprise us. Because each of us is unique, much of what we consider to be predictable in our own thinking can appear fresh to others. But predictable ideas are the result of thinking according to our habitual patterns of thought. They are usually very specific, very doable—and very safe. They are the path of least resistance (a form of bad habit, really), and by consciously opting for a different path, we are doing our creative selves a favor.

To increase our creativity, we need to move to the right on the spectrum and come up with ideas that surprise us. Surprising ideas may tend to be more directional than specific in nature, and they can appear as fuzzy, vague, or semi-formed thoughts— thoughts we are conditioned to devalue. But many innovations in the world have resulted from someone holding on to a vague notion—a direction in thinking—and working in that direction until the idea crystallized and then became an innovation. Edwin Land's daughter launched him in a new direction when she said, "I wish I could see the picture you just took . . . now." That direction led to the research that eventually produced the Polaroid camera.

Surprising ideas are not easy to come by. Accessing them requires confronting and overcoming self-censoring blocks and venturing into the strategically creative and un-governed end of the where ideas come from spectrum. It takes hard work; it often takes courage, as well.

Whenever possible, allow time for employees and teams to solve tricky or cre-ative problems.

Ideas that are acted on. The final row of the model, ideas that are expressed or acted on, represents when we actually articulate a thought or act on it. It is here that the poten-tial threat to our ideas escalates. We can become subject to ridicule; we can fail. Acting on ideas is a subject for another article, but it is important to point out in this context that anticipating potential threats can dissuade us from ever forming or recognizing those ideas in the first place.

Understand the level of radicalism you are looking for. Does the idea you are acting on reach that level?

ELEVATING CREATIVE RESPONSE

As we grow and negotiate the world around us, we latch onto certain patterns of think-ing. Soon those patterns become such automatic, unconscious habits that we are no lon-ger able to question their efficacy. At Synectics, we have observed that certain patterns of thought are in use more often in creative work than in everyday business-as-usual thinking. In our research with participants in our courses, we have created exercises to strengthen these creative patterns. When you go to a gym and exercise unused muscles, you find your entire body functions better over time. Similarly, we find that when people use these exercises, they reclaim parts of their ability to think creatively, and their minds begin to work more effectively over time.

Creativity exercises. The thinking skills involved in the following exercises underlie the idea-generation techniques we use with clients. These exercises tend to increase the creative acuity of our clients. They have also been shown to have a positive impact on individuals' creativity scores in research studies.[1] We have room to include only a few examples in this article.

Imagery. This exercise uses a complex of thinking patterns—excursion, improvi-sation, analogy, and metaphor—but it relies primarily on imagery. You can bring this technique to any personal or professional dilemma you face. Imagine the problem as a scene in a movie. Picture the entire scene in your mind. Who are the main actors? Who are the secondary ones? What are their relationships? What is the main plot? The subplots? Now play with the scene. Imagine new plot twists, different roles for the char-acters. Do you gain any new insights or perspectives on your problem?

Wishing. Recall how extravagant your wishes were as a child. As we mature, we learn to wish increasingly within the limits of the possible. People become accustomed to judging ideas, not wishes. Re-instituting the act of wishing brings us back to our child-hoods, when more things seemed possible. In this exercise, consider a problem you are confronting. Set aside ten minutes to wish for the seemingly impossible. Come up with at least twenty-five wishes; stretch for a few. Can you think of any new approaches to the problem on the basis of those wishes?[2] Wish yourself. Ask employees what they wish for, too. Don't throw out intriguing but so-called impossible ideas. Put them on the back burner, but leave the flame on.

Excursion. By following this pattern, individuals can strengthen their connection-making mechanisms and force new ideas into being. The pattern is fivefold:

1. Put the problem out of mind

2. Allow new, seemingly irrelevant information to occupy your attention (if you get stuck, just look around you and pick something that intrigues you)

3. Consider the object for a couple of minutes (What's its use? If it were alive, what would it say to you? How was it formed? Imagine the factory or environmental forces that made it)

4. Find ways in which the new information connects to the problem

5. Work on the connections to build a new idea for a solution to the problem.

The examples in the table show the idea-generating mechanism at work (see Figure 2, on next page). Using analogy, metaphor, and absurdity allows the mind to forge new connections. You can apply the same structure directly to issues you are considering in order to come up with new ideas.

Reframing evaluation. Learning how to come up with new ideas is critical to developing creativity, but it is also important to examine how ideas, once gotten, are treated. As we have acquired our habits and patterns of thought, we have also acquired a pattern for evaluation to help us negotiate life. We are taught to evaluate ideas for relevance and feasibility, and the more rapidly and sensitively we do that, the more efficient we become at making the hundreds of decisions we need to make daily. This pattern, like the other unconscious thinking patterns, has to be adjusted when creativity is our goal.

When it comes to evaluating ideas, we fall into a pattern of fault-finding, which is rooted in the scientific method: Build a hypothesis, attack it with vigor, and repeat until a hypothesis can stand all attacks. Any new idea can be considered a hypothesis. Imagine the effect on our self-censor and self-image when our ideas are under constant attack. No wonder we give up the fight to be original. If we wish to become more creative, we need to learn to treat our new ideas in a friendlier way.

One way we can do just that is by deferring decisions. In a study of art students, Getzels and Csikszentmihalyi[3] identified a pattern of behavior, which they termed problem-finding behavior, that correlated strongly with the students' tested levels of creativity and with professional success later in their careers. The students that tested high for creativity and success were more likely to change directions, to go wherever a new idea took them. Final decisions were put off. A work was seldom, if ever, considered finished; rather, it was just put aside for the moment.

ANALOGY	METAPHOR	ABSURDITY
Process: 1. Forget the problem for a few minutes. 2. Find examples of matching things from the world of animals: **Examples found:** • Mating • Climate and body protection • Kids and dogs • Predators and population 1. Choose one that is intriguing and run a scenario about it in your mind. I'm thinking about predators and population — how the match seems so appropriate after the balance is achieved. I picture deer and wolves. Too many wolves and some starve. Not enough wolves and deer overpopulate and starve. There are other factors that enter in and keep the balance. 2. After a few minutes, think about that example (matching process in nature) and the original problem. See if you can find a way the same mechanism can be transferred over and articulate a new idea from the exercise. Idea: Look for industries where there are a lot of companies but not a lot of newness — say a commodity industry. Suggest tools for new thinking to each player as a way to survive the mutual starvation.	**Process:** 1. Forget the problem for a few minutes. 2. Look for three or four things that represent your problem. • None of the furniture in my office matches. • My computer doesn't really fit well on my round table. • My 4:30 AM to 10:30 PM daily schedule is a poor fit for my wife's 6:00 AM to 11:30 PM schedule. 1. See if each example (metaphor) can point the way to a new approach to your problem. Even though a poor match, the function of the furniture is appropriate. Beginning idea — maybe I should look for industries that seem ready to absorb new thinking quickly and easily (functional approach). The round table is a poor fit, but that's where I like to work. Beginning idea — just concentrate on the companies and industries that interest me personally — maybe the extra energy I have in these areas will translate to market acceptance. Beginning idea from third bullet — by working with each other's schedules, my wife and I each have concentrated alone time and more focused together time. Final idea — Make the software available in bite-size pieces so people can easily "reach for it" when the mood strikes them — and just pay for those times. This leads to an idea for an Internet or per-use fee — maybe a lower yearly subscription instead of a higher one-time-buy price.	**Process:** 1. Forget the problem for a few minutes. 2. Develop several absurd ideas to solve your problem. • Use a marriage matchmaker. • Put ads in the personals. • Drop little disks from airplanes and watch who picks the program off the ground. 1. Now use each absurd idea to create another idea that is a little more useful toward solving your problem. First idea (from marriage matchmaker) — Interview ten successful entrepreneurs, ask how they would go about finding the right match for a program like mine. Follow the three suggestions most frequently offered. Second idea (from personals) — Choose a city and offer the software free in the local business news. Calculate response rates and pursue the most frequent in other cities. Third idea (from airplane) — Put the software out free on the Internet for six months — the cost of using it will let me know who you are and the business you are in. In six months, go after the most-frequent-user business areas.

Figure 2. Example: Find a way to match our company's brainstorming software to the right audience.

Deferring closure on a solution allows more time to be spent exploring a variety of approaches. It promotes creativity by leaving the issue open to increasing connections and a greater degree of richly unresolved ambiguity. Still, the benefits of exploration and discovery have to be weighed against costs in terms of the budget and the production schedule. There is a tension. Deferring closure "contradicts common management practice. Decisions are made and frozen in order to implement those decisions throughout the organization and coordinate multi-functional tasks."[4]

Two exercises can help individuals think creatively about a problem while forcing them to defer deciding on a solution. The first is the forced-plus exercise. Write down two potential solutions to a problem, each at the top of a sheet of paper. List four pluses, or benefits, for each idea. Think again about each solution. Do you see them in a more positive light?

The second is the next-step exercise. Write the two solutions for the same problem, each at the top of a sheet of paper. List the next steps you would take to execute the solutions. Think again about the solutions. Do you see either of them in a more positive light?

These are good exercises for managers who must approve or disapprove proposals and ideas.

THE DRIVE AND VISION TO CREATE

Creating new things is inherently fun and, for some, necessary. But any new way of thinking requires continual practice, and some clients who complete our program in creativity lose their skills in a matter of months because they stop flexing their creative muscles. In much of the world—and the business world, too—there exists considerable hostility to creative ideas and efforts. One firm we worked with even had the terms "career-limiting idea" and "career-terminating idea" in its lexicon. A 1991 study by P.A. Holland and colleagues[5] shows that groups of new employees, hired to be more creative than existing ones, eventually stop using their creative abilities and come to resemble their less creative counterparts. Why? Our hypothesis is that a complex set of expectations and norms were already in place in the organizations. As the new employees brought fresh thinking into the establishment, they threatened established norms. In order to protect those norms, other employees brought increasing levels of judgment to bear on the new ideas until they brought the "creative" group into line with the existing organization. Much, but not all, of the change wrought in the more creative group was found to occur through attrition. First, new employees exhibited coping behavior, then distress and job dissatisfaction; finally, many left the companies.

▲ Understand the climate for creativity in your company, your division, your group.

▲ Find ways to make each climate friendlier. What's your level of control? Can you manage up? How can you make each group you manage friendly to ideas? Many of the clues are in this article.

▲ This is a never-ending activity. Make creativity public. Keep proselytizing.

A few creative thinkers find ways to persevere in the face of such hostility, and it is from that small group that innovative ideas emerge. How can individuals nourish their drive to create? How do you make creativity stick?

Identify what's important. Make a short list of the things you want most in life. (For most people, money is only a means to something else—what is that something?) This is no easy task and can take days or even weeks. Exercises can help. What would you like to do before you die? Collect metaphors or images about your ideal self, extract thoughts from those metaphors, and put them on your list. Who are your heroes? What qualities or accomplishments do you most admire in them? Put those on your list. Write your obituary—what would you want it to say? Robert Fritz, who has spent much of his life thinking and writing about the creative drive, suggests that you consider adding three things to your list if they are not already there: be true to yourself, choose freedom, and be the predominant creative force in your own life.

Identify what keeps you from reaching those goals. For many people, knowing what they want—and trusting in that—is enough. They believe that their own drive will bring them there eventually. Some techniques in this article may be helpful in accelerating their arrival. For others, there are roadblocks: physical, psychological, or structural restraints that get in the way of their ever moving toward their ideals: "I can't do that now; I have responsibilities," or "That would be great, but I can't do it because of religion/children/phobias/money." Each of us has a calculation to make about the importance of the goal and the importance of the roadblock. Reality plays a part; again, courage may be called on.

Use creativity to find new ways of reaching your goal of a more creative self. Or identify the roadblocks and, one at a time, use some of these techniques to find new ways to overcome them. Remember, too, that in some cases there is no arrival. Freedom means reaching for the goal. It lies in the direction, not the destination.

▲ This section was written for you, the manager. If you aren't committed to a more creative self, so that you learn about creativity daily, then you will not be able to convince others in your organization.

▲ This exercise also works for employees interested in improving their creative selves.

CREATIVE INDIVIDUALS, INNOVATIVE ORGANIZATIONS

Most individuals and most organizations have similar goals regarding creativity—both want more of it. And organizations know their ability to innovate lies in the creativity and abilities of their people. The individual needs to understand and adopt internal thinking processes that increase the potential for new thinking. Organizations have to do the same. The processes and patterns are different when applied organizationally because they have to account for a collective diversity. But the same underlying mechanisms can produce creative individuals and innovative organizations.

ACKNOWLEDGMENT

I would like to acknowledge my indebtedness to George Prince, the founder of Synectics and the chief researcher behind the creativity and innovation techniques used at the consulting firm and in this article.

Suggested Reading

Amabile, T.M. *The Social Psychology of Creativity* (New York: Springer-Verlag, 1983).

Fritz, R. *The Path of Least Resistance* (New York: Ballantine Books, 1984).

Gardner, H. *Creating Minds* (New York: Basic Books, 1993).

Mauzy, J., and Harriman, H. *Creativity, Inc.* (Cambridge, MA: Harvard Business School Press, 2002).

Perkins, D.N. *The Mind's Best Work* (Cambridge, MA: Harvard University Press, 1981).

Perkins, D.N. "Creativity and the Quest of Mechanism" in *The Psychology of Human Thought*, Sternberg, R.J. and Smith, E.E. (eds.) (Cambridge, UK: Cambridge University Press, 1988).

Endnotes

1. S. R. Grossman, "Seven Operating Principles for Enhanced Creative Problem-Solving Training," *Journal of Creative Behavior 27* (1993), pp. 1-17; R. J. Sternberg, *How to Develop Student Creativity* (Alexandria, Virginia: Association for Supervision and Curriculum, 1996).

2. Conrad Paulus, manager of new product development at AT&T, came up with an innovative idea using this technique. "I had made a wish for a product," he says, "a 'conference in a box' (the invitations and stuff you pack together and send out to set up a conference call). The wish originally came from my problem of how to sell more conference calling. I took it to a colleague of mine, and we decided to try it as a joint venture. We've never been able to do it—the idea blows up in all our new product research—and I still wish I could do it."

3. Jacob Getzels and Mihali Czikszentmihalyi, *The Creative Vision: A Longitudinal Study of Problem-Finding in Art* (New York: John Wiley & Sons, 1976).

4. Elizabeth Deane, executive producer for public television, WGBH TV, Boston (from interview notes).

5. P.A. Holland, I. Bowskill, and A. Bailey, "Adaptors and Innovators: Selection Versus Induction," *Psychological Reports 68* (1991), pp. 1283-1290.

Chapter 2

The Prepared Mind Versus the Beginner's Mind

by Mark Stefik, Research Fellow, Palo Alto Research Center
and Barbara Stefik, PhD, Transpersonal Psychology, Private Practice

Many breakthroughs—those great "Aha!" moments—emerge when experience is both deep and broad. However, some breakthroughs, as Mark Stefik and Barbara Stefik emphasize, only occur when people move away from past experience—changing activities, trying ideas that shouldn't work, and failing quickly and regularly.[1] Innovative success cultivates this dynamic tension, balancing the tried and true with the unanticipated.

CREATIVITY OFTEN EMERGES out of the tension between two seemingly irreconcilable properties that a design or product should have. Sometimes, a higher-order synthesis of the opposing properties is needed in order to find a creative solution.

There is also a tension of opposites in methods for creative work: cultivating a "prepared mind" versus cultivating a "beginner's mind." Advice for the prepared mind says, Develop and use your experience. Advice for the beginner's mind says, Discard your previous experience. How should we effectively use these seemingly opposing pieces of advice?

The great nineteenth-century scientist Louis Pasteur once said, "In the field of observation, chance favors the prepared mind." At the moment of a breakthrough, inventors experience a highly charged feeling of "Aha!" This happens when one insight rapidly follows another in a sequence. Crucially, this burst of rapid insights is possible because the mind is well prepared. After the preparatory work, the mind is fertile and ready. All that is

17

needed for sudden creativity is a catalyst—a chance observation—which triggers the insights that build on each other. In this mode of creativity, preparing the mind is crucial.

Creativity can also arise without specific preparation. In academic settings and research laboratories, professors and head investigators often say, I love to give hard problems to graduate students. They solve them because they don't know that the problems are impossible. This parallels a quote from San Francisco Zen master Shunryu Suzuki: "In the beginner's mind, there are many possibilities, but in the expert's there are few."

As we work in an area, we gain experience and acquire particular patterns of thinking. A mindset is a pattern and a set of assumptions that guide our thinking. Over time, these patterns of thinking become deeply ingrained. Without noticing it, we become very efficient at thinking "inside the box." When we're faced with a novel situation, these built-in assumptions can cause us to overlook inventive possibilities and potential breakthroughs. Shifting mindset helps us to loosen the tenacious hold these patterns have on our thinking.

A good way to shift mindset is to cultivate a beginner's mind. This involves quieting the parts of the mind that get in the way of creativity. The beginner's mind is open to fresh perspectives, considering unconventional ideas that an expert might say were silly or illogical. The beginner's mind is the opposite of trying too hard and getting agitated. The beginner's mind is lighter and more playful.

THE PREPARED MIND SETS UP THE AHA! MOMENT

Science offers many stories of chance observations that led to important discoveries. One of the most celebrated is Alexander Fleming's 1928 discovery that a particular mold culture growing on a Petri dish in his laboratory secreted a juice that killed bacteria. Around every culture of the mold, all the bacteria had died. That mold was Penicillium, and eventually Fleming's discovery led to the "wonder drug" penicillin. Fleming's prepared mind recognized an opportunity in the patterns of dead bacteria on the Petri dish. Absent a prepared mind, Fleming could have dismissed his discovery and thrown away the sample without realizing its potential as an antibiotic. This story is a classic illustration of Pasteur's idea that in the field of observations, chance favors the prepared mind.

Preparation is essential. It brings the necessary ideas to the mind at the same time so that they can be combined in novel ways. When the combination happens, there is a sequence of insights and then the Aha! experience of discovery.

People describe their Aha! experiences with a sense of wonder, saying something like, "It just hit me," or "I know the answer!" Such accounts give rise to the misunderstanding that inspiration comes simply and inexplicably from genius, without previous work. In his book *Thinking in Jazz*, Paul Berliner describes a similar misunderstanding about improvisation for jazz musicians.

The popular conception of improvisation as "performance without previous preparation" is fundamentally misleading. There is, in fact, a lifetime of preparation and knowledge behind every idea that an improviser performs.[2]

Alan Kay once said that "point of view is worth 40 IQ points."[3] One way to look at repeat inventors studying across disciplines and jazz musicians studying across types of jazz is that they are preparing their minds for invention by accumulating points of view.

PREPARING THE MIND WITH CROSS-DISCIPLINARY STUDY

Invention involves combining ideas—especially points of view from different fields. Different points of view bring new ways of thinking. New points of view can lead to shortcuts, such as solving a problem in one field by drawing an analogy to a problem solved in a different field.

Pattie Maes is a professor at the Media Lab at MIT. Maes is acutely aware of the importance of finding new ways of looking at things. She takes inspiration from fields that study complex systems. When we spoke to her, she was on a sabbatical from her teaching responsibilities and was using the time to take courses in other disciplines.[4] I often put two very different things together—a technique from one domain, for instance, used on a totally different type of problem. For example, I may take an interesting idea from biology and marry it with a problem in artificial intelligence.

I started paying attention to biology about fifteen years ago and over time have been looking at other fields. I usually don't attend conferences in my own field, except if I have to present a paper or give a talk. I prefer to attend talks and conferences in other areas. When I was working at the artificial intelligence laboratory with Rodney Brooks, all of us—Brooks included—would study other fields, specifically biology and ethology,[5] the work of Lorenz and Tinbergen. Those ethologists had very sophisticated models about how animals decide what to do and how they learn. They take extensive observations and then make models to explain what they see. Their models were unknown to the artificial intelligence community and rarely exploited in computational systems. That was a rich area to explore and to get inspiration for artificial intelligence and for building computational systems.

THE AHA! MOMENT

Like jazz musicians, inventors gather several distinct kinds of ideas. All the preparation and work of gathering ideas pays off in an exciting way when there is a breakthrough, or Aha! moment.

What does an Aha! feel like? What is the experience of the moment of discovery like for people who have prepared their minds? Many inventors have told anecdotal stories about this event. We can explore this by using a thought experiment.

There is a fable about the invention of chess. Versions of this fable often take place in India, in China, or in an unspecified exotic kingdom. In one version of the fable, a clever traveler presents the king with the game of chess. The king is so pleased that he asks the traveler to suggest a possible reward for presenting the game. According to the fable, the traveler-inventor says he would like a grain of rice on the first square of the board, double that number of grains on the second square, and so on for all the squares on the board. He arranged to come back each day to pick up the next install-ment of rice.

The king thinks this is a very modest request and asks his servants to supply the rice. As agreed upon, one grain of rice is the award on the first day. Two on the second. Four on the third. Eight on the fourth. The amount of rice to be picked up in a week (27 or 128 grains) would fit in a teaspoon. In two weeks, however, the daily reward was about a half kilogram. This is about the time that many people get a mini-Aha! When something doubles repeatedly, it grows to an enormous size very quickly. By the end of the month, the daily installment would be 35 tons. Although the stories vary on the fate of the king and the traveler, the real lesson of the fable is the power of doubling. The amount of rice to fulfill the request—264, or about 1.8 1019 grains of rice—would cover the land mass of the Earth.

This chess fable is well-known to students of mathematics and computer science. The story is taught to develop intuitions about exponential functions and large num-bers. Something like it crossed the mind of Kary Mullis[6] in 1985 when he invented the polymerase chain reaction (PCR). Mullis had a PhD in biochemistry and was working in molecular biology for Cetus, a company that makes synthetic strands of DNA for use by molecular biologists. From his work at Cetus, Mullis was aware of the need for good ways to "amplify" or make multiple copies of DNA. Like geneticists everywhere, he knew about the polymerase enzyme that is employed by living cells to copy DNA. Cycles of heating and cooling are used to trigger each doubling cycle of the polymerase.

According to his account, Mullis was driving through the mountains north of San Francisco with his girlfriend asleep in the car when it occurred to him.[7] He recognized that he could apply the polymerase reaction to copy a sample of DNA. Then he real-ized that he could repeat the reaction over and over again, doubling the DNA each time. Then he realized that ten cycles would give him 1,024 copies; twenty cycles would give him a million copies, and so on. Mullis later received the Nobel Prize for his invention of the polymerase chain reaction now used widely in molecular genetics.

In his description of the event, Mullis writes about how one insight followed the next in a series of exciting revelations—the Aha! experience. This rapid sequence of under-standings is the same pattern that many others have described.

People remember their Aha! experiences. Every creation has some mini-break-throughs, as insights arise to meet the challenges of the problem. But big insights—the Aha! moments—happen much less frequently. We count ourselves lucky if these hap-pen a few times in a lifetime. Ahas are the juice of creation; the excitement of major insights motivates us to keep on trying. What Mihaly Csikszentmihalyi[8] calls "being in the flow" is a strong motivator for focused concentration.

The archetypal journey of the inventor—the movie version—centers on a brilliant individual who has an insightful dream and struggles against great odds before realizing the dream. This myth reflects some truths. People have moments of keen insight. These moments inspire them.

What is forgotten in the simple versions of the invention myth is that preparation precedes insight. Preparations bring key ideas into the mind, where they can be combined rapidly—almost like a polymerase chain reaction itself. Preparation saturates the mind with ideas. Then, when the right problem or the missing link is provided by a situation, the Aha! chain reaction can occur.

THE BEGINNER'S MIND BREAKS MINDSETS

Breakthrough inventions are exactly the ones that do not arise incrementally from what has been tried before. They break from past experience. In breakthroughs, the hard part is finding the insight. People say that breakthroughs require "thinking outside the box."

Breaking Out by Changing Activities

Cultivating a beginner's mind is about letting go of grasping and cultivating spaciousness. Too much alertness—trying too hard—leads to agitation. The beginner's mind has a sense of playfulness, lightness, and receptivity.

But how do you relax when you are trying too hard? Ben Bederson is a prolific inventor in the field of human-computer interactions, especially in zooming user interfaces. A professor at the University of Maryland, Bederson is the second director of the Human-Computer Interaction Laboratory founded by Ben Shneiderman. In reflecting on his own experience, Bederson recalled something he noticed early in his research career.[9] I noticed that 90 percent of my best ideas arose when I was riding my bike over the Brooklyn Bridge. I was in a balanced state of alertness—alert enough to be careful about how I was riding, and not trying to solve my problem of the day. I'd be playing with ideas at the back of my mind. That was when insights tended to arise.

Other inventors take a break or go for a walk to clear their heads. Sometimes inventors, like other creative people, cultivate alternate states of consciousness to see what comes to mind. Some people have noticed that just before we go to sleep there is a state of mind when we can see visual patterns. The patterns arise, fade away, and are then replaced by other patterns in a series of images. This state, known as the hypnogogic state, has been correlated with enhanced creativity in various research studies.

Breaking Mindset by Trying the Opposite

When inventors search for solutions, they often start by following their first ideas. Sometimes, what they try first turns out to be the opposite of what is needed. Ted Selker, a professor at MIT, recalled an example of trying the opposite when he was working on the TrackPoint invention, the eraser-like nub near the H-key in laptop computers used as a pointing device.[10] One of the ideas we had along the way for speeding up user interaction was to build in momentum. In the physical world, if you push or throw something in a particular direction, it tends to keep going that way. If a pointing device is going in a direction, we thought it would be likely to continue going in that same direction. We built momentum into the cursor movement routines. In fact, somebody had a patent on that.

It turns out that adding momentum to the logic makes a pointing device harder to control. In fact, the opposite idea works better. It works better to amplify how movements are changing rather than amplify the current movement. In other words, you take the derivative of motion and amplify the change. When you start moving the pointer, it starts faster and when you slow down, it stops faster. This is the opposite of momentum. The idea is basically ABS brakes[11] on a pointing device. Amplifying the derivative is the invention. The good news is that it makes a 15-percent improvement in control.

Another example of trying the opposite comes from stressed metals in material science. In the silicon fabrication processes for making computer chips, one of the steps is the deposition of metal to ultimately create wires for circuits in the chips. The metal is initially sputtered on to the silicon surface during fabrication to form a metallic film, followed by other processing steps. There is always some stress in the metal—potentially causing it to lift up from the surface. Because such lifting is undesirable for chip operation, the fabrication process is controlled to minimize stress in the film.

David Fork is a materials scientist. We interviewed him about two inventions involving stressed metals: "the claw" and "kissing springs." In these inventions, the inventors saw the potential of going in the opposite direction of conventional wisdom—deliberately using stress to create three-dimensional structures with the metal.[12] Don Smith got the idea for the claw when he was writing a chapter in his book about thin-film stress and sputtered material. Thin-film stress has been the bad guy for many years, and in the minds of many process engineers it still is the bad guy. Conventional wisdom says that if you can't make the stress zero in your process equipment, then something is wrong. In contrast, the claw invention actually relies on very large mechanical stresses engineered into the material. So it was turning lemons into lemonade, in a way, to get some three-dimensional self-assembly to occur as a result of intentional stresses built into the material ahead of time.

Normally, a lot of bad things can happen when the stress in a metallic film isn't zero. It can crack or de-laminate and do other bad things. But it can also result in interesting structures, such as microscopic springs or coils. The springs form a bunch of cantilevers that pop up off the surface of a wafer. We call this the "claw."

Selker's and Fork's examples show how conventional experience can sometimes be turned around. Trying the opposite can lead the mind beyond the conventional.

Uncovering Assumptions by Talking It Out

One of the great joys in creative life is having good colleagues to talk with. Mark Yim, a professor at the University of Pennsylvania, describes how this practice has worked for him.

When I am stuck on something, I often take a walk down the hall. Usually, I run into someone and start talking to him or her. I explain the problem. In the process of explaining it, an insight or a new approach may come up. It is rare that a problem has no solution and remains frustrating.

It doesn't have to be an expert or even someone on the project team. Talking it out works with almost anyone in the lab.

Progress comes episodically. Sometimes, we work on something for months without making progress, and then an idea comes up in conversation. We say, Oh, here's an idea. Why don't we try it? We try it, and in three days we have it working fantastically. It may not be along the lines we were thinking before. It may be a completely different approach and one that really works.

The process of explaining a problem or an idea to someone can fundamentally aid in thinking outside the box. Interestingly, this talking-it-out process can work even when the second person is not an expert on the problem. The reason is that unconscious assumptions that are hidden to ourselves can surface when we explain a problem to a scientifically minded colleague. In the practice of working alone, unconscious assumptions can remain invisible for long periods of time. When our assumptions are articulated in conversation, we sometimes notice them for the first time, making it possible to discard or soften them. In general, the less familiar a second person is with our original problem, the more explanation we need to give. In this way, explaining a problem to someone else can help us to cultivate beginner's mind and enable us to see the problem differently.

Exploring Efficiently by Failing Quickly and Often

Gary Starkweather, a researcher at Microsoft, invented the laser printer when he was at the Palo Alto Research Center in the late 1970s. He characterizes effective research as learning to fail quickly: "The secret of research is learning how to fail fast. That gets you to the right answers quickly. You measure good research by how fast people are making mistakes. It's the one organization in a company whose job is to explore."[13] Starkweather's dictum emphasizes the rate of exploration. Most new ideas are bad. From this searching perspective, a strategy for research is to search alternatives quickly, without fear of failure.

Starkweather's story is similar to an anecdote reported from Linus Pauling, a Nobel laureate for his work in chemistry and later, a recipient of the Nobel Peace Prize. Pauling was asked by a student, "How does one go about having good ideas?" His reply: "You have a lot of ideas and throw away the bad ones."

Learning to fail early and often is a tenet of industrial design and a theme practiced in the Center for Design Research at Stanford University. Director Larry Leifer puts it this way:[14] In design, we tend to use the phrase fail early and often to describe the method of generating many ideas or concepts early in a product design or development cycle. This helps to make later stages relatively error-free. Even in structured models of design through phases, we move on to the next version quickly—again failing early and often. In this way, that attitude dominates our design practice.

In some of our principled research studies of design practice, we have found evidence that failing quickly actually matters. These were double-blind studies to judge the quality of a design outcome and correlate that with the design practice. We measured the design quality with an external panel that did not know which team did the designs. We measured design practice by using an analysis of a design transcript. We used the rate of adding noun-phrases as a stand-in for introducing new design concepts. In other words, we counted the number of noun-phrases people used as a measure of the number of ideas they generated. We also looked at the rate of asking certain kinds of questions, which is a stand-in for criticism and the number of ideas they rejected. Groups that failed early and often generated and rejected more ideas than the others. The results of the experiment showed that these metrics were a good predictor of the design quality. The more rapidly a group generates and discards ideas, the better the resulting quality of their design.

The virtue of failing quickly is counterintuitive for people who expect designs to unfold directly from a principled linear process. The practice requires letting go of perfectionism and developing confidence in a process of trial and error.

THE PREPARED MIND VERSUS THE BEGINNER'S MIND

These accounts of the prepared mind and the beginner's mind suggest opposite advice for creativity. The prepared-mind advice says, Accumulate and use experience, and the beginner's-mind advice says, Discard your previous experience. One way to reconcile these seemingly contradictory ideas is to recognize the difference between routine and novel problems. The advice about having a prepared mind works well for routine problems, and the advice about cultivating beginner's mind is for novel problems. For routine problems, previous experience helps us to work through the problems effectively. For novel situations, however, our experience can get in the way of having a breakthrough.

For people facing a mixture of routine and novel problems, the methods of the prepared mind and the beginner's mind are the yin and yang of creative problem solving. We start out by trying to apply knowledge from past experience. Sometimes, previous experience also works spectacularly for new kinds of problems, as when insights acquired from different disciplines come together for a major Aha!

If the old experience doesn't seem to work, we face an impasse: "I've never seen a problem quite like this one before!" "I see a couple of alternatives, but neither of them works, and I don't know what to do." This impasse is a signal to cultivate the beginner's mind. When old knowledge doesn't work on new problems, cultivating a beginner's mind can free us from our preconceived notions. We can notice this and put aside those sensible assumptions that block the path to creative solutions.

Sometimes, our work activities are so busy there seems to be no time for either preparation or play. In these situations, all this talk about prepared mind and beginner's mind may seem out of touch. "We need answers now! Isn't necessity the mother of invention?" In our experience, such creativity as can be found in these tense situations draws on our bank account of previous preparations and arises in part when we are able to relax in the middle of the urgency. Creative thinking dries up when we fail to replenish the source.

Creativity has a rhythm. Recognizing the rhythm—and the signal of when to change the beat—is a higher-order synthesis that honors the essential elements of the two kinds of advice. Play is most crucial when creativity is most crucial. Without play, the joy drains out of the work. It becomes harder to hear the inner voice and to engage in novel ways of thinking. Play is an essential part of the method for first-rate creative people. For repeated creativity, we need a balance—sometimes working very hard and sometimes playing, sometimes drawing on our experience and sometimes putting it aside. We adjust the rhythm to serve both the routine and the creative challenges of our work.

Endnotes

1. The material in this article is drawn (with permission) from Stefik & Stefik, *Breakthrough: Stories and Strategies of Radical Innovation* (MIT Press, 2004). This book draws on interviews with about fifty creative inventors, designers, and researchers.

2. Berliner, Paul F., *Thinking in Jazz: The Infinite Art of Improvisation* (Chicago: The University of Chicago Press, 1994, paperback edition), p. 17.

3. Many variations of this quote have been cited. Friends of Alan Kay at PARC remember the quote starting out at around 10 IQ points. Recently, versions with numbers as high as 80 IQ points have appeared. In any case, Kay's point is that a point of view can provide a real advantage for having insights and reasoning by analogy.

4. Pattie Maes's story is based on two interviews. The first was with Mark Stefik on June 28, 2001, and the second was with Barbara Stefik on September 7, 2001.

5. Ethology is the study of animal behavior.

6. Mullis documents his discovery in his book *Dancing Naked in the Mind Field*, published in 2000 by Vintage Books. The discovery was reported in Mullis, K.B. et al., *Cold Spring Harb. Symp. Quant. Biol*, 51, 263–273 (1986).

7. He says that the insight occurred at mile marker 46.58 on Highway 128.

8. Csikszentmihalyi, Mihaly, *Creativity: Flow and the Psychology of Discovery and Invention* (New York: HarperPerennial, paperback edition, 1996).

9. Based on a personal communication on April 19, 2001.

10. Ted Selker's story is based on an interview recorded on April 18, 2001.

11. ABS brakes for cars are designed to modulate brake pressure on slippery roads and to do other things to give a safer response for a driver.

12. Dave Fork's story is based on an interview recorded on August 25, 2002.

13. From an interview by Kristi Helm ("Redefining the PC") in the *San Jose Mercury News*, Saturday, January 11, 2003.

14. Larry Leifer's quotation is from a personal communication on March 10, 2003.

Chapter 3

When You Build in the World, You Build in Your Mind

by Robert Rasmussen, Director, Business Development, Tufts Center for Engineering Outreach, Principal, Robert Rasmussen & Associates

With their multiple perspectives and insights, teams bring added value to resolving all manner of business challenges. But only if the dynamic among team members is collaborative, motivated, and informed. Robert Rasmussen reviews how Lego Serious Play facilitates this positive interaction and allows managers to tailor "real-time strategies" for moving through various kinds of decision-making situations.

"I AM WILLING to give this merger a chance, but I want to let you know that I brought my weapons just in case."

This was the opening statement from one of the managers in the service department of an entertainment company for which we were conducting a two-day merger workshop. This company had decided to merge two of its departments, but the climate between the two was hostile and untrusting. One department felt its contribution wasn't being valued, and the other tended to behave more like an acquiring company than an equal partner.

This was in 2001, during one of our real-life tests of LEGO Serious Play,[1] then in its final stages of development. Serious Play was the result of a challenge we had set for ourselves two years earlier: to design a thinking, communication, and problem-solving technique for teams.

But first:

WHY WORK IN TEAMS AT ALL?

Why do we gather designers in groups to deal with opportunities and challenges? We do it because we believe that working together in teams brings more value to the business than working as individuals. Teamwork offers the possibility that the insight and knowledge of each team member eventually becomes the insight and knowledge of the whole team and that this makes the team more confident in achieving its goals. However, increased insight and greater confidence don't bring value to the organization unless everyone on the team also commits to act as part of a shared effort. The goal of LEGO Serious Play, or LSP, is to encourage each individual's desire to make that commitment.

Our job is done when:

▲ New insights have been uncovered and the experience, knowledge, and understanding of each member have been accessed.

▲ Team members feel more confident and motivated to act on the knowledge that has been shared.

▲ Team members feel more committed to shared action.

▲ The team is better prepared to respond optimally to the unknown.

The central theme that emerged from our tests of the LSP idea was the importance of helping groups to see the entire system they are a part of in order to be better prepared for the future. By using this approach to build a complete picture of their current business system, including team roles, relationships, and culture, and by testing the system with future-specific scenarios, team members can gain insight, confidence, and commitment in dealing with complex business challenges (Figure 1).

Figure 1. "It made it easier to describe complex relationships in a complex process." . . . "LSP gave us a tool to have fierce conversations, interrogate reality, provoke learning, tackle tough issues, and enrich relationships." . . . "It equalized diversity and differences that were inherent in the group."

And as for the merger workshop, those two teams managed to successfully disarm themselves and remove all weapons from the table.

THE CONCEPT

Kjeld Kristiansen, owner and CEO of the LEGO Company, found himself dissatisfied with the results of his strategy sessions with LEGO staff. Although his business was about imagination, the results from these sessions were decidedly unimaginative. At the same time, Johann Roos and Bart Victor, professors at the International Institute for Management Development (IMD) in Lausanne, Switzerland, were noting similarly poor results in companies using traditional strategy development techniques. (The LEGO Company had for several years used IMD for executive and leadership development purposes.) When Kristiansen, Roos, and Victor connected, they noted their similar dilemmas, as well as the values they shared—which saw people as the key to company success and strategy as something you live rather than something stored away in a document.

In 1999, I was director of research and development for the educational division of the LEGO Company. I was asked to head a project to investigate the feasibility of applying LEGO bricks to the process of strategy development. When we realized that this idea could be more than just a hypothesis, our work moved into the development phase. Over the course of several years and after more than twenty iterations, our team made LEGO Serious Play the reproducible and robust methodology it is today.

TEAMS IN ACTION

The following example captures many of the organizational experiences that drove our work with the development of LSP.[2]

Let us consider a project team consisting of four persons. They gather in a meeting room. Here they interact, meaning that their individual effects multiply. We can illustrate the overall impact of the interaction through multiplication: $1 \times 1 \times 1 \times 1 = 1$.

In real life, however, things do not work that way, given the perceptions and beliefs that people have about one another.

Imagine a situation in which the first person to enter the meeting is a 50-year-old Finnish engineer, Jaska. Jaska is technically at the top of his game, but he's somewhat of an introvert and not comfortable with spoken English. As he comes in, he is thinking about 32-year-old Mark, an Australian engineer. Like many Aussies Jaska has known, Mark is incredibly self-assured and articulate—a man-of-the-world who believes he knows everything. Actually, Jaska finds him arrogant; he never listens, particularly to someone like Jaska, who is pretty awkward with spoken English. These thoughts make Jaska's entrance rather subdued. He comes into the room having lost some of his excitement and energy, with the result that 30 percent of his "edge" vanishes. He enters the room as a 0.7 rather than the 1 he should have been.

Mark approaches the room through another corridor, already demoralized by his expectations of this meeting. Finnish guys are such a depressive lot. They might be pretty good technically, but you would expect them to be able to say something without having three beers first. I'm tired of sitting in saunas all the time just to have a discussion. Let me try to be a little provocative today. Even so, by the time he walks into the room, Mark has shrunk to a 0.9.

The next team member to enter is Paula. She's a financial controller, who feels she always must act like a "tough broad" and finds that irritating. Of course, she can play that part, but she does it at the cost of some of her sensibilities. In truth, she is a 38-year-old loving mother of two fabulous children, but she can never talk about them with these guys, who seem to be so tough and task-oriented all the time. She, too, enters the room at less than a 1—let's say an 0.6.

The last to show up is John, a 54-year-old senior vice president of marketing. He's a bit weary already at the prospect of meeting with these young and hungry lions. They believe they command the world. He himself is not quite as eager as he once was to board the next plane to Hong Kong. He sighs, thinking, You would expect there to be some respect for experience in our company, and enters the room as a 0.8.

Each of the team members enters the room as less than a 1, and their interaction results in an outcome that can be summed up as follows: $0.7 \times 0.9 \times 0.6 \times 0.8 = 0.30$—a far cry from the $1 \times 1 \times 1 \times 1 = 1$ they could have achieved.

Imagine if it could have gone like this:

How lucky it is that Mark could make it to the meeting, thinks Jaska. Mark is so quick on his feet, and so articulate. And because Mark knows Jaska isn't all that comfortable with the English language and with situations in which you have to impress a lot of other people, he tends to cover for Jaska, who is now able to enter the room as a 1.3.

For his part, Mark is thinking he's lucky to have Jaska's technical expertise on his team. Jaska is shy and even a bit innocent, but he has tremendous integrity. And it feels great to be able to help him out in the language department, Mark thinks. When I was working in Australia, it never occurred to me that I was particularly articulate, but it sure helps here. Mark's thoughts give him a boost of some 20 percent, and he enters the room as a 1.2.

Imagine if Paula and John also enter the room uplifted by the projections they have of one another—adding another, let's say, 30 and 40 percent. The team's interaction multiplies the effects: $1.3 \times 1.2 \times 1.3 \times 1.4 = 2.83$.

THE KEY TO OPTIMIZING TEAMWORK

We have found that LSP builds a 2.83+ capacity into teams—and that teams can use this capacity to improve the quality and speed of their ongoing decision making, which again leads to faster and better implementation of solutions.

All too often, executive, design, and management teams work sub-optimally, which results in the following:

▲ Valuable knowledge remains untapped in team members.

▲ The team makes poor decisions based on illusion rather than reality.

▲ The team reacts to events unconsciously rather than consciously and
    with intention.

Using the LSP technique, individuals build three-dimensional models using a special mix of LEGO bricks designed to inspire the use of metaphors and story-making.
They build in response to questions on relevant challenges—everything from "What's
your vision for this project?" to "What's your worst nightmare for this design outsourc-
ing initiative?" to "How can we benefit from this technology?" Once the model is built,
members share its meaning and story with the rest of the team (Figure 2). The use of
metaphors, imagination, and story-telling is integral to the process. The culmination of
the whole exercise is a scenario-testing phase, which leads to action plans and guiding
principles for the team's decision-making on the fly.

Figure 2. This team felt they had a unique new technology product (symbolized by
the panda), but it wasn't selling. The LSP workshop helped them to realize what the
problem was. The team was very proud (the pink house) of their invention, but they
were also afraid of copycats, so they had become too protective (the panda in a
cage, fences all around, the team acting as guards in a last defense). The team could
see the customers (in the glass hut) and the customers could see the team, but the
two couldn't communicate with each other. Once the team understood the problem,
they could start playing what-if games (scenario testing). What if we removed the
guards? Who would be getting closer to our panda? What would happen to our panda? What could our guard people be doing instead? Would the fences be enough?
By playing out the consequences, the team was able to decide the best way in which
to get the panda out of its isolation and into the hands of the customers.

People naturally want to contribute—to be part of something bigger than themselves and to take ownership. And leaders don't have all the answers. Their success depends on hearing and engaging all the voices in the room. Design processes that allow each individual to contribute and speak out result in a more sustainable business. And the more people know about the system they are a part of and how they fit in, the more impact they can have in terms of input to discussions and decisions (Figure 3).

THE SCIENCE OF OPTIMIZED DESIGN TEAMWORK WITH LEGO SERIOUS PLAY

Research shows that people are changed significantly and irreversibly when movement, thought, and feeling fuse during the active pursuit of personal goals.[3] Learning is deeper and the experience becomes memorable, almost hard-wired. The limbic brain gets engaged. LSP users make use of multiple intelligences—visual-spatial intelligence, linguistic intelligence, and bodily kinesthetic intelligence—and discover what they didn't know they knew in a very direct manner. Quite simply, users bring the unconscious to the conscious by building, giving it meaning, and telling others the story of what they've built (Figure 4).

Figure 3. These team members had a hard time understanding the actions of their colleagues. Building a team system enabled them to see what was going on: "We all have responsibilities" (symbolized by the hats); "we each work with different tools" (symbolized by the tools); "there are external factors that affect us . . ." (the gear wheels) ". . . and force us to turn" (the meshing gears); "and although 'blue helmet' reports to 'red cap,' she is affected" (turns) "when the middle man" (top hat) "moves." From here, it was easy for the team to decide who should interact (mesh) directly and which in-between wheels could be moved or removed entirely.

Figure 4. In a team improvement workshop, one member built this model as her answer to "What is my best on this team?" Her story: "It depends on which of my multiple heads is most appropriate for the situation." When the facilitator asked her why she had placed all the heads on top of her real head, she reflected for a minute and then said, "I guess that must mean I believe I am at my best when I can use all my heads all the time."

LSP was greatly influenced by work done by Seymour Papert, a founding faculty member of MIT's Media Lab. Papert gave us the theory of constructionism, which proposes that we gain knowledge when we construct something external to ourselves. Papert was also interested in concrete thinking—thinking with and through tangible objects. Research has shown that the use of objects as part of an inquiry process can make hidden thought more discussable. Building external models that can be examined, shared, and discussed makes it easier to construct internal mental maps. When you build in the world, you build in your mind.

LEGO Serious Play uses an etiquette that ensures all participants have a chance to express their own viewpoint before being influenced by the rest of the group (Figure 5). In a meeting, when a question for group investigation is posed, some members of the group typically think and speak more quickly than others. This immediately determines how the conversation proceeds. Often, the rest of the group do not finish their own thinking or express their thoughts. Having everyone in the group "build" an answer to an initial question avoids that short-circuit, while simultaneously providing an enriched way for individuals to express their thoughts. Use of physical constructs enhances the

Figure 5. This is a metaphor used by a designer to express that the company's decision-making was inefficient and dominated by outdated thinking and turf wars. LSP focuses attention on the model, not on the creator of the model. Hence the environment remains safe, even in the face of emotionally charged issues. LSP allows "dark spots" in the conversation to be more openly discussed by separating the speaker from what he is saying. He is, after all, just describing a model.

depth and clarity of individual contribution to the conversation. Our experience with LSP has shown that the best insights in a team come from the individuals who don't normally share what they are thinking.

REAL-TIME STRATEGIES

My colleagues at LEGO originally posed this question: How can we be better prepared as a design team to respond intentionally and optimally in the moment, all the time? Here's what we learned: Develop and use real-time strategies to support your ongoing decision-making process.

Most design teams, as well as other executive teams, live in an unpredictable environment, where changes happen faster than the speed of planning. It is difficult to plan ahead and make predictions about the future. Yet to run a successful business, you need to heed the landscape continuously and be prepared for the unknown so you can decide to change directions in the blink of an eye (Figure 6).

A real-time strategy is expressed as a dynamic and continuously changing set of simple, guiding principles that improve the speed and quality of the team's day-to-day

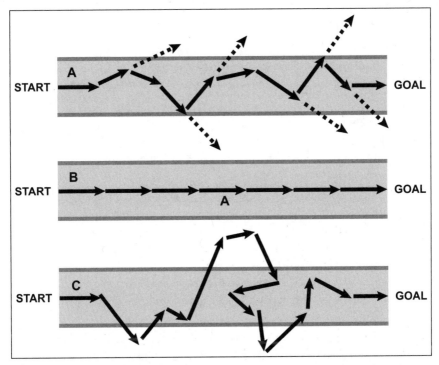

Figure 6. (A) Real-time strategies are for teams that need to continuously strategize. The real-time strategy informs the team when it is time to change course and in which new direction the team should aim. (B) What we like to believe is possible—and which can indeed be the case when the landscape is highly predictable. (C) What the reality often looks like—a situation that easily leads to frustration and conflict.

critical decision-making and helps the team stay on track when deciding on a choice of action. They are not instructions that tell the team and its members what to do or how to do it. Instead, they specify where to look, and in what spirit and direction solutions must be chosen in order to achieve the goals.

HOW TO DEVELOP A REAL-TIME STRATEGY

A design team can have multiple real-time strategies, each one guiding decision-making pertaining to a specific field. Examples might be blending in-house and consultant staffing; dealing with the expanding breadth of expertise needed; communications with customers and within the design group; or how to keep staff motivated, creative, and up to speed on design trends.

Getting to the simple guiding principles for your real-time strategy happens through a one-to-two-day tailored LSP workshop. It is a four-step process for the team, in this order:

1. What is going on right now? This step involves building and defining the current identity and nature of the issue and the landscape of the business system it is part of. It is a bit like a complete, real-time SWOT (strength, weaknesses, opportunities, threat) analysis in 3D.

2. Imaging the future. This is what-if brainstorming, imagining what could happen in the future that might have a direct or indirect impact on the issue—something that, if it happened, would give us opportunities to act or force us to act.

3. Scenario testing. We imagine that the future what-ifs happen today and use the 3D LEGO landscape to play out the impact. We test which decisions and actions we would take and why we would choose those decisions and actions.

4. Extracting simple guiding principles. By playing out and scenario-testing which decisions affected the systems favorably and studying why that was the case, the team can extract the principles they want to guide their future decision-making. These become the guidelines that can ensure that each design team member makes wise decisions, even when situations are complex and new. They are the team member's beacons of light in stormy seas, a tool that allows for the group to act optimally and with intention in the face of the unexpected.

Here is what the management team in a company facing severe competition and a sharp decline in sales extracted as their "beacons of light" for improving their competitiveness in an uncertain future:

▲ Tip the sacred cows.

▲ Take risks with good intent.

▲ Improve technical skills.

- ▲ Mobilize ten brains instead of only one.
- ▲ Build trust, build trust, build trust!
- ▲ Make sure we can implement.

On their own, these simple guiding principles as a real-time strategy can seem like basic platitudes. How do they specify "where to look, and in what spirit and direction solutions must be chosen?" The deeper meaning in each statement is only understood by the team members, who extracted them through the four-step process explained above. The statements below capture the lessons they learned from their scenario testing.

Tip the sacred cows: Embodies the strategic discovery that new solutions radically different from those the team currently favor played out much better than expected. Moving forward, the team therefore wanted to make sure they constantly challenged current practice and looked for radical new ways of operating.

Take risks with good intent: The scenario testing showed that a strategy aiming for radical changes to current practice meant taking risks. This simple guiding principle should remind the team that it is okay to take risks, as long as you continuously heed and assess those risks.

Improve technical skills and mobilize ten brains instead of only one: This part of the real-time strategy captures the insight that coming up with radical new ways of doing things requires prioritizing the use of resources, including time. Priority should be given to improving technical skills to avoid wasting valuable time by working in isolation.

Build trust, build trust, build trust: Playing in the workshop, the impact of the best scenario decisions revealed the high importance of the human factor. Trust emerged as the glue that could keep the business system from collapsing under the heavy load of changes (Figure 7). Whether a decision increases or decreases the level of trust should therefore be top of mind again, again, and again.

Figure 7. Build trust, build trust, build trust.

Make sure we can implement: The management team discovered during the workshop that coming up with new radical operating ideas was easy. Playing out various implementation approaches exposed the weak ideas. Consequently, the team realized that checking the implementation strategy early on would be a good way to weed out the less promising ideas.

A real-time strategy's simple guiding principles are a dynamic strategic tool. They need to be continuously checked for usefulness. Six months on, the team ran such a check and replaced three of their original principles with others they found more helpful in dealing with new situations.

SUMMARY

Results from dozens of organizations over the past five years have lived up to our aspirations for LEGO Serious Play and the real-time strategy idea. This approach is particularly adept at leveling the playing field so that the power of a team's diverse resources and competencies can be realized. The depth of knowledge and wisdom in groups is typically left untapped. Groups have access to plenty of information, yet it is knowledge that businesses lack—information applied to a specific context. And even more than knowledge, organizations yearn for the wisdom that builds confidence and commitment to shared action.

It is my experience that the most motivated and effective teams are those that embrace the ever-changing nature of their roles and responsibilities. They operate in a highly dynamic and constantly changing business landscape, where it is almost impossible to predict the future with any degree of certainty. One can prepare for the unexpected by constructing new knowledge, by sharing meaning with others, and by maintaining an open, poised, and curious attitude toward change. LEGO Serious Play is a process tool that prepares teams emotionally to embrace change.

Endnotes

1. LEGO® and Serious Play™ are trademarks of the LEGO Company.

2. Thanks to J. T. Bergqvist, a senior executive in the Nokia Corporation, for help with this story.

3. Wilson, Frank R. *The Hand: How Its Use Shapes the Brain, Language, and Human Culture.* New York, NY: Pantheon Books, 1998.

Chapter 4

Driving Creativity and Innovation Through Culture

by **Anne Archer,** Manager Account Services, Optima USA
and **Doris Walczyk,** Brand Strategist, Optima USA

An organization's traditions and values can inspire people to excel. At Optima Group, Anne Archer and Doris Walczyk explain how the consultancy guards its inclusive, flat structure as a way to attract the best talent. The company recognizes and rewards all those who contribute great ideas. Business and social activities overlap to nurture trust, respect, community, and out-of-the-box thinking that support exceptional client results.

CORPORATE CULTURE IS made up of a complex mix of the employee and corporate beliefs, attitudes, values, rituals, and behaviors that permeate a company and give it its unique personality. It has surfaced as one of the most compelling factors in characterizing, leading, and managing any organization.

Culture can attract the best employees and maintain their loyalty. It can rally people around an important belief or shape the definition of a corporate brand. Despite its impact, corporate culture is not always given sufficient weight or consideration, and its effects are underestimated primarily because they are difficult to measure.

In cases in which a culture springs organically from the nature of a passionate and focused leader, the company's whole existence hinges on its cultural heritage. On the other hand, many companies struggle to define the values that underpin their cultures, and many more wrestle with how culture should be articulated within the organization—beyond dressing up or down on Fridays.

CULTURE AND CREATIVE INSPIRATION

The design industry relies heavily on a strong corporate culture. Nowhere does culture have a more direct impact than in a company where creativity and innovation represent the livelihood of the organization. At the same time, the mechanism that inspires creative people to come up with the perfect design is hardly the same as the one that inspires a salesperson to make a big sale. Creative inspiration, unlike a sales commission, is something that cannot be artificially generated or demanded.

Management expert Peter Drucker observed that knowledge workers (also known as creative workers) do not respond to financial incentives, orders, or negative sanctions. Drucker writes that the key to managing these workers is to treat them as people whose commitment is highly contingent and whose motivation comes largely from within. In order to generate genuine inspiration or passion naturally, a company has to start at the core.

CULTURE AND COMMUNITY

Optima Group USA is a brand identity firm located on the North Shore of Chicago. From the start, the company's culture is taken very seriously. This is because its ability to attract and retain gifted creative people is a direct result of the culture it has created. From the outset, applicants are evaluated not only for their skill set but also for their ability to fit into the group. From this perspective, the ideal cultural fit is a person who has respect for others, a sense of community, and that good old Midwestern work ethic. "It doesn't matter if we're filling a design position or an administrative position—we want good people with a sense of humor. We're not so much about individual accomplishments as we are about team accomplishments," says Ann Werner, one of the founding partners.

To this end, Werner and partner Lyle Zimmerman encourage group activities that help build a strong bond among its twenty employees. Themed potluck lunches are a staple, and summer months are full of activities such as annual Cubs baseball and Ravinia Music Festival outings. Bowling night is a fun way to incorporate families and significant others, and children and dogs make frequent appearances in the office. From a more professional viewpoint, the founding partners have taken into account the fact that Optima is not located in Chicago's downtown, where culture, shopping, and entertainment are always a short walk away. The company tries to counteract this in several ways. Whenever we grow and need to relocate, we make sure we find a space close to a train line so that the employees who live downtown (and in Wisconsin!) have a convenient way of getting to the office. The company even bought scooters for employees who motor down to Lake Michigan in good weather. "We want our people to be fulfilled and happy," says Zimmerman, "and we've become like an extended family. We care about them as individuals, not just as employees. It's all about quality of life."

Each year, two designers, on a rotating basis, attend a major design conference in order to learn about design trends and renew their creative spirits. One staff person is currently on sabbatical on the West Coast. Optima has design partners in Latin America, Europe, Asia, and Africa, and plans are forming for a work exchange program.

OUR WORLD IS FLAT

Two fundamentally interrelated traits mark the corporate culture at Optima.

First, we are an organization that is very flat. All our employees are privy to CEO-level information regarding how the company is doing, plans for the future, and so on. We try to be as supportive and employee-focused as possible. We believe that good ideas can come from anyone.

Second, we operate under an atmosphere of mutual respect, social consciousness, and uninhibited creativity. By stressing the underlying value of individual creativity, Optima has made itself extremely attractive to both demanding clients and talented employees.

The employee-focused, uninhibited, values-infused culture is a direct product of the personalities, visions, and efforts of the company's founders. They started the business conscious of their own dissatisfaction with traditional management practices and the limitations placed on creativity and personal fulfillment. "I don't think you can get the best out of people when they feel uncomfortable, stifled, or devalued," says Zimmerman.

Social consciousness and respect for others permeates the organization at many levels. Optima participates in projects that contribute to the community and bring greater personal meaning to the everyday work environment. "We're not just about brand identity. We're about human relationships, and those have to be recognized at many different levels. If we can be good people while doing our job, so much the better. And that's what everyone here aspires to be—good people, and then good designers," Werner notes.

It is an attitude that informs everything the company does. "My most critical personnel challenges have been in relation to marketing and sales personnel, whose view of our business and of our company's role with our clients can be very different from our own view," says Zimmerman. If an account exec attempts to please clients by giving them what they want, rather than challenging them to find out what they really need, the company runs the risk of missing out on an opportunity to realize a brand's potential.

OPTIONS FOR REWARDING SUCCESS

Optima team members are rewarded on multiple levels. The more promise an employee shows, the more decision-making options are open to him or her. We let employees guide their own destiny. One senior creative director, who had been in the business for years and who had helped build the company, decided she wanted a more flexible schedule. She has Fridays off. She earned that.

An open-forum structure encourages proactive efforts and free exchange of ideas. Individual efforts are continually recognized and credited in order to promote growth and success for individuals and the group. In other words, the more successful the team becomes, the more successful the team members become, and vice versa. A good model for this was the Chicago Bulls championship team. Even though the team relied on individual stars such as Michael Jordan, the focus was on elevating the entire team, which in turn yielded much greater rewards than any single player could have ever achieved by himself.

Each individual feels important, and each is treated with the same respect, regardless of status in the company. We are all friends, and we take care of one another. We believe that good ideas can come from anyone. Consequently, when we have brainstorming sessions, everyone participates, not just the designers. Similarly, everyone is given a say in the types of clients we go after. For example, our new business director recently asked each employee for a wish list of dream clients. Those are the companies she's concentrating on. The list included traditional consumer packaged goods companies, cosmetics companies, sporting goods firms, and wineries. Each person's list reflected his or her own personal interests and backgrounds, and there weren't many overlaps!

THE FORCE OF THE FUTURE

To ensure a steady course, Optima consistently adheres to the values and practices on which it was founded. Without fail, employees receive recognition and respect for their individual talents, and as a result clients consistently receive superior service and creativity. By listening carefully to employees and clients, Optima is able to remain relevant and competitive in a difficult and crowded marketplace. Because change is taken seriously, careful thought is given to any changes that could break down what we've built through hard work and dedication. For us, culture has become a way of life.

LEVERAGING CULTURE FOR A COMPETITIVE EDGE

High-profile projects are thrown open to every designer on staff, not just the ones with the most seniority. Everyone contributes to the conceptual development phase; this way everyone feels he or she can contribute to key jobs, and the client has the benefit of the widest range of thinking and experiences possible. It would be safer not to do it this way, but if we didn't, individual growth would be hampered and wonderful solutions "from the mouths of babes" might otherwise go undiscovered.

Clients count on a strong creative product, and the only way for a team to deliver it is for every member to feel vested in every project. In order to make this a reality, Optima's designers are given the freedom to explore without unnecessary constraints that might stifle individual expression. The company's flat, open organizational structure avoids making people feel micro-managed or hindered. Designers are encouraged to work in free-flowing teams, as long as they stay on track with the project's objectives.

Optima recently worked on a project for a brand that had no clear identity and had found itself competing with private-label brands. The competition was doing a much better job at communicating to, and connecting with, the consumer. The client needed to bring new consumers into the franchise without alienating its existing and loyal user base. At the same time, consumers were unsure what this brand stood for.

The challenge was to make the package more relevant to consumers without over-promising.

Optima had created some designs, and the client had evaluated them but had no plans for further research. Because the brand had no equity to speak of, Optima suggested a revolutionary packaging change. The client had worked with another design firm on a previous "refreshing" of its packaging, but that design had been too incremental, and it failed to move the needle in terms of sales. Optima strongly believed consumer input was crucial, and at the eleventh hour, the client agreed to get the packaging concepts in front of consumers. Concepts were tested to see which ones delivered a stronger "flavor story" and made the brand more relevant to core users (lower-income, mostly rural families). But in addition, the client wanted to bring new, younger users into the franchise.

This is where things really got creative. The first thing Optima did was to put an ad on Craig's List looking for respondents. This mega-popular Web site was a bold experiment that paid off big in terms of getting a lot of respondents quickly. In the first 24 hours, we had 101 responses. Staff members also called friends, family, and neighbors in the target market, and within two days we had written a discussion guide and recruited about thirty people for one-on-one interviews. The client was impressed that we were able to pull research together so quickly.

As sometimes happens, the project was put on hold before the design was finalized so that the client could make some capital improvements needed to support the relaunch.

Case Study: Miller Lite

Miller Brewing Company's introduction of Miller Lite changed the beer industry forever with its invention of a light beer in 1975. However, within several years competition had driven Lite from first to fourth place in market share. Miller hired Optima to update its secondary packaging (cartons, six-pack carriers, and so on). However, after the briefing and some initial investigation, Optima realized that a much bigger opportunity was available and proposed that Miller drastically reposition the brand instead.

Young Optima staffers hit local bars with video cameras to meet the consumer where he drank and to bring back real-world consumer insights, not contrived focus-group data. This guerrilla-style research was encouraged by Optima's partners and embraced by the staff. They gained a real understanding of the brand's positioning, personality, equities, and consumer perceptions. What they found out was that Miller Lite was considered "my dad's beer." Miller had lost relevance with their target consumers—21- to 27-year-old males.

At the initial creative presentation, Optima presented Miller management with badges that read, "I'm not the target market." This gently humorous reminder helped everyone lay their personal preferences aside and get down to the business of rebuilding

Although the first true light beer, Miller Lite's competitors had caught up with it. Optima helped Miller to update its packaging so that it was no longer "my father's beer."

the brand. The result of this outside-the-box approach to design was a bold, dynamic new look that infused the brand with energy and modernity and pushed it back up to the number two position among all light beers.

Case Study: Bun Meals

Our client, Forkless Gourmet, was in a fix. The preferred design and part of the product flavor profile for their new Bun Meals were in question. The product launch was imminent; they didn't have time to do the research, hire a firm, or wait for the results, but Forkless Gourmet was not comfortable moving forward without talking to consumers. In one-and-a-half days, Optima pulled thirty women aged 25 to 50 into the studio for research. We contacted mothers, sisters, friends, and neighbors within the target audience and interviewed them on-site in our conference room. Once we got through twelve of the respondents, it became clear which design system was the winner and which flavors the consumers liked.

Being flexible and fast and thinking out of the box helped our client to make important decisions. The company debuted at the Fancy Food Show in Chicago last year and received a lot of media attention.

Case Study: Axe Body Spray

Corporate culture is more than just casual Fridays and bowling parties. It's a state of mind that shapes your perspective, your thinking, and your actions. It's how you see and interact with the world.

For example, when Axe, the world's number-one-selling deodorant for men, made the bold move to launch in North America, it had no road map, no precedent, and no fixed set of rules to follow. On the other hand, to become a leader, you cannot follow. It might sound trite or overly simplistic, and of course it's easier said than done.

Optima, because of its unique corporate culture, was able to help Axe write its own rules. The company's challenge went beyond merely introducing a new brand. It had to create a new category for the US—men's body sprays—and change the way consumers think about personal hygiene. No small task.

No one in North America had ever heard of body sprays and they didn't care about Axe. Not yet. Axe was not about controlling odor and wetness; it was all about smelling awesome and getting the girl. So new rules were written and new methods adopted, along with new ways of working, gathering information, and reaching decisions. Con-

Body sprays for men was a new idea when Axe targeted the North American market. Optima's research into a young and male target demographic helped to make Axe a huge hit.

ventional corporate culture was abandoned. Axe was all about young men: fickle, skeptical, unpredictable, unconventional young men.

Research took place in dorm rooms. Focus groups were pizza parties with video games and Web surfing. House parties were held to see how young men interacted with young women in a real-life setting. Brand managers got a new perspective. Armed with firsthand knowledge of what makes young men tick, they launched the brand in the US. Packaging supported high-impact point-of-purchasing displays and advertising that is now legendary. Axe was a huge hit, and within a few years, competitors started popping up on shelf.

CULTURE IN ACTION

Naturally, not all agency-client collaborations have happy endings. If their corporate cultures are too disparate, they may not mesh, and both client and agency end up feeling frustrated. It's a lot like dating. Sometimes it takes one or two projects, working together, to get to know each other, to build trust and a comfort level. And, also like dating, sometimes those differences create a positive tension and opportunity for growth. Other times, it's a recipe for disaster.

If both agency and client are too rigid in their approach, the project may suffer or stall altogether. Flexibility, openness, and respect for all participants are important. Finding a common connection is key. Timing, workflow, tolerance for risk—all contribute to a successful collaboration.

Equally important is knowing when to say when. Both agency and client need to understand their roles and duties and to stick to them. "We once turned down a huge project from an important client," explains Zimmerman. "It was a tough decision, but in the end we felt it was just not a good match for us. The project did not allow for the creative latitude we needed to do the job justice. It was a lot of money and it was difficult to walk away. In the long run, we benefited by earning that client's respect and ultimately more work, as well."

"If I had to sum up our corporate culture, I'd say, 'We have fun,'" Werner adds. "For one client that was marketing a sports drink, we created a special suitcase-sized sales kit for the product that was housed in a stadium-like box with crowds of people inside. Hidden within the crowd were both myself and my partner, our studio manager, and two of our creative directors. It was just something frivolous and fun to do, keeping spirits light and not taking ourselves too seriously."

Chapter 5

Integrating Design Into Organizational Culture

by **Thomas Lockwood,** President, DMI

This is a story of design in action. Referencing several mini-case studies, Thomas Lockwood demonstrates the integral relationship between design and corporate success. Of even greater value, however, is his distillation of seven ways organizations can approach design to make the most of this resource. Moreover, because one option does not preclude the others, executives and managers can use all seven!

ASK 20 BUSINESS executives whether design is a business resource, and if the answer is not "What?" it probably will be "Yes." But ask how design can best support business strategy and innovation or how design and other business activities should interact or how to measure the impact of design on the bottom line or how the benefits of design can be infused throughout the corporate culture, and you'll find that answers to these questions are much harder to come by. And yet it is these answers that make design a business resource, with the power to affect business objectives in tangible ways.

To help us to get better, more practicable answers to these questions, I interviewed several design managers about using design as a business resource and about the integration of design into business culture. These managers came from many of the companies that emerged as design performance leaders in my PhD research on integrated design management (see the sidebar on page 50, "Design in Business Global Top 20").

Since we've all seen examples of successful design work, I decided to focus on the ways design management can successfully lead the design output in order to make it a business resource. There are many ways to use design organizational success. Here are seven examples.

Levi Strauss: Design That Became an American Icon

Since 1873, Levi's has been the original worker's jean, and an icon of design.[1] Icons, which often align with rebel subcultures, represent collective human experience and a collective conscience. So how does an iconic design like Levi's jeans remain meaningful to today's customers? The answer is the continuation of good design.

And design comes in all sizes and shapes—literally. At Levi's, design is research-based and customer-centric. According to Caroline Calvin, vice president and creative director at Levi-Strauss, "We recently redid all our fits and construction features, undertaking a meticulous fit-testing process—something like 15,000 fit tests. That led to a complete redesign of the product line: refitting, reconstructing, making the jeans tougher, and making our design details more pronounced." The result is a resurgence of interest in the Levi's brand, with increased equity measures.

The design management process at Levi Strauss is integrated within the company's brand values: "It's synergistic," says Calvin. "The Levi's brand has a persona based on

At Levi's, designs like the Superlow 534 help the brand link between their traditional design and materials and the new styling of fashion design. (Photo courtesy of Rethmeyer Photography)

our design, and our design starts with our brand values." But at the same time, this makes innovation a challenge for Levi's. As the category originator, it's difficult to maintain the company's heritage and still meet the expected values of current customers, while also innovating and attracting new customers. Therefore the Levi's design management process includes core design teams to maintain the base styles, but it also takes on strategic, "quick-release" projects, allowing the company to release something new every six weeks. That's six weeks—from trend analysis to concept design, to fit design, to manufacturing, to distribution, and into stores throughout the United States.

And it seems to work. For example, according to Levi's, the incredibly widespread fashion of "low-rise" jeans originated with Levi's design. The development of low-rise was a liberation of functionalism, and in this regard, Levi's design is akin to a continuation of the Memphis design movement. It is a blending of sociology and marketing in the development of iconic Americana jeanswear and a blending of styles, from functionalist to cosmopolitan. At Levi's, design is a strategic resource.

Heineken: Innovative Packaging Design and Aluminum Bottles

At Heineken International, design is a business resource. According to Martien Heijmink, director of design and innovation, "It's about managing the coherency of the brand." Heijmink doesn't worry much about what he calls "design cop" jobs, "like the company calendar or the company tie," but he pays serious attention to the contribution of design to the objectives of the organization. Through best practice in design management, focus groups called "brew sessions," and comprehensive briefs, the Heineken brand is on the road to becoming iconic. Heijmink claims Heineken is the only beer brand that is focused on design, and he has results to back up his claim.

The innovative use of materials and design, such as the new aluminum bottle and keg-like cans enable a tactile dimension, so that consumers have a full sensory experience with the Heineken brand.

DESIGN IN BUSINESS GLOBAL TOP 20

For this study I developed a Design Performance Leadership™ model, which is a method to evaluate brands based on their design performance. The results suggest that one brand is the best in the world at using design as a business resource.

BMW was the only company to score well in all seven categories measured. During the research period from 2002 to 2003, BMW increased its brand value, received numerous awards for product and communications design, and was consistently ranked as outstanding by four different peer group measurements.

First Place

BMW	Germany

Only one company scored well in all seven categories.

Close runners up

Adidas	Germany
Apple	United States
Armani	Italy
Harley-Davidson	United States
Nike	United States
Samsung	S. Korea
Starbucks	United States

All of these brands scored well in six categories.

Honorable mentions

Canon	Japan
Caterpillar	United States
Dell	United States
Heineken	Netherlands
FedEx	United States
IBM	United States
IKEA	Sweden
Microsoft	United States
MTV	United States
Nokia	Finland
Prada	Italy
Sony	Japan

All of these brands scored well in four to five categories.

These twenty companies represent the best-of-class brands. Each has demonstrated exceptional performance in applying design as a business resource.

DESIGN IN BUSINESS GLOBAL TOP 20

Research Methodology
To attempt to measure the effectiveness of design in business, seven data points were evaluated in three criteria categories.

Business Performance Criteria
The first screening criteria were companies that merited a place on Interbrand's Global 100 Brand Scorecard; they ranked in the top 100 for global brand value. A second brand performance measure was added by also scoring those brands that had increased their brand value ranking over the previous year.

Design Performance Criteria
A second criterion was determined on the basis of design awards received and peer recognition. Methodology included product design awards from IDSA, communications design awards from Communication Arts magazine annuals, and a survey of design managers of different disciplines from the US, Korea, and Italy offices of Design Continuum, a leading international design consultancy, regarding each company's performance in design excellence, design innovation, and design synergy.

Design Management Performance Criteria
A third criterion was determined on the basis of design manager peer recognition. Methodology included a survey of design managers attending the 2002 DMI annual US conference, the 2003 DMI annual European conference, four design manager focus groups, and a survey of design managers from PARK, a leading design management consultancy, regarding each company's performance in design excellence, design innovation, and design synergy.

Future Research
My intent is to continue to refine this research model, and work with the Synergy Design Lab™ to further evaluate the contribution of design to business performance and the triple-bottom line, for both large organizations and SME's.

The author acknowledges that this study represents only a sample of the universe, and some of the measurements are interpretive by the respondents. Nonetheless, a disciplined methodology was applied and numerous independent data points were collected.

Recently, Heineken introduced two new packaging containers that have made measurable contributions to revenue. A new aluminum can, distinctively shaped like a little keg barrel, is now shipping all around the world. Heijmink explains, "When we introduced the new design, we had lots of people in the production areas asking why. But the package form not only delivers a new tactile dimension, it also immediately provides an opportunity to distinguish the brand from its competitors. It's easily recognized by sight and by feel, and it contributes significantly to the brand experience. The design resonates at the functional, aesthetic, and emotional levels." Although some might see changing the container packaging of a production line that produces five million units an hour as a bit risky, Heineken is truly committed to design.

A second Heineken package design now coming out in stores worldwide is an aluminum can shaped like a bottle. It's a beautiful form, with the company's simple red-star logo on a green and silver background. The container was first test-marketed in France with tremendous success. "It was only available in super high-end outlets," says Heijmink, "and it made beer relevant again for trendy young consumers. It brought beer to places where it never had been." There is something gratifying about the fact that by superior design management and superior design execution, Heineken is able to sell more beer in France, of all places!

Microsoft: Sub-brands, Usability, and Common Platform Design

Microsoft uses information design as a resource. It uses a sub-brand architecture: an endorsed identity system, with eight different sub-brands. Generally, in a sub-brand architecture, the sub-brands each have their own individual design style.[2] For example, although many GM cars share parts, from a visual point of view there is little in common among Chevys, Cadillacs, Corvettes, Pontiacs, Saabs, and Saturns. Not so at Microsoft. Although each sub-brand has unique design elements, they all share a common visual style, which is intentionally consistent for the benefit of their users.

According to Jeff Boettcher, creative director of branding, Microsoft has "distinct business groups that are empowered to build their own brands, product experiences, innovative technology, and designs. It's a very entrepreneurial environment. But to realize the full potential of these brands, the design has to overlap," in common user interface and icon design. Whether the products are for home users, business users, or professional IT personnel, they all share a certain visual style, communicated via a pictorial system of icons.

Nadja Haldimann, art director and product design lead for Microsoft Office, says that Microsoft looks at icons as if they were type fonts, pictures, or pictograms. The trick, she says, "is to decide on the essence of the feature, then determine how to visually demonstrate that essence. The metaphor must be precisely correct." Imagine a tiny sixteen-by-sixteen-pixel pictogram on a toolbar, which must communicate a specific task or function by linking the image with your memory of the actual experience of that thing. Now multiply this by more than 6,000 icons for Office, Windows XP, and various server products, and it's easy to understand the complexity of this design management challenge. Branding director Boettcher describes this task as one of utilizing virtual brand and design teams, integration teams, and engagement managers to "make things fit together."

Of course, humans have been transmitting information through wordless signs for some 30,000 years, so this isn't a new idea. Even so, I think the idea of using interface and icon design to provide a better experience for your customers, regardless of brand architecture, is utilizing design as a business resource.

British Airways: Increased Market Share With Design

British Airways turned to design to increase its business-class customer traffic. Led by Mike Crump, head of design management, its first task was to study the needs of its long-distance-travel customers. The resulting outcome was the first business-class seating arrangement to allow customers to lie down and sleep on a fully flat surface—a real benefit for long flights, and one that has helped grow market share in business-class travel. BA launched Club World seating on several routes and soon found its revenue increasing on those routes by more than 30 percent. As Crump points out, "The seating design redefined the business-class offering and revolutionized the sector. It helped British Airways realize the influence design could have on business performance."

British Airways is committed to good design throughout the organization. Design was a key factor in the building of the company's new headquarters, which was meant to act as a catalyst for culture change within the organization—to create a more open and trusting working environment. The architecture of the building has a "village street" central feature, which helps to ensure human interaction. According to Crump, "The customer, as well as the employer, is at the heart of all our design programs. Customers are engaged from initial research and throughout the design development program."

Throughout the flat-bed-seating project, BA created a small "customer family" team to help with the design and development. Involving customers, says Crump, enables the design team to really understand customer needs and aspirations, and is helping the company to maintain its position as global leader.

StorageTek: Design Improved Employee Creativity

When I was the global brand and design director at StorageTek, we used design as a business resource to improve employee creativity and to build corporate culture. In 2003, a human resources professional, a facilities expert, and myself, representing brand and design, formed a small cross-functional team. Our objective was to overhaul all the common spaces at our headquarters campus. This consisted of 1.8 million square feet of industrial and office facilities, including ten buildings, eighty-two conference rooms, twenty-four lobbies, three cafeterias, customer and training areas, and a maze of corridors.

We named the project Great Company, Great Place. We knew we could drive design improvements that would make employees proud. What we didn't predict was the measured improvement of employee creativity as a result of our interior design project.

With limited resources, our strategy was to focus on paint, carpet, lights, and art—lots of art.

First, we secured corporate approval, expanded the work team, developed a contemporary color palette, and painted everything in sight. Then we had all the carpet replaced with colorful carpet tiles, creating interesting patterns and diagrams, and built structures at department thresholds. Next, we improved the existing lighting and added new lighting to showcase the 400 pieces of art we brought in. Now our collection has grown to over 800 pieces, including 330 originals from Colorado artists.

The result? StorageTek was selected by the Colorado Business Committee for the Arts as the leading supporter of the arts in Colorado. Our CEO accepted the award at an important community banquet. What's more, we've measured the results with two employee surveys. More than 50 percent of our employees say that the corporate art program improves their creativity at work, 72 percent say it reduces stress, and 84 percent say it improves their mood or attitude. In this way, design is becoming a more meaningful part of our corporate culture. We have an art curator, Ted Jobe, who summarizes, "The art program provides a visually stimulating workplace that increases employee creativity and productivity."

Design can be a resource in many ways. As this demonstrates, the results can be measured by employee creativity, satisfaction, and corporate reputation.

Nike: Corporate Culture and the Sport of Design Competition

Nike is one of the few corporate brands that claims superior design performance as a core value. The company sponsors quarterly Design Days, maintains a dedicated design library, and supports an executive Corporate Design Council. What's more, company executives at the highest levels endorse design excellence as key to achieving Nike's corporate goal: the "endless pursuit to make the right product to improve athletic performance." Nike gets it.

Design is not only a resource, it's also a big part of the competitive nature of Nike's culture. According to Ron Dumas, creative director for image at Nike Golf, "If you are not on top of your design game, you're not going to be playing, and you are not going to design a successful product. It forces the entire team to step up and be demanding. We love the challenge, and that's what makes our products better. I mean, if you can make it for Tiger Woods, you can make it for anybody else."

Nike's design management process has a nice balance between formal and informal. The company has innovation sessions it calls "sandbox meetings." Management develops concepts and then forms three-person product development teams consisting of a designer, an engineer, and a marketer. Once a project is well defined, says Dumas, the design team is expanded to include industrial design, engineering design, and graphic design specialists. "We get inspiration from all aspects of culture," he explains. "We look at other objects that are beautifully designed. We try to understand the values and traditions of the sport we're designing for, and then we add innovative materials to increase performance. In the end, it's all about using design to increase performance."

One example is Nike's new Slingshot golf irons. Senior designer Carl Madore notes that "the center of gravity, the CG, of most golf clubs is within the club face. However,

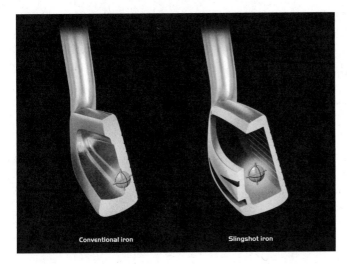

Products like the Slingshot club, shown in ideation phase and final design cut-a-way, help Nike to realize the benefits of its commitment to innovative design.

Conventional iron   Slingshot iron

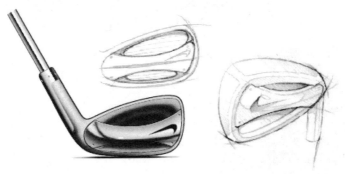

the CG of the Slingshot irons is suspended in air beyond the thickness of the face. This launches the ball higher and makes it easier to square the club face. It's all made possible by the use of a custom material that makes the face thinner, stronger, and faster. The weight savings is repositioned further back, which enhances perimeter weighting and results in a greater moment of inertia and less twisting." Here is a design that's true to brand values—a strategic resource.

Starbucks: To Own Your Brand is to Own Your Design

What do a good cup of coffee and good design have in common? At Starbucks, just about everything.

From the blends of its coffees, to its packaging, to its espresso equipment, to its store fixtures, furnishings, and graphics—the entire experience is all designed by Starbucks. It's a simple corporate philosophy: If you want to own your brand, you have to own your design. As vice president and creative director Robert Wong explains, "At Starbucks, the experience drives everything. So we design the experience. Design is part of our inner DNA—it's a strategic advantage. Because design is core to our business, we've invested in our design group."

As a result, Starbucks has developed very sophisticated design management processes structured to enable the right design—not just to follow design standards. Design management at Starbucks believes that culturally relevant brands need to be alive. The company's design system is based on shared knowledge, and the design department's work process is based on frequent interactions among design teams. Says Wong: "To support a charismatic brand that is alive and evolving, the process must be one of high contact. We look at all the work, together, every week."

If your business is all about experience, why wouldn't design be a business resource? And here's an interesting brand "guardrail." Yes, Starbucks could add more merchandise to its stores, and add more signage to promote it. After all, the store is there anyhow, and so is the customer. But Starbucks has discovered how to manage design very carefully in order to create the correct experience for its customers. Not more, not less, but just right—by design, because design is core to that corporate culture.

Analysis

While there are many ways in which corporations can use design as a business resource, I have identified seven common themes that emerge from these mini cases, from the easiest to the most difficult to achieve.

Organizational Structure

In each of these seven cases, the design functions were located appropriately within the organizational structure to enable effective design. For this to occur, each company must first recognize that design has a strategic value to the business. As Peter Drucker has pointed out, organizational structure is key to determining organizational performance.[3]

Design Management Processes

Each of these companies has instituted design management processes that are appropriate, whether they are formal or informal. W. Edwards Deming has described management as a set of processes that keep complicated organizational systems running smoothly.[4] Important aspects of design management, as with any management function, include planning, budgeting, organizing, staffing, controlling, and problem solving.

This raises the issue of design management versus design leadership. Deming claims that management's objective is evaluation, improvement, and matching management strategy to business needs. But what leaders do is prepare organizations for change and help them cope as they struggle through it. Each case I examined involved change, and today building design into the corporate culture is more about design leadership than traditional design project management. At Heineken, changing high-volume packaging required leadership from many functions in the organization, including design management.

Design to Enable Change

Supporting a design culture requires organizational openness to change. While most corporations talk about change, few organizations change enough to realize intended strategy. However, if they are to be successful, organizations need to embrace continual change[5] as they seek to reduce costs, improve the quality of their products and services, locate new opportunities for growth, and increase productivity. All of these processes require change, and all of them require design. StorageTek realized a change in employee attitude and creativity as the result of improved interior design.

Design-Facilitated Corporate Strategy

Good design brings commercial success, which is, after all, the purpose of corporate strategy. For all the companies highlighted in this article, design is an enabler of corporate strategy, whether it is used as a visualization tool or for the delivery of actual products. British Airways wanted to increase business-class bookings on long-distance flights. It realized its goal by providing customers with better seating design.

Design solutions should be aimed not only at satisfying market requirements, but also at exceeding customer expectations. Almost fifty years ago, economist Lawrence Abbott stated, "What people really desire are not products but satisfying experiences."[6] Today, many companies work to define, craft, and deliver those experiences to customers through design.

Design to Realize Innovation

The primary purpose of design—any design—is to create something new. It may be a completely new creation, or an improvement on something that already exists. Successful organizations use design to realize new innovations and then to establish parameters for further development within that context, whether it's a product, an environment, an identity, or a form of communication. Nike is all about innovative new products, which is why it is so committed to design. Design is a key resource to enable innovation, because innovation may be defined as creativity (idea) plus design (applied).

Design Teams and Collective Purpose

For an organization to transform its vision into reality, it must start with a shared vision of corporate strategy and implementation. And part of this is a shared vision about design—what Robert Bradford calls "designer collectivism."[7] Paul Odomirok supports this proposition,[8] arguing that the core of organizational success is collaborative purpose: the collective, cooperative, and co-owned beliefs and aims of the individuals who are part of a team. The model of collaborative purpose applies to groups of two or more people who work together on joint activities. Each of the foregoing design management case examples falls into this category and required such a collaborative team.

The management of collaborative purpose should be a part of design management, because project success won't be repeatable without well-defined processes to align individuals and teams. Further, since coordination includes teams and team management, the notion of "it's not what you know—it's who you know," and the power of social networks, cannot be underestimated. The argument is that the real work is done in most companies informally, through personal contacts. Therefore, design management has to consider critical linking roles in order to achieve alignment and desired results.

Design-Minded Corporate Culture

A corporate culture that embraces good design is a necessity. Often design-minded corporate culture is led by executive management. Often it comes about as the result of a "moment of truth," during which the company realizes a business success directly related to design.

Presumably, all design managers agree with Paul Rand's 1987 phrase, "Good design is good business." The trick is to convince business executives and nondesigners. Even harder is building a corporate culture in which design can flourish and realize its potential. All the companies showcased in this article benefited from a design-minded culture. Each appeared to recognize the value of design as a business resource and therefore managed design as part of its standard business process.

CONCLUSION

The stronger an organization's culture for design, the greater its commitment to using design as a resource. Businesses need to develop their own design culture by applying design leadership and applying effective design management practice in order to produce effective design and achieve business results. Only then will the idea of design as a business resource achieve its true power as a means of reaching business objectives. These seven themes are critical for company-wide design success, and are the foundation of my Integrate Design™ International consultancy.

ACKNOWLEDGMENT

Several of the case examples for this article, and much of the Design Performance Leadership Measurement research, are part of my PhD research about integrated design management, and I would like to recognize my academic supervisors, Dr. Alison Rieple and Dr. Richard Harding, as co-authors of this article.

Suggested Reading

Borja De Mozota, Brigitte. *Design Management: Using Design to Build Brand Value.* New York: Allworth Press, 2003.

Bruce, Margaret, and Bessant, John. *Design in Business.* Harlow: Pearson Education, 2002.

Cooper, Rachel, and Press, Mike (eds.). *The Design Agenda.* Chichester: John Wiley and Sons, 1995.

Gorb, Peter. *Living by Design.* London: Lund Humphries, 1978.

Endnotes

1. See Aaron Betsky (ed.), *Icons: Magnets of Meaning*. San Francisco, CA: Chronicle Books, 1997.

2. See Wally Olins, *Corporate Identity*. Boston: Harvard Business School Press, 1989.

3. See Peter Drucker, *The Practice of Management*. New York, NY: HarperCollins, 1986.

4. See W. Edwards Deming, *Out of the Crisis*. Cambridge, MA: Massachusetts Institute of Technology, 1986.

5. See Gary Hamel, *Leading the Revolution*. Boston: Harvard Business School Press, 2000, and John P. Kotter, *Leading Change*. Boston: Harvard Business School Press, 1996.

6. Lawrence Abbott, *Quality and Competition*. New York: Columbia University Press, 1955, p. 25.

7. Robert Bradford, "Strategic Alignment," *Executive Excellence* 8, 2002.

8. Paul Odomirok, "The Power of Collaborative Purpose," *Industrial Management*, 2001, p. 28.

Chapter 6

The Making of Design Champions

by Mark Barngrover, Director of Design, Procter & Gamble,
Geneva, Switzerland

Innovation is always about ideas. It is also, as Mark Barngrover makes clear, always about people. At Procter & Gamble, the role of design has shifted from being brand support to being a strategic brand feature. It is a transformation that has strengthened the value of brands, as well as consumer understanding and loyalty—bottom-line changes driven by the increasingly important contributions of design champions, design managers, and design consultants.

FOR PROCTER & Gamble, the work of creating a vital and vibrant design organization is an ongoing process both globally and in Europe. Our challenge as design managers is to build an organization that can provide design leadership for our brands, providing a new source of innovation for the evolving goals of the company. Having worked to build organizational structures in Japan and in Europe, I have faced the challenges of growing skills and creating a positive culture within the design function, and one thing I've learned is that partnerships with design consultancies are fundamental to our success. Most critical to my work, however, is a challenge that, if left unattended, would negatively affect everything else I do. I have learned the importance of creating design champions at the highest level in the company.

Members of the Procter & Gamble design department on retreat in Boisbuchet, France, where, as part of a team-building exercise, they constructed silhouettes of themselves and posed by them—a visual representation of the challenge of building an organization.

P&G: TOUCHING LIVES, IMPROVING LIFE

Design at P&G has always focused on brand identity development, but now we include aspects of research and development as well. Our growth is exciting, but we definitely feel growing pains at times. Four years ago, we had just seven more design managers in the company than we had when I joined the company in 1988. In 2002, we doubled that number; in 2003, we added 50 percent more again, and in 2004 we've more than tripled the 2001 number. In Europe, we have grown at a similar rate, and we still have numerous positions to fill worldwide.

I am located in our European headquarters in Geneva. We have national offices across Europe, and research centers in Belgium, the United Kingdom, Italy, and Germany.

The company was founded in 1937 by two immigrants: William Procter, a candle maker from England, and James Gamble, a soap maker from Ireland. Based in Cincinnati, Ohio, P&G is organized by global business units (GBUs), market development organizations (MDOs), and corporate functions (CFs). Our GBUs focus on fabric and home care, baby and family care, beauty care, snacks and beverages, and healthcare. Our MDOs focus on local market knowledge and include Japan/Korea, greater China, North America, Latin America, Western Europe, and Central and Eastern Europe, the Middle East, and Africa.

Design is now a corporate function—a new development, and a significant show of support. At the same time, creating a space for design in such a vast structure is daunting.

THE INNOVATION CHALLENGE

P&G is committed to leading innovation and embracing sustainability. Our research and development facilities are, as always, making products better and better. For 150 years, that's how we have differentiated ourselves. We remain good at this type of enterprise, and pretty good at marketing these superiorities, as well. We make strategic choices toward innovation and always have. Our existing innovation model, however, evolves from technology and efficiencies.

Design was not central to this model. Rather, it was seen as a late-stage activity or brought into the work through narrowly defined tasks. In fact, within the efficiency-driven and marketing processes, design was often seen as a barrier rather than a benefit. We make packages that fly down the manufacturing line; it's an important component of our economic model. But we've learned that if you let the machines rule, everything ends up in the shape of a brick or a cylinder. Bricks and cylinders are stable and easy to fill, but in this more-sophisticated marketplace, if the package isn't distinct, it suggests that what's inside is a mere commodity.

Our products are unique and compelling, but design wasn't allowed to tell that story. It wasn't even asked to serve the brand in that way.

THE DESIGN-DRIVEN INNOVATION MODEL

Our new innovation model is more design-driven, and it shows. The designer is now part of a holistic approach to product development, and the designer's voice is heard from the earliest stages of discovery through development and launch.

Kandoo, an extension of the Pampers brand, is a splendid example of the new model. Pampers spends a lot of time and effort making connections with moms and their kids. But once the kids grow out of diapers, those connections are lost. Through Kandoo, and as a result of the early influence of the design function in the development pro-

Kandoo is an example of design-driven innovation. Basic product technologies aren't the only story behind the product; aesthetics and functionality serve the young target audience through deliberate design.

cess, we have extended and expanded that relationship and created a new market for toddlers three to five years old who are beginning to attend to their own personal-care needs. Kandoo products include flushable moist wipes and foaming hand soaps. The brand uses existing P&G knowledge and technologies and tweaks them a bit to make them more appropriate and sensitive for young skin. Design, however, plays the central role in actualizing the brand's benefits. The aesthetics of the brand, as well as the functionality of the products, serve this young constituency through design.

Pringles is another design-driven story. The product formulation remains the same. What is different is design's role in taking newly identified, unmet consumer needs and developing formats for different usage occasions. Not everyone wants to carry a can of Pringles around all the time. The Snack Stack is an aesthetically pleasing, functional solution that builds on core brand equities.

Tampax also shows the benefit of the investment in design. Armed with insight into the needs of teens just entering this market, the designer has come up with a package that is small and discreet but also "fun" and fashionable. Even the paper selection is deliberate, based on a material that tears quietly (avoiding the scenario of everybody in the school bathroom hearing the tampon wrapper being torn). While product performance is tailored to these consumers' needs, it is design sensitivity that enhances the product offer and makes it compelling.

A final example is Pantene. Unlike previous shampoos from Procter & Gamble, this brand invests in shape differentiation. The early involvement of design is also demonstrated through attention to detail in things like embossing and decoration. This raised the bar for Pantene and the entire category by delivering an elegant identity for the brand. The presentation counts at two distinct "moments of truth" in the life of the product: the purchase and the actual use of the product. Both are served by design. Human factors such as grip and dispensing are addressed, while the aesthetics still delight. (And, by the way, our manufacturing lines still move very quickly.)

Tampax is a design-sensitive brand. Everything from the brand's aesthetics to the choice of material for the product wrapper (which is quiet when torn) contributes to the well-being of the teenage market audience.

Our new innovation model has paid off. Procter & Gamble's success in expanding our brand portfolio and turning many of our businesses into billion-dollar brands with design partnership is noteworthy. A.G. Lafley, our chief executive officer, regularly talks to the business and financial press about the role of design in P&G's turnaround. He is the company's number-one design champion.

A COMPANY OF DESIGN CHAMPIONS

As noted earlier, I serve a vast organization. At Procter & Gamble we have fifteen presidents—one in charge of every major business unit. Each market development organization also has a president. It would be great to be able to state here that every one of these leaders was an early adopter of design strategy and understands its business impact. This, of course, is not the case.

It was demonstrated to me early on that enrolling managerial leadership to create advocacy is absolutely key to the success of establishing design leadership, and this became a primary part of my job. I knew that if I got leadership talking about design, their organizations would accept that design is important, and eventually this would elevate the importance of design throughout the company. You soon begin to see people who have been at the company only two to five years starting to care about design in a deeper way. They know their leaders care, so they at least know they need to learn more. Eventually, finance people, research people, and other constituencies will become sensitive to the business power of design. In fact, I believe this enables them, since as consumers they also appreciate products that are thoughtfully and intelligently designed. Sooner or later, they will recognize design as a tool to help elevate P&G products in consumers' eyes.

By creating design champions in senior management, we create a positive "virtuous cycle." Champions set priorities and create energy. This leads the design community to feel empowered and to take risks. If great design leads to a great business, then we see this feeds on itself and becomes sustainable. It's a challenge to get this in place, but when it works, it works well.

One of my early successes involved a P&G president who was approaching design in a tactical way, dictating scale, proportion, and color. You can imagine what this did to the organization—not just to design, but to everyone involved in the brand-building process. In spending time with him, I was delighted to learn that he wanted to know what success in enabling design in his organization would look like. I spoke of the importance of behavior and role modeling—things such as never reviewing design without having the design manager in the room, and staying involved directly with the designer, since we've seen that if design is managed at a lower level in the brand organization, it will be seen as unimportant work. Further, I suggested that he speak about design regularly in his work. When he discussed objectives, goals, strategies, and measures, he should be sure to include design strategy.

This president's business has improved significantly, and this is one of the strongest management/design manager relationships we now have at P&G.

Recognizing that design strategy had served the business was a breakthrough and one of my first insights into the role of design champions. Business leaders are often tactical in the way this president was because they don't know another way to approach design. I find such leaders very open to suggestions about how to establish design leadership in their organizations. We can do better than make them design-tolerant. With care, we can make them design champions!

DESIGN CULTURE

As we begin to create design champions throughout the organization, we must develop a design function that is sufficiently robust to serve the needs of our expanding constituency. Design at P&G has always focused on brand identity development, but now we include aspects of research and development, as well. Our growth is exciting, but we definitely feel growing pains at times. Four years ago, we had about forty-five designers in the company, globally. In 2002, that went up to sixty-four. In 2003, we doubled, and in 2004 we stood at 150. In Europe, we have grown from six to twenty-four, and we now have forty positions to fill worldwide.

With all this growth within the design function, a lot is expected of our designers. We need to have a deep understanding of our target consumers and use that to provide new ideas and design leadership for our brands. There is a lot of organizational focus on our designers right now, and that's great. The design function is building credibility within the marketing and R&D organizations and beyond.

In Europe, the design function has grown from six to twenty-four people. We are still bringing people into the organization. We are looking for strong, independent people who can work collaboratively.

However, this has led to challenges within the organizational structure of the design function. When I joined the company, the highest title in the design community was associate director. Today, we are led by Vice President of Design and Strategic Innovation Claudia Kotchka. She is a great leader and a strong advocate for the business value of design, and she has been extremely effective in communicating it throughout the company. The function has assumed its appropriate role in brand building under her leadership.

We are bringing new people into the organization and recruiting for the first time at senior levels. (Historically, P&G has recruited out of colleges.) Bringing many new and experienced people into the organization in a brief period is bound to have an effect on the culture of the P&G design function. We want to take the best of what new people bring, and yet we need to ensure that they fit into what we feel we already have working effectively. We soon found that we needed to understand the elements of our culture that mattered most and spend a lot of time thinking about what kind of organization we want to be before we added new employees.

We knew we wanted to be about great design. Driving and delivering design excellence is the reason we exist. We needed to make sure that we care about our people and that they know it. We thought a lot about what that behavior looks like and the importance of modeling it to others. We also wanted to be a learning and sharing organization—this was crucial for effective and robust growth in business capabilities.

This, I might add, is consistent with Procter & Gamble's overall culture. Our principles, values, and policies are posted in every meeting room. We talk about honesty, fairness, and the belief that people are the most important thing.

The individual design management skills we look for are subservient to the realities of working within a company of 100,000 employees. Collaboration is a key skill. You must be an effective communicator and you must be able to draw people to your ideas in a positive way. You are, in fact, expected to participate. If you don't participate in meetings, you won't be invited back. That's an important point for designers to understand.

The design function is also looking for leadership. I'm not certain this was recognized even five years ago. You cannot create design champions if you cannot talk intelligently about design—if you cannot persuade people and train the organization in what design does.

At the same time, rest assured, there is room for quirkiness and independence. If you are only 200 people in an organization of 100,000, you need to develop some unique skills and embrace others. Our design managers often sit in business units all by themselves. If they are not strong and independent, they can get swallowed up and pushed around. Quirkiness is a trait that can serve the creative voice well at times.

Maturity is another critical issue. We are hiring people with ten to fifteen years of experience, which serves the point about independence. You cannot be independent if you are not confident. A level of experience can create confidence.

The design function has become a great learning and sharing organization. In Western Europe, we invest in creating community through regular meetings. All our meetings follow a general agenda around the businesses, the consumers in each country, and other dimensions of demographics. We spend a lot of time in stores. We share successes and failures. We give each other advice on overcoming challenges; all this goes toward developing, expanding, and growing our design management capabilities.

DESIGN PARTNERS

I have also noted the importance of design partners. A few years ago, Procter & Gamble was not necessarily a desired client for design consultants. Design consultants are now seen as partners—and our partners tell us that their best designers now want to work with P&G businesses.

This is another example of the benefits of the virtuous cycle. It's much easier to sell design within an organization when it's done well. A great design partner understands our challenges and helps us grow. Our partners anticipate our needs and help us coach younger members of the design organization.

SIX THINGS I'VE LEARNED

After doing this on three continents over two decades, I've noted six things that a design organization must do in order to create design champions and achieve success.

Lesson 1—You can't get there if there isn't pull.

You cannot create great business-building design if the company isn't supportive. P&G is becoming a design-savvy company. By creating design champions, we will grow and expand our virtuous cycle.

Lesson 2—All the nonbelievers can be converted (almost).

Every time I am informed of a senior manager who doesn't value design, I find it is because of a misunderstanding. When talking about the importance of their behavior in supporting design, managers usually ask how to support design in their organizations. Senior managers in a company like Procter & Gamble are smart, and they are successful for all the right reasons. They didn't get there by not understanding and valuing. Getting design into their thinking process is almost always possible; I've had only one failure.

Lesson 3—You can't do it by yourself.

You need support to build an organization. A community of practice that supports and nurtures is a must.

Lesson 4—A great organization is about great people.

Great organizations equal great people. Every great design consultancy I work with says it is great because it has great people. The same thing is true of corporate design functions. Investing in culture and valuing people leads to a successful organization.

Lesson 5—The real work is in teaching and enrolling to change beliefs and behaviors.
I have learned that managing the design function is about teaching and enrolling. By changing beliefs and behaviors, we create design champions (see lesson 2).

Lesson 6—You must keep it positive when things are negative (a mantra of our department).
Managing a high-performance enterprise of any type is demanding. There are days when things don't go well. As leaders in design, we must strive to stay positive, even when there are many reasons to feel frustration. I have found over the years that if you stay positive, even negative people will come around. Operating on a positive level is a benefit to your company and to yourself.

P&G is about its people. It's a great time to be a designer at Procter & Gamble because design is exploding all around us. We don't even know where this growth will end, in number or in role. I love the work and am proud of being part of this story. By investing in people and making design champions of our business leaders, we will continue to create a virtuous cycle.

COLLABORATE

There is always a duality related to the creative endeavor. On the one hand, it is about freedom—looking at challenges from multiple perspectives, exploring new frontiers, proposing unexpected relationships. On the other hand, it is about framing—filling in the background, defining limits, distilling truly effective associations. In both areas, creativity involves people, and most importantly, people working collaboratively.

The thoughts shared in this section address this second aspect of corporate creativity. They put creativity in context. They identify the processes and players critical to success. They integrate strategies related to accountability and management. Ron Sanchez probes how design and its creative focus can contribute to the strategic direction of a business. In a fascinating analysis, Nicholas Ind and Cameron Watt elaborate on the balance of tension and trust in collaboration. Michael Schrage shares thoughts on prototyping as the venue for a creative discussion. Then, in another chapter, Ind and Watt bring closure to the notion of the creative dialogue by suggesting that a company's brand can be a sounding board to help generate the criteria essential to making decisions about creative options. Dimitris Lamproulis offers insights on managing creativity, exploring the topic of leadership; Leonard Glick provides practical tips on optimizing the creative process; and Naomi Gornick considers the special role of consultants in the creative effort.

The lessons here are threefold:

The creative energy of designers makes them critical partners in shaping corporate strategy. Designers have the crucial ability to empathize with customers. Often this leads to a unique wisdom about markets and current as well as potential customers. Designers understand the importance of the service and personal interaction that are increasingly part of any company's offerings and a foundation for enhancing brand loyalty. They sense what consumers are willing to invest in terms of time and energy, and what attributes they value. They can help prioritize the allocation of resources and streamline business processes. In these and many other ways, designers can be collaborators in making sure a company achieves its long-term objectives.

Interaction with different points of view and boundaries is vital to the creative effort. Creativity blends structure and autonomy. It is contained and expansive. It should be self-directed and managed from the outside. Companies must discover ways to foster these dualities. They also have to establish arenas in which creative alternatives can be critiqued, reshaped, and assessed. Ultimately, organizations should promote a challenging combination: the freedom and excitement of exploring, layered against strong criteria that help identify promising pathways. This evaluative backdrop can include brand, proprietary content, and unique insights about consumer needs.

Creativity can and must be managed. This is about crossing the threshold from theory into reality—a must in the world of business. There are many models for doing this. Some companies have extensive research divisions. Some invest in small firms that become incubators for creative ideas. Some empower all employees to generate and share creative options. Still others ask consultants to offer their insights and wisdom. Of course, combinations are also inevitable. What they all share is the following: leadership that articulates a vision; a collective team approach to problem-solving; a culture that values the individual; an emphasis on learning and growth; and a willingness to take risks. These are the qualities that stimulate creative interaction and collaboration, in order to develop an innovative organization.

Chapter 7

Lessons for Managing Creative Staff

by Leonard J. Glick, Faculty, College of Business Administration, Northeastern University

To "turn talent into performance," Leonard Glick's advice is to pay attention to motivation, abilities, and culture. Assign work so that people identify with the complete product. Increase the significance of tasks. Provide constructive feedback early and often. Ask staff to do things they haven't mastered as a way to learn and grow. Help those on the creative team understand the organization's design and corporate culture.

PERFORMANCE = (MOTIVATION) x (ABILITY) AS MODERATED BY THE ENVIRONMENT (CORPORATE CULTURE)

Experts have been writing about management for a long time. In 1949, in his book General and Industrial Management, Henri Fayol offered what is arguably the classic description of the work of managers: They plan, organize, staff, direct, and control. Management is also defined as "getting things done through people." More recently, Buckingham[1] posited that the job of management is to "turn talent into performance." I believe this point of view is an extremely useful way for managers of creative staff to think about their role. It raises the question: "What can I do that converts the talent of my staff to performance?" Here is a formula that begins to answer the question.

$$\text{Performance} = (\text{motivation}) \times (\text{ability}) \text{ as moderated by the environment}$$
$$(\text{corporate culture})$$

So now we have a framework from which we can derive lessons for managers of creative staff. They must motivate their staffs—or more precisely foster the conditions in which staff feel motivated. Second, they must develop them—that is, enable them to increase their abilities. Third, within their group, they must create an environment that fosters creative work that is useful to the business. Further, because the environment within the creative group is typically different from the larger corporate culture, creative staff must understand these differences so that they can bridge them. Within the context of a business, it is not enough to inspire creative work, although clearly that's important. That work must contribute to the business.

Motivation

Raise the topic of motivation, and people quickly focus on money and other tangible rewards, such as stocks, trips, promotions, and the like. For sure, these so-called extrinsic rewards can shape behavior. People behave in certain ways in order to win them. Here, though, I'd like to focus on intrinsic rewards—rewards that are generated from within. Of the many theories of motivation, Herzberg's dual-factor theory addresses this most directly.[2] A basic tenet of the theory and an important lesson for managers is that the primary source of motivation is the work itself. If people don't like the work they do, they cannot be fully motivated. This is a built-in advantage for managers of creative staff because most of their employees have chosen this field over others; in other words, they are doing what they love.

That's a good start, but managers have more to do as they create jobs, which in essence is finding ways to share the work among creatives. So, what do people like about jobs? If, as Herzberg's theory argues, one's work is the primary source of motivation, what features of a job are most motivating? The job characteristics model, from Hackman and Oldham, helps answer this question and provides direct advice to managers of creative staff.[3] According to the model, there are five dimensions of a motivating job:

1. Skill variety—the use of different skills in one's job

2. Task identity—requires completion of a whole (or identifiable) piece of work

3. Task significance—impact on the organization and/or larger society

4. Autonomy—amount of freedom, independence, and discretion

5. Feedback—ability to tell how well one is doing from the job itself

While each feature can be translated into dos and don'ts for managers of creative staff, I'll focus on task identity and task significance because managers seem to underutilize them and therefore miss opportunities to increase the motivation of their creative staff.

To oversimplify, task identity is affected by the way work is assigned, and task significance is affected by the way work is explained. The principle behind task identity is straightforward: If you expect people to identify with—and therefore really care about—the complete product (or service), they must be involved in the complete product. The form of involvement can vary, ranging from literally doing all the work from beginning to end to doing some of the work but having visibility to and influence on the rest of the work. In other words, the greater the task identity, the greater the creative employees' effort and satisfaction. Imagine alternative ways of managing a marketing campaign that includes several components, such as brochures, mailers, and displays, as well as visits to trade shows and major customers. In the low-task-identity alternative, each designer stays in a cubicle working only on his/her assignment—for instance, one brochure. In the high-task-identity alternative, designers would have broader work responsibilities. In addition to their direct work output, they would also meet about, have influence on, and contribute to the total campaign. The assumption is that in the first, low-task-identity alternative, each designer would care primarily about—and only about—what she/he directly worked on. In the second, high-task-identity alternative, the assumption is that because they have broader involvement, they will identify and care about the total campaign, and therefore their performance will be better.

Lesson: Assign work so that creatives can identify with the complete product. Specifically, broaden their jobs: provide visibility to and enable involvement in all the work that affects the complete product.

Task significance complements task identity. The notion is that motivation increases when people understand why they are doing what they are doing, as well as its impact. Without task significance, people merely go through the motions—doing something because it's their job. With task significance, there is meaning, and with meaning there is increased motivation. In my experience, this notion is true but unfortunately the work of many people in the workplace lacks task significance. Why do I say this? When I ask people about their work, they are comfortable describing how they do what they do. But, when I ask them to explain why they do what they do, they become vague and uncertain. For example, they often aren't sure how they affect other groups, customers, business results, corporate goals, and so on.

Managers of creatives materially affect the level of task significance. At one extreme, if they merely say, Do this, and focus solely on the specifications of the task, the work will have minimal task significance. At the other extreme, if they provide the big picture behind the assignment (more details below), then it will be more than just something to do. Creatives understand the significance of their work, which, in theory, should affect the quality of their work. On the basis of discussions in the course I teach, there is opportunity here. My students, who are managers, often admit that when they assign work, they could spend more time on context—on helping their employees to understand the implications of the assignment.

Lesson: Increase the task significance of assignments by:

▲ Explaining the larger project (purpose, goals, and so on) to which the assignment contributes (the big picture)

▲ Explaining the role of the project to the company (the even-bigger picture)

▲ Naming the desired outcomes of the assignment—its contribution and added value

▲ Identifying the implications of doing it well (and of blowing it)

▲ Encouraging creatives to learn more about the overall project, by asking questions, attending meetings, and so on

Ability

In addition to motivation, good performance requires ability. To increase the abilities of their creative staff, managers need to provide feedback so that staff members know how they are doing and where they need to improve and opportunities for staff to learn new things and improve abilities. It is much easier to write (or say) how to give feedback than it is to actually give the feedback—especially when you want to say something that will be difficult to hear. Managers of creative staff often believe this task is particularly difficult because creatives are sensitive to criticism, idiosyncratic, and personally invested in their work—and that work is often more subjective than other types of work, and therefore difficult to judge.

While one may argue these points, let's assume they are essentially true. What, then, should a manager do? First, it is especially important to clarify expectations and criteria. The challenge is to make the subjective as objective as possible and to separate what matters and what doesn't, what's negotiable and what isn't. For example, such things as deadlines, milestones, desired impact, and integrity of brand need to be clarified so that there's a foundation of agreement on which feedback can be based. For sure, there will always be some element of subjectivity (there is in many fields), but the fact that you will not achieve total objectivity should not prevent you from striving for more objectivity.

Second, the feedback should be as descriptive as possible (for example: "You missed the first milestone by one day and the second by three days," rather than, "You are always late," or, "In our tests, the colors did not create the desired image," rather than, "You made a poor choice of colors"), to take as much subjectivity out of the conversation as possible so that a constructive discussion can take place. Third, provide feedback early and often so that problems can be detected—and hopefully corrected—early. Further, most people develop a skill of accepting feedback if they receive enough of it. If feedback is ubiquitous, each occasion is not as big a deal as when it is given annually. While some people are more sensitive to negative feedback than others, on the whole everyone's sensitivity should diminish, paving the way to more open and productive discussions.

Lesson: Lay the foundation for constructive feedback by establishing and clarifying mutual expectations and objective criteria. Discipline yourself to provide descriptive (rather than evaluative) feedback early and often.

Feedback informs employees only about the strengths and weaknesses of their abilities; it doesn't improve their abilities. Employees do that in many ways, such as trial and error, attending class, reading books, observing a "master," and the like. I frequently ask people this question: "What has been your most developmental experience—that is, when in your career have you learned the most?" Virtually everyone has the same answer: "When I had to do something I hadn't done before." The implication for managers is unmistakable: Ask your creatives to do something new. Those new experiences, coupled with constructive feedback, will increase the abilities—and the performance—of your workforce.

Clearly, neither the abilities nor the performance improve instantly. That's the price managers pay when they assign work to someone who isn't fully skilled. (Looking at it in another way, the price is an investment in their future capabilities.) This poses a dilemma to managers who are under pressure to get work done as well as possible as soon as possible; they have to balance learning versus performance. If they always tilt toward learning, performance will suffer, and vice versa. I certainly do not recommend that all or most of the work should be new to the creatives, nor do I recommend that managers ask inexperienced creatives to do the work that has the most at stake. What I am saying is that when managers always assign work to people who already are highly skilled in that area, the person who does the work will not learn, and neither will the people who can't do the work. In the longer term, the development of creatives will be arrested and the performance of the group will not be optimized.

Lesson: To increase learning, be sure all employees have some "stretch" assignments—that is, ask them to do something they haven't mastered.

Culture

Consistent with the previously cited formula, managers turn talent into performance within the context of the organization. In other words, because the corporate culture greatly affects performance and results, managers and creatives must understand that culture so that they can work successfully within it. When I asked senior design managers what managers needed to know, "helping employees to understand and work within the corporate culture" was high on everyone's list. They—and participants in my seminar—

underscore the fact that the design culture is typically very different from the corporate culture and that creatives must learn how to live and work in these two worlds.

What can a manager do to help? As a concept, culture is somewhat amorphous—it's often defined as "the way we do things around here." That's a start, but there are also two frameworks that can help make sense of culture. The first illustrates that there are different levels of culture: observable (artifacts) and unobservable (underlying values and beliefs). The main point is that while one experiences and senses the observables (the way people dress, how they interact, what is talked about, the physical surroundings, what gets rewarded and recognized, and so forth), to really understand culture, one must identify the few critical underlying values and beliefs that explain what is observed.

For example, in organization A you might observe charts that highlight outcomes, conversations asking about deadlines, rewards for results, and the like. In contrast, in organization B conversations focus on how the project is being managed and who will be involved, deadlines are readily extended, and members of project teams are asked how things are going. You could conclude that one component of organization A's culture is an underlying belief that "the only things that matter are results," whereas members of organization B may believe that "it's most important to follow procedures." Suppose a designer comes from a B culture to meet and discuss a project with people from an A culture. If the designer is unaware of these differences, he or she runs the risk of talking process and procedures to people who are only interested in results. The outcome could be disastrous and lead to escalating mistrust and bad feelings.

The second framework distinguishes between the espoused beliefs/values and the enacted beliefs/values (beliefs/values in use). The former are the beliefs that the organization claims to follow; they are often written in the annual report and on plaques. The latter are the beliefs that can be inferred from the observables, as already discussed. In some organizations, the enacted beliefs are essentially the same as the espoused beliefs—in other words, the company does what it says. For example, the company might espouse "we value the ideas of all employees" and, in fact, managers continually solicit—and use—ideas from employees. In others, they are quite different, with the company espousing certain beliefs yet behaving otherwise. Such a company may say it values the ideas of all employees, but it rarely asks for them, and when it gets input, it tends to ignore it. Gaps between espoused and enacted have organizational consequences; for starters, they increase cynicism and reduce commitment. For the purposes of this article, the main point is that managers of creative staff should understand that the real culture—the one they and the staff needs to understand and navigate—is the enacted culture, not the espoused one.

Lesson: Help creatives understand the enacted beliefs and values of both the design culture and the corporate culture so that they are more likely to navigate and succeed within them.

SUMMARY

Starting from the premise that a manager's primary role is to increase the performance of his/her staff, we looked at three levers: motivation, ability, and culture. Managers of creative staff can foster the conditions for heightened motivation by increasing certain job components such as task identity and task significance. They can enhance ability by providing constructive feedback and giving stretch assignments so that creatives are essentially forced to learn new skills and build on existing ones. Finally, managers can help creatives understand the differences that exist between the design culture and the corporate culture and how to deal with these differences. By doing so, managers of creative staff can turn talent into performance.

Endnotes

1. M. Buckingham, "What Great Managers Do," *Harvard Business Review* 83 (2005), pp. 70–79.

2. F. Herzberg, "One More Time: How Do You Motivate Employees?" *Harvard Business Review* 46 (1968), pp. 53–62.

3. J.R. Hackman and G.R. Oldman, *Work Redesign*. Reading, MA: Addison-Wesley, 1980.

Chapter 8

Teams, Trust, and Tribalism

by **Nicholas Ind,** Author and Consultant
and **Cameron Watt, PhD,** Innovation Consultant, Muse

*Collaboration is the norm in design management. Nicholas Ind and
Cameron Watt explore the nuances that help companies get the most
from this strategy. They believe that creativity and productivity are
optimized when there is "equitable tension," respect, and trust among
stakeholders—a balance of structure, or process, and autonomy; of
boundaries and expansive thinking; of active management and self-
direction; of homogeneity and diversity.*

IN THE LITERATURE on creativity, there is considerable emphasis on the enhancement of individual potential. Yet in most commercial contexts, even if there are individuals who inspire the rest, creative outputs result from a team process. This immediately
changes the approach to creative thinking because the vital element becomes the ability
to generate and manage effective teams that have the courage to think in new ways.
Our research demonstrates that the key antecedent to effective collective creativity is
trust. The importance of trust should not be surprising, but both within the group and
outside, in relationships with internal and external clients, trust is often taken as a given.
This is misplaced. Trust needs to be earned over time if the seemingly natural tendency
toward tribalism in organizations is to be mitigated.

DESIGNING CREATIVE TEAMS: KEEP IT SIMPLE

Creative teams must balance the need for order with that for self-expression. Overly rigid structures can unbalance the dynamic illustrated in Figure 1, bringing about demotivation, conflict, and lack of cooperation. Such imbalance occurs because traditional hierarchically based structures reduce personal freedom and encourage political behavior, reducing trust, altruism, and risk-taking. However, overly informal structures can also hinder the creative process by failing to provide support, focus, or leadership. Without formal structure, teams may feel vulnerable, confused, and isolated, and they may oscillate between defensive and aggressive behavior. As economist Ernst Schumacher once argued, we always need "freedom and order."

The argument in favor of order may appear to run against a great deal of research that advocates high levels of team autonomy. We agree that autonomy is vital, but we believe that structure and direction are required for it to actually occur. We do not recommend that creative organizations introduce traditionally structured teams in which decision-making and idea generation are directed from a single team leader or board director. Neither do we argue for the implementation of specific role responsibilities; such a system can lead to pigeon-holing of staff, a lack of diversity, and reduced motivation. What we do suggest is that organizations should provide simple supportive structures that reinforce key organizational objectives and systems, as well as identify broad spans of responsibility for team members.

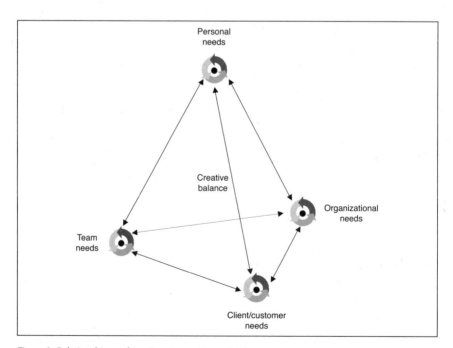

Figure 1. Relationships and tensions in creative projects.

As an example, let's take online gaming company Funcom (producers of Anarchy Online and The Longest Journey).[1] At Funcom, the focus of team members is primarily on the game they are developing. Individuals are motivated to deliver the best within their specific remits, but they also need to connect with other team members, whose skills may fall into a radically different area. A visual artist who is creating a fantasy world set 30,000 years in the future might need to connect with a software engineer whose primary concern is how the detailed programming will work. Both have to be willing and capable of learning from each other and to solve problems together without reducing efficiency. In describing the culture of Funcom, founder Gaute Godager says, "It's innovative, self-examining (not taking anything for granted), and cooperative, and it involves teamwork. Everyone says they like to work in teams, but we're 110 percent dependent on them. For a product to work, there needs to be one person in each area who knows what's going on. There needs to be creative discipline, but within that framework there also needs to be a lot of freedom. Meeting these two demands is quite difficult."

The key factor that Godager and his managers recognize is that effective teamwork and the management of tensions can be realized only through trust. To achieve this, the company tries to recruit people with high levels of skill in their specific disciplines. This is important because team members need to have trust in one another's capabilities; after all, no one person can micro-manage the detail. Godager sees his own role as one of inspiring people about the game idea and of setting the boundaries of creativity. He knows he doesn't have the technical expertise to oversee the specifics, so Funcom's employees are allowed as much creative freedom as they can handle. The value in this is that the individual team members feel a strong sense of project ownership, since it is their own individual and collective creativity that defines the game. In part, this is an issue of scale. Whereas a company like Disney can employ highly specialist individuals, Funcom needs people who can cover bigger areas and input their creativity into the detail. It is also an issue of philosophy—a view that the ability to express creativity is fulfilling.

In well-balanced organizations like Funcom, structure acts as a flexible template that allows team members to work flexibly within broad constraints. This balance enables diversity within a paradigm that is fundamentally homogeneous in terms of core values, objectives, and systems. Individual needs are met and managed within a framework of shared values and goals that facilitate trust.

GETTING THE RIGHT BALANCE

Our research supports the commonly held view that teams made up of diversely experienced people help facilitate creativity. Although none of the companies we have worked with highlighted size of team as a key issue, it is interesting to note that all the firms involved usually formed teams of between three and six people. In such a context, the development of socially based informal interaction is more likely to occur, since members often work in the same space. We are neither suggesting that small teams will ensure creativity nor that large ones will prevent it. However, we do assert that the possibility of need imbalance may increase within larger teams, as more stakeholders become involved and associated need-tensions increase. In particular, in larger teams, the importance of personal needs can be reduced in favor of team or organizational needs, resulting in negative perceptions, demotivation, and formation of internal tribes. Our experience suggests that, as with larger organizations, larger teams often require more control from management, with the needs of certain stakeholders prevailing over others. Again within the context of Figure 1, such a lack of equality can lead to problems in stakeholder relationships and reduce the potential for achieving creative balance. This inflexible approach to design can result in the personal needs of senior managers and senior designers dominating the internal environment, reducing the value of team and individual needs. In addition, large teams can increase the distance between clients and customers and those members actively engaged in the project. Such layering reduces personal contact and involvement, increasing the potential for misinformation and misunderstanding. Such a climate can quickly reduce trust, intrinsic motivation, and benevolent behavior and negatively affect the creative process. This is not to say that such stakeholder dominance will never occur in smaller teams. However, it is often easier to identify, making it easier to manage the situation before damage is done.

As well as size of team, the other key component in achieving a balance is diversity. In general, diversity is desirable, but it is particularly important that such a group has points of commonality derived from clear accountability and a shared perspective or shared values. The view on diversity is supported by a number of key writers,[2] who all argue that variety in both skills and personalities is key to generating energy, interaction, and a creative climate within organizations. Without differences in knowledge, styles, and personalities, teams can quickly develop what Irving Janis described as group-think, in which perspectives and debate are confined in a static framework of understanding. Without the tension of diversity, the creative climate can become de-energized and demotivated. In this context, maintaining and developing creative relationships may prove difficult, with negative feelings and perceptions among stakeholders reducing trust. We believe it is critical to understand and balance different styles, philosophies, and skills among groups to maximize diversity, yet minimize the potential for conflict. Without the right balance, constructive discussion and idea generation can dwindle. Debate, fueled through a diversity of perspectives, is a key part of the creative process within teams.

We suggest that the answer lies in balancing the needs for diversity and homogeneity. Too much diversity in personalities and experience may not provide a common frame of reference for the team, making trust-building, relationship development, and the generation of relevant ideas difficult, as well as increasing the potential for conflict and tribal behavior. By the same token, too much homogeneity can lead to group-think and creative stagnation.

The challenge for managers in getting this balance right is to recognize how much creativity is needed. At certain times, real blue-sky thinking is required; at others, the boundaries of creativity are more limited. As an example of these diverse needs, Tate Modern (the world's most visited modern art gallery) in London used teams in different ways as management planned the gallery's launch in 2000. A distinctive aspect of Tate Modern is the curation of its art collection, which is based around themes rather than chronology. The definition of the thematic approach was the result of a small and cohesive core team comprising Lars Nittve, director of the gallery, as well as two curators and an education curator. All of them wanted to challenge people's perceptions about art. However, having developed this idea, they were still determined to avoid group-think. To overcome this possibility, they expanded the group into a think tank augmented with artists, philosophers, and art historians. In an interview with us, Nittve said of this diversity, "I think we valued different voices and we also knew that we all came from the same direction. And it's not given that that is the only direction. At certain moments in processes, it's good to have some friction because it breaks up patterns and models of thinking. Sometimes you're moving too automatically. . . . Also, we wanted to move toward having different voices in how we displayed and talked about the collection . . . to move away from this institutional voice to a more multiple voice."

At this stage, the boundaries of creativity were defined by the vision for Tate Modern, but within those boundaries there was considerable latitude. Once the team had agreed upon a thematic approach, the members defined a new goal: Flesh out the basic themes and test the viability of delivering them. Whereas the first think tank required diversity of background, the new groups, who would explore the themes, needed to have diversity of knowledge but within a cohesive field. Consequently, a series of bigger groups was formed, with curators from the Tate's central collection. These people used their specific expertise to define how the four themes could be realized from the works the museum owned. Finally, once the bigger groups had reached agreement, a small group was formed to fine-tune and detail each room within the themes. This tighter group was less about diversity and more about unity. Nittve says of the last group, "When you install the collection, it has to have a similar tone of voice. It's enough that you get different positions and statements in the works of art, because you have different artists. If the mode of installation and presentation were different from room to room, it might just turn chaotic. That's why we had a smaller team under one person who was responsible for bringing that together."

This accordion-like process within Tate Modern was designed to adapt to the requirements of creativity—providing different levels of diversity and homogeneity at different times. At the earlier stage, when creative boundaries were at their broadest, diversity was encouraged to help create connections that might not have been seen by a narrowly defined group. However, when the level of creativity became more detailed and the boundaries narrower, homogeneity was more valuable. At that point, the requirement was not to question the fundamental approach to curating the museum, but rather to provide creativity in the specifics of installation.

One last word on team balance: It is vital that clients and customers (whether internal or external to the organization) are seen as part of the team. Too often, organizations maintain a them-and-us attitude toward such relationships, forgoing the potential for insightful contributions and key opportunities for gaining essential buy-in and feedback. IDEO, Quiksilver, and Levi's are organizations that champion such thinking. They are committed to breaking down the traditional barriers that exist between customers and designers. They employ a clever use of free-flow networks that encompass a wide variety of customers who are heavily involved with their brands, testing new concepts and living with existing lines. These semiformal networks have been built up over many years and include opinion leaders within fashion, sports, and lifestyles, as well as passionate amateurs and successful professional boarders, surfers, and skaters. Quiksilver customers, for example, are in continuous contact with Quiksilver staff, who themselves are all essentially members of this network, feeding back information on products, trends, and prototypes. Such communication is not limited to occasional formal marketing reports, but instead takes the form of a constant conversation with stakeholders—hence the notion of free-flow.

WHAT DOES MANAGING CREATIVITY MEAN?

A major challenge facing managers is how to balance the tensions within the team dynamic to foster a creative climate. The model in Figure 2 indicates how this can be achieved. Managers have to deal with and balance external organizational and client pressures within a team context. The model details the forces at play and identifies internally driven pressures relating to specific team needs, such as trust, support, and enjoyment, which match those of individuals. However, there are additional needs and tensions that are more specific to a team dynamic than a personal one, and it is these that this section will focus on.

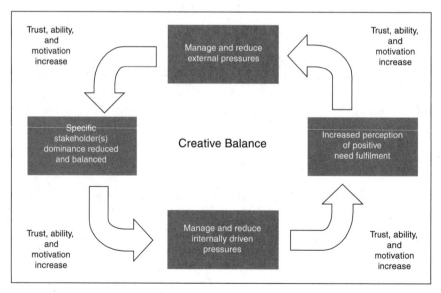

Figure 2. Managing for creative balance.

Benevolent Dictatorship

The previous section highlighted the need to develop teams in the form of self-organized networks of integrated teams supported by a core organization. The challenge facing managers is to balance this concept with the external pressures placed upon the team by clients, organizations, and other stakeholders. It is important that teams be allowed to develop ideas in their own way—a point well highlighted by philosophers Gilles Deleuze and Felix Guattari. Deleuze and Guattari wrote about the concept of nomadology, in which groups form not because they are put together by a hierarchy, but because they are responding to change, immanently. The conceptual space that groups occupy is not predetermined but is a result of sense-making and the movement of the group in response to inputs. This approach helps ensure that changes in the internal or external environment are sensed quickly and that reactions are fast and creative. A nomadological approach also suggests that creative acts are less likely to be "royal" (to come from senior figures in the organization) and more likely to be nomadic (from within the organization).

However, achieving client and organizational objectives is just as critical. At IDEO, managers relish engagement with external stakeholders because they realize that cultures cannot become creative if they remain locked in ivory towers. IDEO attempts to involve clients at all stages of a project and espouses the idea of co-creativity as a way of making the process of innovation as transparent as possible. Tim Brown, CEO of IDEO, believes that "if you do it in a complete enough way, expectation management becomes a self-managing thing. The more 'black-box' you make the process [of creativity], the more you have to worry about expectation management. There's no visibility—they [the clients] can't prepare themselves, and they can't prepare you. So that's why we've tried to move toward being more transparent and more open; there's more participation, involvement, and buy-in." At IDEO, managers work with clients to set and agree on key objectives and to define the boundaries of creativity. The setting of boundaries is critical because the process is delicate and requires a high level of skill and emotional intelligence.

If managers are to use emotional intelligence, they must ensure that they manage emotions ethically, delivering what they promise to staff. Otherwise, they may damage their reputations. It is important that managers do not seek to manipulate but instead look to develop partnerships with team members. Over-control or the implementation of inflexible or too tight boundaries appears to be the most common problem. This often takes the form of creative direction or decisions made from outside the team environment. High levels of external control can reduce the possibility of a team generating a shared and meaningful vision or goals relating to the project and the development of the team itself. The development of a shared vision is a key element in directing and bonding a team, for without such a vision members can feel disenfranchised and devalued, leading to problems of trust and demotivation within the team.

A second common way managers constrain their teams is through the introduction of a process model that prescriptively describes how projects should be approached. In such a situation, the team can perceive its role as one of technician or supplier, rather than expert or consultant. Lacking freedom to express ideas, teams can become predictable and uncreative in their thinking. Managers need to understand that although process parameters can be useful as a guide, ensuring the team has enough autonomy to develop and agree upon project goals and objectives is vital. Such self-organization is important because it communicates trust from senior management and is a powerful way to develop team commitment. The team begins to feel it has the potential to control its future and to affect change.

Without facilitative and supportive management, teams find it difficult to develop integrated, trust-based relationships as they return to more-traditional roles. Design company Design Bridge, as well as Funcom, provides good templates for the management of creative teams. The focus for both companies is on creating a supportive learning environment, which allows individuals the freedom to experiment within an emotionally safe context. This view appears to extend to the way in which teams are organized and managed, relying on a high degree of trust and interdependency among team members and managers. The objective is to create a network-based team structure that balances diversity and homogeneity and that can support itself by drawing upon the skill sets available. Once the team has been chosen for a project and key objectives agreed upon after discussions among team members, managers, and the client, senior management steps back and assumes a hands-off, monitoring role. The team is given the freedom to explore and develop ideas with the client without significant interference from internal hierarchies. Senior management is involved at key internal meetings and in monitoring and mentoring, but not in client meetings unless requested. This process appears to work for a number of reasons. First, the high level of client involvement enables the team to gain a better understanding of their needs, as well as build trusting relationships and communicate more easily and directly about design issues. Second, the resulting high degree of trust between stakeholders internally and externally results in positive perceptions and benevolent behavior. Third, due to the high quality and diverse nature of the team, members possess the breadth and depth of skills, knowledge, and experience needed to manage complex projects. Fourth, team members are aware of their areas of responsibility and, although encouraged to be involved in the whole process, remain focused. Finally, project management staff provide a protective framework within which the team can work without significant distraction or fear.

KEY LESSONS FOR DESIGN MANAGERS

Understanding which forces create tensions within the team dynamic, what the consequences could be in terms of perception and behavior, and how best to manage for balance are critical management tasks. Favoring the needs of one stakeholder over another can create an unbalanced team dynamic, resulting in the prevention of benevolent creative behavior.

We recommend that organizations do the following:

▲ Move away from traditional role designation and hierarchical forms to a far more fluid network-based model.

▲ Provide clear boundaries and support structures, but do not micro-manage.

▲ Do not pigeonhole staff; rather, allow them to step out of character and offer new perspectives on projects they show interest in.

▲ Develop the correct balance between diversity and homogeneity by choosing diverse personalities, experience, and skills, while maintaining the existence of a set of shared core values that provide the basis for a team's culture.

▲ Accept that the team management role is not about control—it is about supporting, protecting, and nurturing teams in an attempt to build high levels of team trust, vision, and motivation.

▲ Provide flexible role and responsibility boundaries within the team and ensure an equitable distribution of power.

▲ Finally, really involve clients and customers. Use informal networks to get continuous, honest feedback and information and get clients working with the team at every point possible.

Endnotes

1. Much of our research has been done on successful creative brands such as Funcom, as well as Quiksilver, Aardman, and IDEO.

2. T. Amabile, "How to Kill Creativity," in J. Henry (ed), *Creative Management* (London: Sage, 2001), pp. 4–10; C. Ford and D. Gioia, "Factors Influencing Creativity in the Domain of Managerial Decision Making," *Journal of Management*, 26 (2000), 4, pp. 705–732; and L. Thompson and L. F. Brajkovich, "Improving the Creativity of Organizational Work Groups," *Academy of Management Executive*, 17 (2003), 1, pp. 96–112.

Chapter 9

Convergence: New Management Imperatives and Their Effect on Design Activity

by Naomi Gornick, Design Management Consultant,
Honorary Professor, University of Dundee

For clients seeking true partnerships, consultants are increasingly positioning their design expertise as part of a larger strategic vision. In interviews with executives at London-based Seymour Powell and at Portland, Oregon-based Ziba, Naomi Gornick probes how this integration has changed the profile of the consulting firms and added value to the services they provide corporate customers.

CURRENT MANAGEMENT THEORY encourages companies to think more creatively. The continuing value of organizational command and control methods is being widely questioned. Innovation in organizations is now paramount and as a result, new types of personnel are sought to bring fresh insight on innovation strategies into companies. The Harvard Business Review noted two years ago[1] that corporate recruiters are now looking favorably on MFAs rather than MBAs—the enhanced conceptual and modeling skills offered by fine-arts graduates can help generate new ideas and find new solutions to problems.

At the same time, designers and design consultancies have begun to recognize their potential to make a broader contribution to business and society with a more complete understanding of client and consumer aspirations and needs.

These shifts point the way to a new world opening up for the design community to enlarge their range of activity. Whether designers choose to take up new roles or not, the expectations of their contribution to business life and to the bottom line have increased significantly. Their opinions and advice will be sought more than ever before.

In the current period of extreme complexity characterized by economic instability, rapid technological advances, social changes, and volatile international politics, how do designers develop strategies for dealing with client uncertainty and change? What changes do design consultancies have to make?

Innovation is clearly an imperative for industrial and commercial companies. Increasingly, more design consultancies understand the new scenario. The standard questions in innovation management apply equally to both sectors: How should the innovation process be structured in the organization? How should a company clearly define a strategic focus that channels its innovative efforts realistically—in ways that will be profitable? How can a company create and sustain a corporate environment that values better performance above everything else? How can the company encourage new behavioral patterns that will keep the innovation process moving on a continual basis?[2] We can begin to see complementary goals and processes emerging between companies and their design consultants, giving their collaboration the unique value of being both creative and strategic. Long-term success goes to the designers who can deliver a fusion of strategy with creativity in their client relationships.

Taking these questions as a lead, I looked at two product design consultancies, Seymour Powell in the UK and Ziba in the USA, that are typical of organizations in their field now undertaking strategic analysis for their clients. Both were among the first wave of consultancies to add strategic analysis as a major client service. I asked their principals[3] to describe their consultancies' strategic focus, structure, processes, and value culture, and I also asked them to comment on the competitive environment in which their organizations operate.

Seymour Powell, established in 1984 by Richard Seymour and Dick Powell, is a London-based group that designs for worldwide manufacturers of consumer goods. The industry sectors in which they operate include automotive, mobile communications, computers, and domestic appliances. Seymour Powell Foresight (SPF), the strategic arm of the consultancy, was established in 1992 and is a research and strategy unit that calls upon a global network of local research and design specialists. SPF's remit includes forecasting social and technology futures, as well as global and lifestyle trends; SPF also studies market dynamics and offers analysis of the competitive marketplace, consumer behavior, and design strategy. SPF has developed a reputation for expertise in specialist areas and now undertakes strategic research for about 50 percent of Seymour Powell's clients, mostly at the pre-briefing stage of design projects. As principal Richard Seymour points out, "SPF is a research company, and to an extent it encompasses work previously done in client companies by consumer research and management consultants." The group, which is currently fifty-one people strong, includes Seymour Powell, Seymour Powell Foresight, administration, and model-making workshop staff.

Ziba Design was also established in 1984. Based in Portland, Oregon, its mission is to align design experience with its clients' brand position by translating brand attributes into three-dimensional objects, environments, and communication materials. Ziba Design has sixty people on staff. The consultancy has been a multicultural, multidisciplinary firm from the day it started, beginning with engineering and industrial design and now including research, design planning, strategic planning, graphics, and communications services.

Tailored multidisciplinary teams are created for every project to ensure that multiple perspectives and options are generated for clients. Says principal Sohrab Vossoughi: "In the first stage of a project, we ask more questions. Now we undertake 80 percent design process strategy work and 20 percent actual design. We are connecting client to target customer, and the leverage from this knowledge is where client companies find value."

STRATEGIC FOCUS

Both Ziba and Seymour Powell were established in the mid 1980s—a time of significant expansion of the design industry, to the extent that a number of leading UK consultancies were listed on the stock market for the first time. Another similarity: The evolution of both consultancies' strategic directions, in the early '90s, came about at a time when recession was hitting the design industry hard on both sides of the Atlantic. It was apparent to Ziba and to Seymour Powell that the best way to respond to the new business environment was by taking due regard of their clients' expanded needs and expectations. In effect, what started as a way of surviving the dark times has since become a key driver of current design activity worldwide.

STRUCTURE

Seymour Powell and Ziba Design followed similar paths in the founding of their strategic direction, but they diverge in the way the consultancies are organized.

With the establishment of Seymour Powell Foresight, Seymour Powell has created a collegiate formula in its organization, with a considerable external knowledge facility. As Richard Seymour notes, "The central gravity of our business shifted when Seymour Powell Foresight was added. We have moved toward encouraging more clarity at the front of a project, before the physical work starts. SPF researchers' roles for each project are based on their various specialties, which include consumer demographics, marketing trends, and ethnography. They carry out much of the vital initial research on which the product development process depends. SPF is now a profit center in its own right, and that has benefited our whole consultancy" (see Figure 1).

For its part, Ziba Design has adopted a team paradigm with multidisciplinary in-house staff. Says Sohrab Vossoughi: "The strategy structure is similar to that of an ad agency. We have a creative director on each team, and two or three client relation managers." All the staff members working on a project develop strategy under the creative director.

Staff members have diverse backgrounds, ranging from industrial design and engineering to architecture, anthropology, sociology, social sciences, graphic design, and business specialties. Only 50 percent of them are designers. Multidisciplinary teams are used on every project; the aim is to ensure that multiple perspectives are reflected in the work (Figure 2).

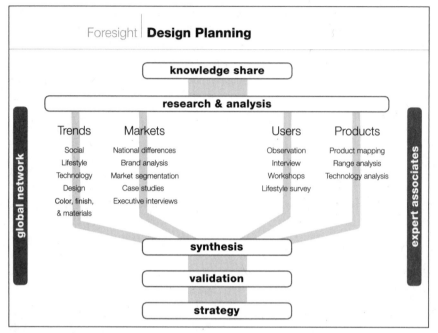

Figure 1. SPF design planning diagram shows elements of a typical project process that combines insight from qualitative user research with analyses of quantitative trend data. SPF strategies are routinely validated by external experts.

Figure 2. This diagram shows a typical Ziba project team. Note the contribution of both creative and account directors, as well as the specialist staff, to a total design strategy.

PROCESSES

Considerable similarities exist in both consultancies' approach to incorporating new work systems in which emphasis on the design process is being transformed. In many projects, research work stands alone. By undertaking more extensive analysis in projects, the knowledge base of each organization increases over the years. This initial in-depth research activity uses a wide range of knowledge and skills, as we can see in the following case studies.

Case Study: Seymour Powell and the ENV Bike

At Seymour Powell, researchers carry out a client company audit before product development begins. This gives the Seymour Powell designers a foundation on which to base their work. Says SPF research team member James Samperi: "We try to make the product design process more informed, so we need to have a clear idea of the client's needs. The investigations themselves include user research; market dynamic studies; and research into social, business, and technology trends; as well as visual design expectations. Research centers on learning about the client's products and the industry as a whole." It also makes it easier to analyze how the client's brand works with the planned product.

SPF researchers consider that their work sits somewhere between product design and marketing. "Marketing people normally carry out the sort of work we now do; designers have not done this sort of research in the past," explains SPF team member Paula Zuccotti. "Advertising planning strategies and product planning strategies affect the brand in the same way. The designers at Seymour Powell can focus their work better when they have the results of our work in SPF."

In 1999, as part of its work with the automotive industry, SPF was hired by Yamaha to research motor vehicle futures. This work led directly to a new project—the development of the ENV (emissions neutral vehicle) bike, created jointly by Seymour Powell and its client, Intelligent Energy, a British energy solutions company. Launched in 2005, The ENV is the world's first purpose-built fuel cell motorbike.

The ENV bike was built around Intelligent Energy's CORE fuel cell, which supplies energy derived from hydrogen and is completely detachable from the bike (Figure 3a, Figure 3b, and Figure 3c). As part of the brand strategy, the name CORE is used to represent a new type of engine. The fuel cell is radically compact and capable of powering anything from a motorboat to a small domestic property. In fact, because the fuel cell is detachable, it can be removed from the bike and used to power another vehicle or deliver electricity to a dwelling. It is particularly relevant for the developing world, where fuel cells offer both easy portability and power delivery at the point of consumption. Even better, this technology emits only water vapor (Figure 4).

"With all the depressing news about climate change and geopolitical unrest, many people look into the future with a sense of dread," comments Richard Seymour on the project. "But designers can't think like that. It's our job to face the future optimistically, and projects like the ENV bike point the way."

Figure 3a

Figure 3b

Figures 3a, 3b, 3c. The ENV (emissions neutral vehicle) motorbike runs on a removable fuel cell the size of a small shoebox. The CORE fuel cell technology allows easy removal of the whole "engine"—a practical, integral, and unique aspect of the vehicle system. The vehicle emits only water vapor.

Figure 3c

Figure 4. The fully-integrated 1 kW fuel cell generator provides power on demand directly to the drive-train. To enhance performance during peak power demand, the fuel cell is hybridized with a battery pack to provide a 6kW peak load to the motor. The result is a balanced hybrid concept that combines the main advantages of the CORE fuel cell, hydrogen storage, and battery technology. Front view of white ENV bike on left, back view of black bike on right.

Case Study: Ziba Design and Lenovo

When Ziba started concentrating on user-centered issues, designers at the company realized they had created a strategic tool. In the first stage of a project, the Ziba team asks lots of questions, Vossoughi says. "We want to create the right experience for the client and the target customer. We connect the client and the customer, and the leverage from this knowledge is where client companies find value," he explains.

For Chinese client Lenovo, Ziba defined and developed a line of products for the company's consumer business segment based on its three technology platforms: desktop, mobile, and cellular. The new products were targeted to Chinese consumers.

Chinese society and economy have changed massively in the last few years, in the face of rapid urbanization and increased personal wealth. It was inevitable that Chinese consumers would seek products with the latest technology. Lenovo realized that to compete successfully, it had to create products that were relevant to this consumer need and had meaning for each section of its varied customer base. The new product-line strategies arose from a comprehensive and rigorous process of internal (company and brand) and external (users, market, and technology) research. Through analysis of the existing marketplace, Ziba discovered that most of Lenovo's products had typically been positioned as one-size-fits-all solutions.

Ziba's research led to the development of a user-centered product opportunity matrix. The matrix defined twelve different product opportunities on the basis of the three technology-based business units and four user segments. The new product strategy also addresses environmental issues. To facilitate recycling, product housing uses virgin, injection-molded ABS plastic, which is inexpensive and easy to reuse.

This project has had a profound effect on Lenovo and the way it now approaches product development (Figures 5–8). The industrial design department, which used to be called in at the last moment to style me-too products, now gets involved at the outset of a project to help define product opportunities and business plans.

Figure 5. The desktop PC's freestanding modular media unit can be attached to a wall for a more immersive entertainment experience. The illuminated LCD indicators keep users informed about the operating status of their systems.

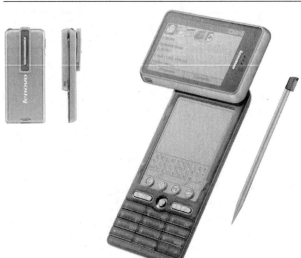

Figure 6. The display rotates 90 degrees to reveal an input pad for Chinese character writing. A convenient stylus is stored inside the phone's housing, responding to the Chinese appreciation for complex details. Software detects display rotation and automatically adjusts pictures and words to fit the new format.

Figure 7. Chinese professionals take multitasking seriously. An optional Bluetooth wireless headset allows hands-free use, a critical need on the crowded streets and buses of Beijing and Shanghai.

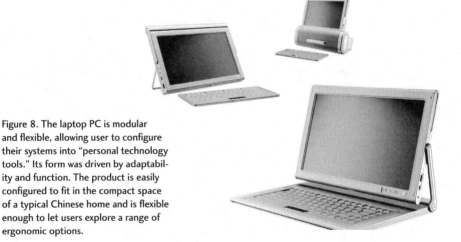

Figure 8. The laptop PC is modular and flexible, allowing user to configure their systems into "personal technology tools." Its form was driven by adaptability and function. The product is easily configured to fit in the compact space of a typical Chinese home and is flexible enough to let users explore a range of ergonomic options.

CULTURE AND VALUES

In the balance between pure product design and strategic thinking, both design organizations have developed new types of consultancy culture. Their tools and techniques are more attuned to client companies' brand values. It is apparent that principals in both organizations spend the majority of their time fine-tuning their organizations' strategic innovation processes with a view to the future. In this way, they are demonstrating a kind of organizational resilience.

Seymour Powell, for example, uses a panel of experts whose composition varies depending on the nature of the work. Panels are made up of independent designers and other consultants who validate research studies. This external panel is a particular characteristic of the consultancy, and as Dick Powell maintains, "We like working in this way." There is no question that the arrival of the consultancy's research department, SPF, has done much to change the culture of the consultancy by providing in-house specialist researchers, thus creating a type of think tank for the consultancy as a whole. Consultancy outputs are mainly product-driven and as such, it is necessary to determine the future of product trends and ranges. Seymour Powell believes this gives client companies a "bigger picture" and a strong direction for new product development.

Ziba Design, like Seymour Powell, has evolved over the years and continues to reinvent and redesign itself. "As we get larger, we need to make sure the message we give to our clients stays coherent and consistent," notes Sohrab Vossoughi. "Visual design or engineering services last only as long as the product. But what we do ties back to the whole idea of brand. We preserve, enhance, and build our client's brand equity so that it continues long after the project.

"We also think we are in the business of innovation management, in that we try to reduce the inherent risks of product development and innovation. We optimize the value of innovation within the context of business and brand."

COMPETITIVE ENVIRONMENT

Comments received from principals in both consultancies indicate a high level of agreement as to where the design profession, in general, should be heading, at the same time recognizing the industry's dilemmas and obstacles to change. As Richard Seymour points out, "All the boundaries we know as designers are dissolving. Designers should take a meta-view of themselves and of the world around them. If design is an industry, it is in peril, because its context is changing, and designers' work currently lacks relevance." Generally, designers' work does not address the larger picture and urgent issues such as demographic change, climate change, and consumer complexity. Principals in both Seymour Powell and Ziba are also conscious of the fact that in the past five years, not only manufacturing but also design and development have moved to the Far East. Designers in the West no longer have the intellectual high ground, Powell maintains. These trends have serious implications for the future of design consultancies in the UK and the US.

Ziba's Voussoghi insists that designers would do well to collaborate with management consultants to improve the work of managing organizational creativity. "In many client organizations," he notes, "brand issues are driven exclusively by marketing personnel. Design and marketing should support each other on an equal basis. More companies are beginning to understand that design can affect decision making on a strategic level."

Unfortunately, Voussoghi adds, many designers still talk about how design looks, rather than how it builds, preserves, and enhances brand—which has become the language of business today. "Design firms that understand the contributions of research and design planning to strategic thinking will be valued," he says. "Design stars will always be there and will flourish . . . but consultancies have to move up the food chain to change."

THE CHANGE DEBATE

Like their business clients, the design industry is going through significant change. Both consultancies' principals believe the design industry has to adapt to the times. As we have seen, major business theorists think a new type of corporate strategy is emerging. Management and design education norms are being re-examined. Richard Seymour asks, "Is the design industry capable of being fast enough on its feet to understand what is needed from it to fulfill client needs?"

In practice and education, both management and design institutions, with a few admirable exceptions, are finding it a struggle to come to terms with the new environment. Of all disciplines, design is expected to be the most adventurous, flexible, and resilient. That there is still a debate as to its future is mysterious. In Guy Julier's book, *The Culture of Design*,[4] many designers were asked about the possibility of integrating the design disciplines more closely with branding, marketing, management, and distribution. They were also asked whether they aspired to orchestrate a complete product in all its aspects so that they might retain a seamless coherence throughout its life cycle. The suggestion here is that designers assume more responsibility for product life cycle and client company collaboration. The majority of respondents considered this unviable; indeed, most did not see it as desirable. These findings appear to demonstrate many design professionals' unwillingness to countenance new activity that would remove them from their traditional pathways.

In contrast, we should consider the 2004 interview Larry Keeley, of the Doblin Group, had with G.K. Van Patter, in which Keeley said, "If you look at design practice and compare it to the average change in the world, we are not advancing our field anywhere near the pace of medicine, computing, entertainment, or scientific research. Design is rapidly becoming a technical vocational field. So we end up with design being overwhelmingly used to give us good style and a hyperabundance of choice.

"We must fundamentally embrace a watershed change in the nature of the role and the source of value that designers contribute today. So many parts of human life need to be reinvented, made more gracious, and understandable. Corporations can't and won't do this in the best ways without being led by people with an acute design sensibility. Thoughtful designers must find one another, and continue to ask the tough questions. So pick an arena and pitch in," Keeley says. "There's important work to be done."[5]

We can begin to see a connected pattern of changes emerging. Management writers exhort their readers to move their enterprises toward more innovative structures and processes and renew their focus on customers, taking a leaf out of designers' iterative processes and lateral thinking. Design consultancies, understanding that they can contribute more, respond to changes in client companies by developing new knowledge and areas of practice that again feed into corporate behavior and systems.

To watch change processes in organizations as they evolve is absorbing, sometimes painful, always rewarding. The evolution of design consultancy has proved that design and innovation are profoundly and inextricably linked. We are now living in the age of the innovation consultancy.

Note: This article has been adapted from a paper presented at the Sixth European Academy of Design Conference, Bremen, Germany, March 2005.

Suggested Reading

Cagan, J. and Vogel, C. M. *Creating Breakthrough Products: Innovation from Product Planning to Program Approval* (Princeton, NJ: Prentice Hall, 2002).

Mau, B., and The Institute Without Boundaries, *Massive Change* (London: Phaidon Press Limited, 2004).

Tidd, J., Bessant, J., and Pavitt, K. *Managing Innovation: Integrating Technological, Market and Organizational Change* (Chichester, England: John Wiley and Sons, 1997).

Endnotes

1. D.H. Pink. "The MFA is the New MBA," *Harvard Business Review*, vol. 82, no. 2, pp. 21-2.

2. J. Tidd, J. Bessant, and K. Pavitt, *Managing Innovation: Integrating Technological, Market and Organizational Change.* (Chichester, UK: Wiley, 1997). and A. Pearson, *Tough-Minded Ways to Get Innovative: HBR on The Innovative Enterprise.* (Boston: HBS Press, 2003), pp. 27-48.

3. Many thanks to Richard Seymour and Dick Powell (principals, Seymour Powell), James Samperi and Paula Zuccotti (research team, Seymour Powell Foresight), and Sohrab Vossoughi (principal, Ziba Design) for their insights and time.

4. G. Julier, *The Culture of Design* (London: Sage Publications Ltd., 2000).

5. L. Keeley, "The Business of New: Interview with G.K. Van Patter," *NextD Journal*, issue 2 (www.nextd.org).

Chapter 10

How Brands Determine Organizational Creativity

by **Nicholas Ind,** Author and Consultant
and **Cameron Watt, PhD,** Author and Innovation Consultant

Creatively defining and managing boundaries—especially the boundaries defined by brand—is essential to innovative success. Nicholas Ind and Cameron Watt explore the sources and nature of these constraints and, using specific examples, suggest how a company can leverage its brand to innovate in ways that strengthen its position in the marketplace and in the minds of consumers.

ONE OF THE core myths about creativity and innovation is that they require freedom from constraint. In this conception, freedom means the ability to make choices without prejudice. This type of pure freedom is, however, a mirage. There are always constraints, whether they are imposed by outside bodies or by internal limitations, and this is true for both individuals and organizations. An organization must recognize that it is limited by its sense of identity, its competitive position, its resources, its knowledge, and its people. However, this limiting of scope is not necessarily negative. Freedom needs order to be successful. Our research among highly creative organizations shows that understanding their constraints provides a focus for their creativity. The positive use of constraints (or as we refer to them—boundaries) enables these organizations to engage members with the idea of creativity and to develop relevant, value-adding innovations. In this paper, we argue that boundaries—largely determined by the idea of an organization's brand—are the key to continuous and successful innovation.

CREATIVITY AND INNOVATION UNMASKED

There has been a great deal written about the nature and meaning of creativity and innovation, and although this paper will not review such literature in depth, in order to provide a conceptual foundation it is necessary to provide working definitions of creativity and innovation. We propose the following definition: Creativity is a complex process based on stakeholder relationships and results in the generation of ideas deemed to be original and valuable within their context. Innovation extends this definition by introducing the concept of implementation and production. In other words, innovation is the realization of the creative idea.

Much early research into creativity and innovation focused on the individual within an educational or military context. However, we have come to believe that context has a greater impact on creativity and innovation, and this has led to our moving away from research that focuses on the individual and toward a greater emphasis on social, environmental, and contextual factors. Indeed, recent research into creativity and innovation has placed greater emphasis on issues relating to leadership style, communication systems, culture, knowledge, social frameworks, and team dynamics.[1]

Our own research has confirmed the importance of contextual factors and their effect on stakeholder relationships and perceptions, as well as the resulting impact on stakeholders' willingness and ability to be creative. We have identified a number of core constructs found in creative cultures: valuing creativity and innovation, trust, a desire to learn, diversity, and fun or enjoyment. However, we also found an important additional factor, common among the organizations we researched: a clear understanding and belief in the brand. This realization led us to pose the question of whether an awareness of the brand among employees forms another core cultural construct in the creative dynamic.

BRANDING AND PEOPLE

We articulate a brand as follows: Although a brand is related to a physical product or service, it is itself immaterial. It is a transforming idea that converts the intangible into something of value. A brand only exists in a buyer's mind, and it is the buyer who has the power to begin, sustain, or terminate a relationship with it. On this basis, we assert that creating a brand is about employees, their perceptions, their actions, and the consequent relationships they build with customers or stakeholders. Organizations and their products and services are defined and communicated by the assumptions, perceptions, and behavior of employees. It is their interpretation of the organizational ideology that determines personal and group disposition that in turn affects actions and relationships. For example, the way in which people interact with brands like Amazon. com, Quiksilver, and Volvo is largely determined by the beliefs of the employees of these companies, who determine what it is that will engage customers. To ensure a relative consistency of delivery for products and services, there needs to be a common view of the brand ideology—as defined in its vision and values. If this does not exist, key business units, such as marketing, logistics, and customer interface, will not be cohesively presented, and external stakeholders will become confused or disillusioned, which in turn weakens relationships and brand value.

It seems obvious that for an organization to be successful, it needs to be genuinely buyer-centric. However, this process requires a significant amount of listening and signaling; it's only partially controllable, and as such cannot be an exact science. The traditional way for an organization to listen is through market research. This can provide insight and help reduce risk, but how good is it as a means of creating genuinely original and valuable ideas? Our research over the past eight years has illustrated that traditional market research cannot always be relied on if brands are to innovate because such research is by definition an abstraction, not a reality. When managers see statistics, they often stop seeing people; they lose their tacit, intuitive understanding of their customers and default instead to the supposed certainty of mathematics. This, combined with the blinkered and inward-looking nature of many companies, creates an organization that is seller-centric. Alan Mitchell summarizes this point, arguing:

The source of marketing ineffectiveness and waste, therefore, lies in its seller-centric preoccupations. Marketers say the acid test of good value is to find out what your customers want and need and give it to them. When it comes to marketing communications, this is the one thing marketers do not do. Marketers seem to believe that the only people who do not need to practice what marketing preaches are . . . themselves.[2]

Our research indicates that another key flaw of market research is that it often relies on customers clearly articulating what they need now or might want in the future. However, we have found that customers are rarely able to understand or articulate complex needs, nor are they always capable of envisioning the future. In addition, the research contexts and processes can often skew answers through biased perceptions of peers or researchers that apply external pressures to customers. We would argue that these issues create particular problems in the area of creativity and innovation because they can hinder the willingness and ability of organizations to challenge customer expectations and to take creative risks.

Even when organizations listen well by openly interacting with their customers, or as managers for sportswear company Quiksilver describe it, "connecting through a free-flowing culture that blurs the boundaries between employee and customer," they have to ensure the brand delivers on its promises. The problem is that many people have become cynical about advertising and other corporate messaging and are more liable to listen to noncontrollable, and perhaps more-authentic, voices.[3] As Figure 1 illustrates, brand messages reach the customer from a broad range of sources. When this is cohesive, the buyer has a clear picture of what is offered. However, if the messages are confused, the buyer either ignores them or is confused, as well. This occurs when there is a lack of clear brand ideology within the organization.

Brands with a clearly agreed-upon internal ideology are more likely to present a clear brand image and interface with customers in a consistent and positive manner.

Figure 1. Sources of brand messages. From N. Ind and C. Watt, *Inspiration: Capturing the Creative Potential of Your Organization* (Basingstoke, UK: Palgrave Press, 2004), p. 25.

Such interaction over time enhances the brand reputation and increases the value of a brand's intangible assets. This is significant when you consider that much of a business's capitalization is contained within its intangible assets: the collective knowledge and skill of employees, the relationships with customers, and the ability to innovate.

To summarize: Having a strong understanding of the brand not only ensures clarity of image but also enhances customer experience. Internally, it increases intrinsic motivation, organizational knowledge, and stakeholder trust—all of which improve internal performance and facilitate creative behavior.

HOW BRANDS, CREATIVITY, AND INNOVATION CONNECT

Branding, creativity, and innovation connect for two key reasons. First, because they are concerned with adding value and delivering a rewarding experience for the customer. To do so, we propose that creativity and innovation need to be framed by customer-focused boundaries. For example, it would not benefit sportswear brands such as Quiksilver, Patagonia, and Nike if the creative output of their designers or communications staff lacked cohesion in terms of ranges, styles, and products. Similarly, if the Tate Modern or Saatchi Gallery started holding exhibitions of twelfth-century religious art, their clear brand positions would be lost. We believe that branding provides the clarity, focus, and boundaries that apply to major strategic decisions, as well as the everyday actions of employees and stakeholders.

The second reason is that brands, creativity, and innovation rely on people and their relationships with one another. As we illustrate in Figure 2, customers can only build relationships with an organization through the ideas and actions of employees. Customers want to be understood, have their expectations met, and be treated as individuals. We argue that this is not achievable with a purely system-based approach that defines and attempts to rationalize behavior. Rather, we propose that if employees are to act in brand-appropriate ways, there must be meaningful employee identification with the organizational brand and that this in turn helps develop and direct organizational culture. The outputs of this connection are increased levels of trust, enhanced employee commitment, a focus on creativity and innovation, an empathetic understanding of customers, significant value creation, and improved performance.[4]

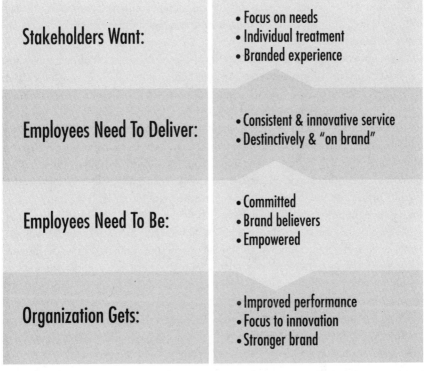

Figure 2. Customer relationship building. From *Living the Brand: How to Transform Every Member of Your Organization into a Brand Champion*, by Nicholas Ind (London: Kogan Page, 2004), p. 54.

FREEDOM AND ORDER

The balance between boundaries and freedom is a delicate one, but it is crucial if creativity is to be encouraged. We suggest that while the brand sets the boundaries for creativity, both strategically and operationally, people should be encouraged to question and test the validity of those boundaries. As Henrik Sjödin argues, "If brands are to remain relevant, marketers and consumers need a certain degree of tolerance for deviants and inconsistencies. If purity becomes a fixation, brands could lose the vigor that companies and consumers require."[5] Tension in a brand is critical because it enables staff to test the validity and meaning of an organization's strategic paradigms and increases perceptions of personal autonomy. In addition, it helps ensure that the organization remains flexible and reflective, thus increasing its ability to compete in highly dynamic environments where there is pressure to differentiate in a significant and meaningful way.

Our work has led us to conclude that defining boundaries is in itself a creative process. Boundaries should focus creative energy rather than limit it by being dogmatic and inflexible. One of our case organizations, the innovation consultancy IDEO, also illustrates our argument. As IDEO president Tim Brown noted in an interview with us:

It's becoming more and more clear that the behavior of products is one of the biggest brand building things that companies have. And also the relationship between products and the brand is absolutely crucial. You have to get that connected loop to work really well . . . we are trying to make sure the innovation is brand driven and that innovation drives the brand too.

What Brown is highlighting is the idea that the brand has always had an implicit impact on setting innovation boundaries, but that as companies have begun to understand the value of their brands and have become self-conscious about them, it has become explicit. For instance, when organizations begin to explore and understand the meaning of their brand, more meaningful innnovation can occur. When a lifestyle brand such as Quiksilver or Patagonia investigates new opportunities, it uses its brand as a benchmark and vision guide. This helps to direct innovation activity and to evaluate the resulting initiatives to determine their validity for the brand. As an example, when Volvo developed its hybrid car, the Cross Country, it used the brand as an explicit input into the process, both in terms of defining a unifying brief that everyone could work to and as a reference point against which decisions could be made. The brief stimulated arguments, but it also settled them. When there was discussion about the cost of the interior of the car, it was the importance of this element to the consumer that determined the resolution. When a feature was suggested that would enable the driver to control the ground clearance manually, there was a safety argument against it—and, because safety is at the top of the Volvo brand pyramid, the idea was rejected. These different thoughts were partly the result of radically different viewpoints that people brought to the project. This encouraged people to fight for their ideas, but because competencies were clearly defined, the team working on the project would tend to defer to expert opinion and to the authority of customer-driven success factors. This was important because brand values in themselves can sometimes seem nebulous. What does it really mean, for instance, to be innovative or challenging? With the Cross Country, attention was paid to thinking through the implications of these concepts. Sara Öhrvall, who was the concept manager on the project, believes this is a major problem in most companies because people don't know how to use the brand values when it comes to product or service development, leading to a gap between the philosophical-sounding brand values and the everyday, critical decisions in a project.

This underlines our core theory that a well-thought-through brand provides constraints that do not hinder creativity or innovation but instead generate clarity, vision, and focus for staff. If the brand is well understood, it should provide the starting point for creativity and innovation and allow for the intuitive decision making that is formed from a deep and empathetic understanding of the brand and its relationship with customers. The brand also provides the benchmark against which decisions are evaluated. Such a paradigm helps organizations balance the tensions between the rational and irrational paradox of the innovation process. In practice, this means that leaders and managers need to encourage the smooth and efficient running of operations while stimulating questioning and creative behavior. Unfortunately, most managers are biased toward the former idea, which focuses on encouraging normative behavior. The outcome of this is a management obsession with quantitative measurements that attempt to categorize the acceptable, punish failure to conform, and rationalize intuitive behavior. But in a creative context there is a problem with this, as Gordon MacKenzie points out:

> Corporate Normalcy derives from and is dedicated to past realities and past successes. . . . To be of optimum value to the corporate endeavor, you must invest enough individuality to counteract the pull of Corporate Gravity, but not so much that you escape the pull altogether.[6]

This belief in rationality is endemic throughout academia and industry. Both business practice and theory often promote quasiscientific methods, laws, rules, and systems in order to justify action or rationalize complex irrational concepts. We would argue that a key leadership role lies in the recognition that reliance on such ideas is creatively harmful and that there is a need to accept that uncertainty and irrationality can be used to generate competitive advantage. We suggest that what the organization believes to be true can and should be challenged; new ways of doing things can and should be found to prevent corporate stagnation.

We are not suggesting that rationality give way to chaos; on the contrary, we believe that structure, boundaries, and systems are key to a successful creative operation. What our research has shown is that successful innovative organizations also inject some irrationality or opportunity for creativity into the organizational culture while using their brand as a foundation, benchmark, and rallying standard. One of our interview subjects, from the online gaming company Funcom, cited the writer Rollo May on creativity:

He said that creativity isn't chaos. Creativity isn't structure. Creativity isn't ideas. Creativity is letting chaos meet structure. That is where creativity is found. To me that's really true . . . It's not the idea itself, it's the meeting with reality, that is true creativity.

DRIVING CREATIVITY: VOLVO

Swedish car-maker Volvo has a clearly articulated brand pyramid, at the apex of which lie its two core values: safety and excitement. These values create a tension because, in some ways, they are oppositional ideas. However, the tension itself is valuable to the brand, because the continuous attempt to resolve it is the fuel of creativity. This creative tension drove the development of a project within Volvo that led to the launch of a hybrid car (a cross between a station wagon and a sports utility vehicle) known as the Cross Country. The idea behind the Cross Country was a perceived need to expand Volvo's appeal to new customers and to make the brand more emotionally (rather than just functionally) engaging. To help the development process and to pinpoint the market opportunity, Volvo undertook a great deal of exploratory research to better understand people's lifestyles and the role transport played in them. This led to the idea of developing an on-road vehicle with off-road potential—something that was explicitly not an SUV, as these had begun to be criticized on the grounds of safety. The briefing process itself was highly detailed. The implications of the brand pyramid and the nature of Volvo-ness were thought through in detail, an exhibition of the target customer's lifestyle was developed, a brand positioning map showing Volvo versus competitive products was produced, and a clay model was created. Sara Öhrvall, who was the concept development manager, notes,

DRIVING CREATIVITY: VOLVO

The project started with the strategy—the role of the car for the overall brand. So innovation is always done within a specific Volvo context. You start with the brand and then you ask: What is the role of this car in the brand? And then: What is the position of this car in the market? How will you position it against other cars?

The value of developing a creative, three-dimensional brief was threefold: It was a source of inspiration for the development team; it provided a customer-focused source of accountability for decision making; and it helped in selling the concept internally to stakeholders all over the world. The brand not only set an overall direction but also influenced the detail. For example, the interior had a distinctive baseball-style stitching on the upholstery that was aimed at delivering emotional appeal and excitement. On the exterior, the bumpers (fenders) were black rather than color-matched to the vehicle—even though some managers disliked it—to demarcate the vehicle as a serious car rather than another of the style-led small SUVs. The twin values also led to ideas being vetoed: When the engineers suggested the idea of enabling the driver to change the ride height of the vehicle, it seemed a clever thought, but as it also led to a reduction in safety, the idea was rejected. As Öhrvall says,

In the brief, there were key success factors, and the law internally was that they had to be defined from a customer perspective. It wasn't a case of "it must be this engine" or "the car has to have 40 centimeters of extra height." It said that the customer must perceive the car as higher than another car, or the customer has to perceive the car as more fuel-efficient. That was done to stimulate creativity.

CULTURAL CREATIVITY: TATE MODERN

Tate Modern is London's major modern art gallery. Like the Guggenheim network, Tate has become a brand in its own right. The original Tate gallery, which opened in 1897, was set up by sugar magnate Sir Henry Tate to house British art. However, as the collection grew in size and stature, it became clear that there was an opportunity for expansion. This led to Tate St Ives and Tate Liverpool, and finally Tate Modern on the south bank of the River Thames. The chosen area was dilapidated and run-down, but rather than choosing to build anew, the Tate trustees acquired a disused 1930s power station and transformed it into a powerhouse of ideas. While the building itself provided a distinctive landmark, the director of Tate Modern, Lars Nittve, and his team had to build a brand.

From the outset, the Tate Modern team conceived of their brand as a place of creative tension: an art gallery that would bring together the modern and the contemporary; a place that would recognize a dual responsibility to artists and visitors; and an experience that would be professional in its delivery but also courageous and challenging. The clear feeling was that if Tate Modern did not deliver on each of these dualities, it would lose its relevance. For example, the gallery could have settled for just showing its collection of twentieth-century modern classics (Picasso, Matisse, Duchamp, Warhol, Rothko, and Pollock, among others). This would have been a safe and commercial choice, but while these artists once shocked, they are now merely modern. To find the "modern" of the future, the gallery had to present the contemporary. This was altogether more difficult. The work might be uncomfortable, its quality more difficult to evaluate, and public interest uncertain. But it could create excitement and dialogue and challenge ideas about creativity. Equally, creating a strong consumer orientation might seem the right thing to do (at least to a marketer), but it was felt that an art gallery should present challenge and a degree of discomfort—there was, after all, a responsibility toward the art itself.

The definition of the Tate Modern brand as a meeting-place of opposites was the source of inspiration for the curation of the gallery, which bucked the norm of chronological presentation, opting instead for a thematic approach based around history/memory/society, landscape/matter/environment, nude/action/body, and still life/object/real life. Within each theme there are also sub-themes and interesting, thought-provoking juxtapositions. For instance, within the landscape theme there is a sub-theme

CULTURAL CREATIVITY: TATE MODERN

of the geometry of nature. What is of particular interest here is the way teams were used to explore the meaning of the brand. The definition of the thematic approach emerged from a small and cohesive core team of Lars Nittve, two curators, and an education curator, who worked to the key principles they had defined. However to avoid group-think, the group was then expanded into a diverse think-tank, with artists, philosophers, and art historians. Nittve says about this diversity:

I think we valued different voices, and we also knew that we all came from the same direction. And it's not given that that is the only direction. At certain moments in processes, it's good to have some friction, because it breaks up patterns and models of thinking. Sometimes, you're moving too automatically. . . . Also, we wanted to move toward having different voices in how we displayed and talked about the collection—to move away from this institutional voice to a more multiple voice.

At this stage, the boundaries of creativity were defined by the brand, but within those boundaries there was considerable latitude. Once the four themes had been realized through this interaction, the requirements changed. The goal now was to flesh out the basic themes and to test the viability of ideas. Whereas the first work group required diversity of background, the new groups, which would explore the themes, needed to have diversity of knowledge, but within a cohesive field. A series of bigger think tanks was formed with curators from Tate's central collection. These people used their specific expertise to define how the four themes could be realized. Finally, once the bigger think tanks had reached agreement, a small group was formed to fine-tune and detail each individual room within the themes. This accordion-like process was designed to provide different levels of diversity and homogeneity at different times. At the earlier stage, when the boundaries were at their broadest, diversity was encouraged to help create connections that might not have been seen by a narrowly defined group. However, when the level of creativity in the later stages became more detailed and the boundaries narrower, homogeneity was more valuable. At this point, the requirement was not to question the fundamental approach to curating the museum, but rather to provide creativity in the specifics of installation.

The success of this approach can not only be seen in the critical plaudits the gallery received when it opened in 2000, but also in visitor numbers: During its first year the gallery received 5.25 million visitors, making it the most popular modern art gallery in the world (in comparison, the gallery at Centre Pompidou received 1.7 million visitors, MOMA in New York 1.2 million, and Bilbao Guggenheim 0.9 million).

COOL CREATIVITY: QUIKSILVER

The sportswear brand Quiksilver exemplifies an approach to innovation that is both intuitive and courageous. Its intuition is a result of long-time employees who have grown up with the company and the close connection between those employees and the sports they serve. As street skater

and Quiksilver creative director Natas Kaupas says, "A lot within Quiksilver happens by intuition. That's because it's a bunch of surfers—people who are unstructured, but very natural. As surfers, they have to adapt to nature and the waves."

Courage is required because Quiksilver has to be a trendsetter in the sports it serves (skateboarding, snowboarding, and surfing); otherwise it would lose its appeal and relevance for its audience of core enthusiasts. This is a fast-moving product area, in which creativity has to be continuous. The implication is that to stay ahead of its competitors, Quiksilver cannot rely on traditional market research or on detailed vision and value statements, but rather has to use its brand as an intuitive spur to creativity. What this means in practice is that innovation is driven by the search for ideas that drive forward the core concepts of quality, innovation, and something Quiksilver refers to as "protecting the roots"—designing and developing authentic products for its customers in a way that recalls the beginnings of the company as the inventor of robust surfing shorts. This approach is embedded into a culture of free-flowing connectivity and co-creativity that encourages listening, sharing knowledge, and experimentation.

As a demonstration of this use of the brand, take the example of the Cell wet suit. Quiksilver learned about wet suits not through research but through the collective experience of employees who surf and through conversations with the professional surfers it supports, as well as from a cadre of enthusiastic amateurs who are treated very much as insiders. As marketing director Randy Hild says, "We believe in the collaborative process, in that

COOL CREATIVITY: QUIKSILVER

input from our riders. If they're not connecting with it, then our consumers probably won't connect with it. . . . It's our job to listen and to adjust." The rider input and the collective sense of the brand, with its imperative for innovation and authenticity, inspired the product designers to rethink how wet suits are designed. The quality failing with many wet suits is that the seams leak, which reduces warmth. To get round this problem, the number of panels on the suit was reduced from 33 to 9, while a new fabric with better stretch was introduced to provide better performance and comfort. The Cell wet suit was then launched through an internally developed and distinctive advertising campaign using Rorschach ink-blob images; this was meant to tease and to test creativity. If the company thought of itself only in terms of a fashion sports brand, the design approach would have tended toward a cosmetic enhancement based on colors and graphics, but Quiksilver knows that its brand credibility relies on an ability to deliver genuine innovation that protects its roots.

Such a strategy is long-term and represents a shift away from the traditional "creative away-days" that let staff escape from the norms of the office environment for short brainstorming sessions. We accept that these may result in interesting ideas but argue that once employees return to their uncreative workplaces, most of these ideas become lost and motivation decreases even further, resulting in a breakdown of trust and potential withdrawal of cooperation. Our research highlights that the ideal is for irrationality and creativity to be incorporated into the organizational culture. Many of the organizations we studied have achieved this through capable and confident leadership and the development of a clear brand ideology.

CONCLUSION

The premise of this paper is that when the brand is clearly understood, it provides the structure and boundaries that encourage creativity and innovation to flourish. It means that people can be genuinely empowered to use their abilities to be creative. And it means overt control mechanisms can be reduced—the brand ideology helps people understand how to set their own controls. In these environments, the brand allows the rational and the irrational to coexist.

Unfortunately, this approach to creativity and innovation is relatively rare. Most organizations and managers still default to a control-conform paradigm either on a day-to-day basis or when they are faced with a new product development project. As Mintzberg, et al., suggest,[7] managers' main concern is ensuring strategies work and are implemented to plan. The control a manager exerts is partially defined by the nature of the operating environment. However, we would argue that it also reflects a philosophical standpoint about trust. If we believe in the ability of the individual to make free and informed choices in line with the brand, we would err on the side of freedom and in so doing capture the intellectual power of all employees. Alternatively, if we do not trust people to act responsibly, we tend to favor a rule-based regime that defines how people should behave. The impact of these negative tendencies can be inferred from research. Take, for example, Gallup's 2000 study of US workers, which found that 74 percent were either not engaged or actively disengaged in their jobs, or the research project carried out by the Tom Peters Company among 700 US business professionals, which found that 75 percent of employees do not support their company's branding initiatives and 90 percent don't understand how to represent the brand effectively.

We believe that corporate order can be delivered by brand boundaries, which leave people free to express their creativity within a defined space. This requires the brand to be determined in such a way that it is inspirational and engaging. And it also requires that employees understand and live the brand. If the definition remains a static, unfulfilled statement, it cannot guide people's thinking and behavior. Such a process also requires a high degree of trust that staff will do the right thing. Unfortunately, many organizations do not trust their employees, which is damaging for the individual, as well as for the organization. When there is a sense of trust, employees' sense of self-worth is enhanced, as are their intrinsic motivation and willingness to collaborate creatively. Such perceptions and actions have a significant impact on performance. In a world where intangible assets are so important, it makes sense to use all the intellectual capacity at your disposal.

Suggested Reading

Amabile, T.M. "A model of creativity and innovation in organizations." In Straw, B.M., and Cummings, L.L. (eds.), *Research in Organizational Behavior* (Greenwich, CT: JAI Press, 1988), pp. 123–167.

Christiansen, J.A. *Building the Innovative Organization: Management Systems that Encourage Innovation* (Basingstoke: Macmillan Press, 2000).

Collins, J.C., and Porras, J.I. *Built to Last: Successful Habits of Visionary Companies* (London: Random House Business Books, 1998).

Csikszentmihalyi, M., and Sawyer, K. "Shifting the Focus from Individual to Organizational Creativity." In Ford, C.M., and Gioia, D.A. (eds.), *Creative Action in Organizations: Ivory Tower Visions and Real World Voices* (London: Sage, 1995), pp. 167–172.

Handy, C. "The Citizen Company." In Henry, J. (ed.), *Creative Management* (London: Sage, 2001), pp. 240–251.

Ind, N. *Living the Brand: How to Transform Every Member of Your Organization into a Brand Champion* (London: Kogan Page, 2001/2004).

Ind, N., and Watt, C. *Inspiration: Capturing the Creative Potential of Your Organization* (Basingstoke: Palgrave Press, 2004).

Sethia, N.K. "The Role of Collaboration in Creativity." In Ford, C.M., and Gioia, D.A. (eds.), *Creative Action in Organizations: Ivory Tower Visions and Real World Voices* (London: Sage, 1995), pp. 100–105.

Endnotes

1. Some of these include work by T.M. Amabile, as well as Csikszentmihalyi and Sawyer, Hennessey and Amabile, Sethia, and Oldham and Cummings (see the Suggested Readings section at the end of this article).

2. Alan Mitchell, *Right Side Up: Building Brands in the Age of the Organized Consumer* (London: HarperCollins Business, 2001).

3. In a study of consumer trust by Yesawich, Pepperdine, and Brown/Yankelovich Partners National Travel Monitor, 2001, US adults recorded a trust figure of only 3 percent for messages received through advertisements.

4. As evidence for the benefits of this, "Commitment: Characteristics, Causes, and Consequences," a global study published in September 2002 by International Survey Research, presented evidence, based on employee feedback from 362,950 employees in forty countries, that organizations with highly committed employees outperformed low-commitment organizations in operating margin by more than 5 percentage points.

5. H. Sjödin, "Dirt!—An Interpretive Study of Negative Opinions About a Brand Extension," paper given at the European Association for Consumer Research Conference, Gothenburg, June 2005.

6. Gordon MacKenzie, *Orbiting the Giant Hairball* (New York: Viking Penguin, 1998), pp. 31, 35.

7. H. Mintzberg, B. Ahlstrand, and J. Lampel, *Strategy Safari: The Complete Guide Through the Wilds of Strategic Management* (Harlow, UK: Pearson Education, 1998).

Chapter 11

Integrating Design Into Strategic Management Processes

by Ron Sanchez, Professor of Management,
Copenhagen Business School, Denmark

Ron Sanchez, analyzing the interface between design and business strategy, identifies the many activities and decision-making points where design expertise has value. He stresses that design managers must expand their understanding of business priorities and processes, and he proposes that by doing so they can positively affect the strategic direction of a business unit and build more productive relationships with their clients' senior managers.

MOST DESIGNERS TODAY occupy positions in their client's value-creation processes that are fairly far downstream from their clients' strategic decision-making processes. In typical engagements, designers are asked to create a good form or a packaging design for a product whose functions and target market have already been decided, or to find good ways to communicate a corporate image or message that has already been defined by senior managers. Growing numbers of design firms today, however, are realizing the significant potential value that could be created for both them and their clients by expanding the role of design-related activities in upstream strategic decision processes of client firms.

To be considered useful participants in strategic management processes, however, designers must meet three challenges. They must understand clearly the issues that managers consider in deciding a strategy; they must identify the ways in which they could most usefully contribute to managers' strategic decision processes; and they must learn how to communicate their potential contributions using language and concepts that strategic managers understand. The goal of this article is to suggest some important ways in which design professionals can meet these challenges.

DESIGN AND BUSINESS UNIT STRATEGY

To explain how designers might connect with and contribute to strategic management processes at the business unit level,[1] we must first answer the basic question: What is a strategy?

To answer this question, it might be useful to explain that the field of strategic management is populated by people from different backgrounds and with different perspectives on what strategy is all about. For example, managers, consultants, and professors involved in strategic management may come from fields as diverse as finance, marketing, organization behavior, operations management, law, and so on. Moreover, given this diversity of participants, the field also has a tendency to generate new terms and concepts at a high rate, often leading not only to debates about key concepts within the field, but also to vocabulary proliferation and terminological confusion. Nevertheless, there is generally a high level of agreement among managers and other strategy professionals as to the essential elements of a business unit strategy, even though individuals may use different terms in referring to these essential elements and may even attach different levels of importance to the various elements in a strategy.

The essential elements of a business unit strategy are shown in Figure 1 under the strategic logic of a business unit, the term for a business unit strategy that my colleague Aime Heene and I use in our book on strategic management.[2] The term strategic logic suggests there are fundamental logical relationships among elements that must be defined and maintained in designing an effective business unit strategy, and we further characterize the role of business unit strategic managers as "designers of organizations as

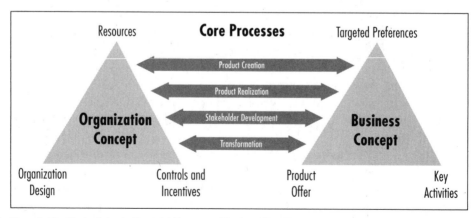

Figure 1. The Strategic Logic: Essential Elements of Business Unit Strategy. (Source: Ron Sanchez and Aime Heene, *The New Strategic Management* (John Wiley & Sons, 2004)

systems for sustainable value creation and distribution." To assist business unit managers in designing effective strategic logics, we also identify a number of system design principles that strategic managers should follow when designing business unit strategies.

Our discussion of the ways in which designers can contribute to strategic management processes at the business unit level focuses on two key activities:

1. Helping managers define the essential elements of a strategic logic

2. Helping managers achieve and maintain conformance to the system design principles that apply to the various elements in a business unit's strategic logic

We organize our discussion of these activities around the three main components of a strategic logic: the business concept, the organization concept, and core processes.

The Business Concept

In a strategic logic, the business concept represents the market-facing side of a business unit's strategy—what we might refer to as management's theory of value creation. The business concept defines the basic who, what, and how questions for a firm: the targeted preferences (kinds of customers) a firm will try to serve, the product offer the firm will create for its targeted customers, and the key activities to be given priority in presenting and delivering its product offer to its targeted customers.

Targeted preferences. Perhaps the most fundamental decision made by the strategic manager is where the firm will compete. At the strategic level, this decision focuses on the choice of market segments the firm will attempt to serve and compete in. As suggested by the term targeted preferences, market segments are not defined by demographics such as age, income, education, or place of residence but rather by the prioritized sensitivities of potential consumers or users of a firm's products with respect to price, performance, speed, reliability, quality, and other aspects of a product offer. Market segments consist of groupings of potential customers who have similar sensitivities with regard to a product category and who prioritize those sensitivities in similar ways.

The first step in the strategy process for business unit managers is trying to figure out what kinds of market preferences and segments currently exist and are in the process of forming within a given product market. Traditional marketing research has developed a suite of techniques (focus groups, expert panels, in-depth customer surveys, and the like) for trying to discover the kinds of preferences that exist or are emerging in a product market. Yet these techniques are clearly not adequate to develop all the possible insights strategic managers need to have today into how customer (and potential customer) preferences are evolving. Indeed, in many firms, market segmentation studies typically focus on quantitative measures of segment size, growth rates, purchase frequencies, and so forth in an effort to provide a basis for assessing the potential profitability of various identified segments. In-depth qualitative insights into the hearts and minds of potential and actual customers are always in short supply, but are critical in strategic decision-making.

Designers have skills and methods that can help strategic managers improve their understanding of the preferences of current and potential customers. For example, designers often employ ethnographic and other research methods based on close observations of and interactions with potential customers in actual product-use contexts, but the critical insights into customer behaviors that can be developed through such methods are rarely included in market analyses that strategic managers receive from marketing research.

Moreover, marketing research is often narrowly focused on investigating how customers perceive the functions, features, and performance levels that currently define a product concept, and as a result may be blind to important evolutions in the ways customers perceive and use different kinds of products. For example, while most producers of home refrigerators focused on researching incremental extensions to existing functions and features in refrigerators, Samsung Corporation asked its designers to take a close look at how American families actually use refrigerators. After installing time-lapse video cameras in the kitchens of a number of American homes, Samsung designers observed that refrigerators also function as communication centers in American homes, typically holding message boards for family members, shopping and to-do lists, phone numbers, and other family information. On the basis of these close observations of refrigerator users, Samsung decided to introduce flat-panel displays in the doors of some refrigerator models to support the important communication function refrigerators have come to play in American homes.

Helping strategic managers understand better how various kinds of customers actually perceive and use their firm's products—and competitors' products—is one of the most important ways in which designers can assist strategic managers in selecting the market segments to serve in their business unit strategies.

Once strategic managers have decided the kinds of customer preferences (market segments) they will try to serve, they must then decide the product offer that the firm will create to serve its targeted customers. The product offer (also sometimes referred to as product offering or value proposition) defines much more than the product a firm will create. It defines and interrelates the ways in which a firm will attempt to create value for its customers and the ways in which it will undertake to manage the costs of ownership and use its targeted customers will incur.

One of the most useful ways of representing the sources of perceived value and cost in a firm's product offer is the net delivered customer value framework developed by Philip Kotler of the Kellogg School of Management at Northwestern University.[3] This framework (see Figure 2) identifies four sources of perceived value (product use, services, image, and personal interaction) and four sources of perceived cost (financial, time, energy, and psychic) that must be managed in designing a product offer to appeal to the specific preferences of a targeted market segment. Designers can provide a number of valuable inputs to help strategic managers define all eight value and cost dimensions of successful product offers.

Net Delivered Customer Value =

Four Sources of Perceived Value	minus	Four Sources of Perceived Cost
1. Product		1. Financial cost
2. Services provided		2. Time cost
3. Image		3. Energy cost
4. Personal interaction		4. Psychic cost

Figure 2. Net Delivered Customer Value framework for representing a firm's product offer.

Designers have traditionally been involved in developing pleasing designs for products whose functions, features, and performance levels have already been decided as part of a firm's strategy. However, as our discussion of market segmentation suggests, designers could become much more active in defining the four value dimensions of a product offer farther upstream in a firm's strategy process. There is excellent potential for designers to become more involved in researching the functions, features, and performance levels a new product could provide to its users, and in helping strategic managers to understand how different kinds of customers are likely to perceive value (or not) in various functions, features, and performance levels.

As more and more firms become capable of offering competitive products today, competitive strategies increasingly emphasize the services a firm provides to its customers as important potential sources of differentiation. Services include all the activities a firm performs to help its customers learn about, evaluate, decide to purchase, purchase, take delivery of, set up, use, maintain, repair, upgrade, retire, and recycle a product. Escalating competition, not just in products, but also in the services that come with products, means it is increasingly important for the services component of a firm's product offer to be designed to deliver services to customers in a growing number of ways and at higher and higher levels of reliability and performance. In today's experience economy, designers who improve the design of a firm's service activities in ways that increase customer perceptions of the value of a firm's services in support of its products can become important partners in helping strategic managers effectively differentiate their firm's product offers in the marketplace.

The image value component of net delivered customer value refers to the value a user of a product will derive from the way other people perceive them when they are observed using a firm's product. Luxury goods, for example, are products that have high image value to people who buy and display them to signal their membership in (or aspirations for) a high economic strata of society. However, image value may come from many kinds of aspirations or affinities that use of a product might signal. Through direct observations of and interactions with product users, designers may be able to help strategic managers sharpen their understanding of the image value users of a firm's products may derive as they use the product to signal that they belong or aspire to some kind of social status.

The personal interaction component of net delivered customer value is the value that customers derive from the human interactions they have in the processes of becoming and remaining a customer for a firm's products. Personal interactions include not only face-to-face interactions, but also a firm's written communications, telephone responses, and Web sites that a customer may interact with. All forms of a firm's interactions with potential and actual customers today can be seen as critical in attracting and retaining satisfied, loyal customers—and therefore should be explicitly designed to create personal interaction value. Designers who can design service processes (and supporting training programs) that elevate the personal interactions a firm's customers experience into strong sources of perceived value are likely to be seen by strategic managers as important partners in imagining new ways of creating value in a firm's strategies.

The four cost dimensions of net delivered customer value must also be designed to minimize targeted customers' perceptions of the costs involved in taking advantage of a firm's product offer. Note that the concept of cost here includes not just the financial costs of ownership and use of a product (on which designers may have limited influence), but also the time, energy, and psychic costs (on which designers may have major impacts) that targeted customers will perceive as they evaluate what is involved in taking advantage of a firm's product offer.

Potential customers for a product are likely to have different sensitivities to the overall costs of a product and also to the timing of various costs. For example, a life-cycle costing perspective suggests that customers will consider not only purchase costs for a product, but also costs of use, maintenance, repairs, replacement, and retirement. However, some kinds of customers will be more sensitive to total costs than others, and different kinds of customers will have different "discount rates" that make them more or less sensitive to future costs of ownership and use of a product. By developing insights into how various kinds of customers perceive and weigh these costs, designers can help managers to design the cost streams associated with ownership and use in ways that can be perceived as minimizing perceived costs by targeted market segments.

Time costs represent the time that potential customers imagine they will have to spend in evaluating, purchasing, setting up, using, maintaining, repairing, and retiring a firm's product. Similarly, energy costs represent the energy that potential customers imagine they will personally have to expend in order to take advantage of a firm's product offer. While strategic managers commonly concern themselves with financial pricing issues, fewer managers have means to imagine how targeted customers will perceive the time and energy costs involved in using a firm's products. In this regard, designers who can interact more closely with targeted customers to develop insights into the relative value those customers place on their time and energy in a given product context can provide strategic inputs to the design of a firm's overall product offer.

The fourth form of perceived cost to be managed in designing a product offer is psychic cost—the extent to which targeted customers will worry about doing business with a firm. Potential sources of worry commonly include concerns about product reliability, durability, and performance, and the level of services and support customers will actually receive from a firm. Psychic costs tend to be important (maybe even more important than financial costs) when a product plays an important role in a customer's lifestyle or business. Designers may be able to help strategic managers to improve their understanding of the range of concerns that potential customers have about buying and using a firm's products, and of the potential magnitudes of the various kinds of concerns and associated psychic costs targeted customers may perceive.

Key activities. Managing strategically means setting priorities, and strategic managers must decide which of the many activities a firm performs should receive top priority in allocating a firm's resources (including management attention). From a strategic perspective, the basis for identifying which activities should be considered key—and thus should receive top priority in allocating resources—is straightforward: Those activities that have the greatest impact on targeted customers' perceptions of the net delivered customer value of a firm's product offers should receive top priority in a firm's resource allocations.[4] Designers who are able to research and understand which specific aspects of the eight dimensions of net delivered customer value really matter most to the kinds of customers a firm is targeting, can provide critical inputs to the strategic decision-making processes that determine which activities a firm prioritizes and how a firm invests its resources in those activities as it tries to create customer value.

System design principles for the business concept. Designers may provide an important service to strategic managers by helping them to assure that a firm always honors the two system design principles for a business concept.

The first system design principle is that the three elements of a firm's business concept must always be logically consistent—that is, the market preferences a firm is targeting, the product offer it has created, and the key activities it is emphasizing should be tightly, logically aligned and make sense together. Achieving and maintaining logical consistency within the elements of a business concept is a constant challenge to firms because the three elements of a firm's business concept are likely to be influenced by different groups within a firm, each of which may have its own world view, priorities, and agendas. For example, a firm's marketing staff may take the lead in identifying and selecting market segments, whereas its R&D staff have responsibility for defining and designing product offers, and operations managers decide how to carry out a firm's activities. Designers who can act as devil's advocates and discover logical inconsistencies in a firm's business concept—for example, key activities that are driven by a goal of cost reduction when the targeted market segment is more per-formance- or speed-sensitive—can help strategic managers to correct design errors in the market-facing side of their strategies.

The second system design principle is that the business concept must always have a clear, credible rationale for superior value creation. In effect, it is possible to have a busi-ness concept whose elements are internally logically consistent, but which will never manage to generate profits. The key concerns in this regard are that a business concept not be susceptible to imitation by many other competitors because competition would then compete away all economic profits and that if a firm's product offer is one that can be imitated by other firms, it should have a lower cost basis than its imitators so that it can operate profitably at market prices. The key role for designers in this regard is again that of a devil's advocate who can offer objective second opinions about the distinctive-ness of a firm's product offer relative to competitors' offers and its relative attractiveness to the kinds of customers the firm is targeting.

The Organization Concept

The organization concept is the inward-facing side of a firm's strategy; it includes the essential elements of management's theory of how to organize to carry out a busi-ness concept effectively. Strategic managers must decide the resources a firm will use to carry out its business concept, the organization design it will use to coordi-nate its resources, and the controls and incentives it will use to monitor and motivate its resources.

The main area in which designers can assist strategic managers in the organiza-tional domain is likely to be in the design of the organization itself. Although strategic managers are responsible for the design of their organizations, very few strategic man-agers have any training in design in general or in organization design in particular. The lack of adequate attention to and skill in creating organization designs is evident in the many firms whose organization designs really do not work very well given the strategy the firm is trying to execute. As a broad characterization, organizations often lack ad-equate communication channels and processes for coordinating the work of different groups in a firm. An important area in which designers can be seen as valuable partners in strategic decisions is helping managers to identify and remedy the missing links in a firm's organizational designs and processes. Accomplishing this means, for example, that designers should be able to help managers to create communications that are not just attractive in appearance, but that also convey the right message to the right people at the right time.

Core Processes

Although firms engage in many activities and processes, at a fundamental level there are four core processes that all organizations must carry out—product creation, product realization, stakeholder development, and transformations. There are some important ways in which designers can help strategic managers improve their firm's performance in all four core processes.

Product creation. Helping firms to create new products has always been the key area of designer involvement with firms. However, as suggested in our discussion of the ways designers can become more strategically involved in defining a firm's business concept, there are many opportunities for designers to become more active participants in researching and selecting market segments and defining product offers that are upstream from traditional design functions. Moreover, many firms today are interested in improving their own design and development processes so that design firms with effective approaches to creating new products may be able to offer consulting services to firms willing to rethink how they approach product creation.

Product realization. Product realization is the current management term for all the activities a firm performs in producing, shipping, delivering, and supporting its products. Today many firms are trying to implement platform strategies[5] that will give them the flexibility to configure and deliver new product variations quickly as markets change. Platform strategies require codevelopment of a firm's products and its processes for realizing its products. Managers who are interested in platform strategies are looking for help from designers versed in modular design methodologies who can help them to define the various process capabilities needed to support high rates of product configuration and change.

Stakeholder development and transformative processes. Stakeholder development is the process of developing the skills and capabilities of the people and firms who provide resources to a firm's value creation process. Transformative processes are periodic transformations that change the way people in a firm think and act—for example, the implementation of total quality management or the adoption of significant social responsibility goals. Both of these core processes require well-designed communications. Stakeholder development can occur only when a firm's stakeholders are adequately informed about improvement opportunities and sufficiently motivated to take advantage of them. To be successful, transformative processes must be communicated internally and externally in ways that make a firm's commitment to a fundamental change in the way it works credible and convincing. In both these processes, designers who can help managers improve their communications to their stakeholders may be seen as valuable partners in helping to design and lead strategic development and change processes in their organizations.

CONCLUSION

This discussion has tried to suggest some important areas in which designers might expand their professional activities in interacting with strategic managers of business units. Some final comments on how managers behave in making strategic decisions may suggest how designers might initiate these activities.

It is important to remember that the field of strategic management really has no orthodoxy of concepts and terminology, and therefore all strategic managers do not use the same vocabulary in talking about strategic issues. However, all strategic managers trying to do their jobs well will have to address the essential questions identified above, and most firms will go through a corporate "languaging" process of creating a vocabulary for discussing its strategic issues. An essential first step for designers in interacting with strategic managers is to learn the vocabulary and concepts the managers use to define and discuss their strategic issues. The essential elements of strategy discussed here can alert designers to the kinds of concerns their clients will be thinking about, and to the concepts and terms they are likely to be using to talk about those concerns.

A second important thing to remember is that all humans—including strategic managers—have heuristics and biases in the way they think. Frankly, given the complexity of strategic decision-making in even moderate-sized firms today, the job of strategic managers is intellectually overwhelming. In such circumstances, those managers do what we all do in our own lives and situations—focus on the few variables we think we understand and can exert some control over. An important way for designers to get the attention of top managers is to let them know they can help to assess some of the softer, more elusive, qualitative elements in designing a strategy, especially those related to what potential customers are really looking for and value most in a product category.

Finally, it is essential to understand that most senior managers are not used to the language designers use. Moreover, because most senior managers inhabit a world in which quantitative and financial analyses of tangible factors ultimately rule the day, many feel uncomfortable with the value system founded on aesthetics that many designers share and with the traditional message from designers about the importance of "good design." Designers who want to connect with strategic managers must not only learn the vocabulary of strategic management, they must also express clearly what they can do to help their clients in the terms that matter to their clients—that is, communicating specific ways in which they can help strategic managers define and implement more successful strategies in their businesses.

Endnotes

1. There are two other levels of strategic management above the business unit level. *Corporate strategy* concerns a corporate parent's "search for synergy" across multiple business units. *Global strategy* considers the additional challenges and opportunities of the search for synergy in an international context. Space limitations do not allow discussion of these strategy levels here, but see Ron Sanchez and Aime Heene, *The New Strategic Management: Organization, Competition, and Competence* (New York: John Wiley & Sons, 2004) for explanations of these strategy processes.

2. See Sanchez and Heene, op. cit.

3. See Philip Kotler, *Marketing Management,* 10th edition (New York: Prentice Hall, 2000).

4. The underlying logic for this view is that if a firm does not succeed in attracting customers because it lacks adequate net delivered customer value in its product offers, then it will not have to be concerned about other activities because it will not have customers or a business.

5. See Ron Sanchez, "Creating modular platforms for strategic flexibility," *Design Management Review*, vol. 15, no. 1 (2004), pp. 58–67.

Chapter 12

Leading Toward Inspiration

by Dimitris Lamproulis, PhD Candidate, Aberdeen University

What are the roles of leaders in creative organizations? On the basis of an in-depth case study that includes examples of client work, Dimitris Lamproulis distills four vital mandates: leaders articulate a vision; they foster a collective, open-minded approach to problem-solving; they nurture the overlap of work and personal activities to reaffirm the commitment to teamwork; and finally, they encourage innovation and independent spirit.

DESIGN COMPANIES WITHIN the competitive commercial world strive for continuous improvement through the best skills of their designers. Leadership, in this effort, is aimed at motivating staff to produce outstanding designs. But how do leaders actually achieve this? For answers, I turned to a leading multidisciplinary design firm located in Glasgow, UK, which I'll call Axon Design. With a staff of eighteen, Axon has been in the market for twenty years, sustaining outstanding growth and completing projects for such clients as the Royal Bank of Scotland. I found that the essence of leadership can be distilled into four principles that enhance the actions and behavior of staff.

LEADERSHIP INSPIRES AN ORGANIZATIONAL VISION

Leaders inspire others with their vision. At Axon, the foundation of that vision is a belief in creativity and its ability to enrich the lives of clients, as well as designers. The result of this is a culture of respect for the ideas and knowledge of everyone on staff, and from that comes trust among employees and commitment to their efforts.

131

My research also showed me that Axon's two founders consistently earn the respect and admiration of their staff because of the imaginative results of their work. The founders (designers themselves) are a point of recognition for the employees, who believe they work with the best. Believing this, Axon's staff is also buoyed with enthusiasm about creating the kinds of high-quality products they know their leaders expect from them.

The corollary to the Axon vision is the idea of creating something new and ingenious. Axon employees tend to be invigorating and "different," but pleasantly acceptable to project clients. Most important, Axon staff expect their projects to be aesthetically challenging for them, as well as for the general public. For instance, the Tinderbox coffee bar (Figure 1), which Axon designed for Matthew Algie and VGF Catering, is an atmospheric and timeless space and emphasizes, like any other of the company's interior projects, the engagement of the space in the activities of the people. With metal and wood surfaces and rich shades of brown, red, gray, and black, the Tinderbox creates a feeling of excitement.

Axon's belief in creativity makes it easy to endorse a diversity of background among employees. Within the staff are graphic designers, interior designers, architects, exhibition designers, and specialists in computer modeling. This variety of expertise offers a breadth of knowledge that makes it possible to carry out innovative projects with high intellectual and commercial value. It also creates a vibrant working environment characterized by the cooperation of equals and a desire to find the best ideas for each

Figure 1. Axon designed the Tinderbox coffee bar in warm but exciting shades of brown, red, gray, and black.

project. This effort is based on the constant sharing of knowledge among employees, who by coming together from different domains transform their learning experience into an interesting and constructive process. Moreover, the mixture of backgrounds advances the self-confidence of the staff, since they feel they are able to approach a design problem from many different aspects. This is supported by Axon's belief that designers who enjoy their work are more creative and innovative. Humor is encouraged in the workplace.

For their part, Axon's leadership does not apply any formal control over its creative staff. They are free to act on their own initiative at any time. The transfer of a vision from the leaders to the staff relies on the freedom of the latter to have their own way of practice. Staff and founders are in a constant dialogue about design and the intellectual effort committed to each project. However, in no way is one person pitted against another; this is not a competition. On the contrary, the idea is to develop the skills of all staff members and encourage their professional growth. For that reason, the founders try to be sure each individual gets the chance to add his or her own value to a project. Axon's founders truly believe that design has the capacity to change the world and make it a better place. This passion for creativity gives shape to their lives, and they share that attitude with their staff.

LEADERSHIP ENCOURAGES COLLECTIVE WORK THROUGHOUT THE STAFF

For Axon's founders, creativity develops and is transformed into innovation through the work of cross-disciplinary teams. Architects, interior designers, graphic designers, and exhibition designers collaborate to reach a solution. In fact, it is a truism at the company that the collective intelligence is greater than the sum of the individual parts, and so staff members are always encouraged to engage with one another. It is the job of company leaders to bring together the appropriate individuals to work on specific design problems. The leaders must also ensure that they provide the right feedback to their staff. In this way, they're able to guide them in the right direction, saving time and effort. In the relationships among staff and founders, there are no boundaries, no walls—anyone can say anything. The leadership aims to generate the dynamic development of ideas within the workplace, hoping this will yield the appropriate conditions for experimentation and for the personal development of each staff member.

My research into Axon's work environment showed me that informal groups are continuously shaped and reshaped during a working day. Employees meet at various places within the organization to discuss difficulties that occur in the course of a project. This generates the exchange of advice and of different stories about similar situations that happened in the past. The founders encourage this; they trust the passions of their staff and their ability to create outstanding work.

In addition, the founders, supporting a collective approach to their work, organize meetings with the members of a project team to discuss the briefing of a client. In these meetings, all opinions are voiced freely; however, the solution that is most realistic, and is supported by all members of staff, will be followed. (This final decision is always unanimous. However, if a member of a project team insists on his or her dissenting opinion, usually one of the founders, but also other employees, discuss their points until all parties reach complete agreement.) Of course, there are often conflicts of ideas, but they are acceptable and occur openly within project teams, and this is seen as a way of achieving the best possible solution. These conflicts are not personal; they bring about the best in a team, the founders say, and the staff operates under that belief.

Brainstorming is another form of collective work encouraged at Axon. It's seen as another way to exchange opinions without criticizing the thoughts of colleagues, and as a way to collect a pool of ideas from which the most viable and aesthetically challenging can be chosen.

Also of interest is the founders' approach to mistakes or failures that happen during a project. As one of them says, "We try to take collective responsibility." In other words, mistakes are the responsibility of the company. Of course, mistakes and failures are examined in order to learn how they were made and thus how they can be avoided in future. Also, the founders ensure that a mistake will not be repeated by actively encouraging the staff to participate in seminars and training courses.

LEADERSHIP ENCOURAGES STAFF TO MINGLE THEIR WORKING LIVES WITH THEIR PERSONAL LIVES

My investigations into the Axon design consultancy showed me that the founders endorse staff interaction outside of the workplace. They believe this encourages solidarity and cohesion. This does not mean that staff members are forced to participate in social events, but it is true that employees willingly meet away from work. The marketing manager, for instance, noted that the office is designed on an open plan and that friendships are often initiated around the common areas. The passion for design is often a starting point for the development of friendships outside the workplace. As a consequence, the performance of each member of the Axon staff is important in his or her private life, as well as at work.

The company's founders, who live together, frequently invite all the staff to their house. They organize regular barbecue parties and often meet staff members to have a glass of wine at day's end. In this way, they express an active interest in their staff, while also establishing a time and a place in which employees can share moments of fun and entertainment.

The staff members are friends, and no one feels excluded. However, as in any group, there are individual friendships that are particularly close. These distinct friendships have a big influence on the development of innovations because they constitute the main networks in the sharing of knowledge among staff members, and that knowledge-sharing is what results in innovations.

Axon's founders try to ensure that employees have enough time to meet outside the working environment. Nevertheless, founders and employees share an understanding that everyone will work long hours and overnights to complete a project on time and of the high quality expected.

LEADERSHIP SUPPORTS A CERTAIN "MAVERICK" ATTITUDE IN THE STAFF

Creative organizations should allow staff members to express their own thoughts and ideas in an independent way. This independence of thought is cherished by the founders of the Axon consultancy. They believe they have hired talented designers for a reason, and once they are on staff they should be encouraged to follow their own inclinations toward what they perceive as superior design work. The founders provide staff with the freedom, as well as the responsibility, to bring their unique talents and creativity into the working environment. Staff members have the autonomy to perform their own research, develop their own thoughts and ideas, and follow the design route they believe is the most appropriate for a project.

This independent spirit is characterized by the way in which employees behave in the workplace. Neither founders nor staff members follow a dress code; in most cases they wear casual clothes. Designers personalize their offices. They are also encouraged to feel comfortable in their interactions. This same autonomy of action applies to their creative work; they can voice their ideas whenever they feel a need to. As a consequence of this environment, the members of this consultancy approach their tasks as their own personal work. Ultimately, it is the passion of the creative employees that drives them to create the best work possible and to express themselves independently in that work.

Collaboration among employees is not hindered by this independent spirit. Axon leadership celebrates individual potential and believes it enhances the collective work.

The creative staff is also encouraged to adopt an attitude of risk-taking in their creative performance—specifically, to move toward unexplored design directions. The founders believe this is the only way a designer can improve his or her understanding about design and will only happen within the development process.

Finally, the independent spirit that characterizes the Axon consultancy is reflected in the inventive, but structured, approach the creative employees are encouraged to embrace. After gathering conflicting and often chaotic information from clients, the founders encourage profound research and the constant refinement of ideas. In this way, they become an example of hard work and efficiency, which staff members imitate by pushing themselves to the best of their abilities.

Many of the projects the Axon consultancy has implemented illustrate its independent and unique approach to design. Consider, for instance, the design of the Tun Ton bar (Figure 2), which was led by Axon's senior interior designer with the support of the company founders. Using light colors in different tones and such materials as mosaic tiles that included glass "gems," he created a space that provides a sense of freedom. The windows are decorated with strips of frosted glass that match the colors used on the walls. The space offers a variety of seating areas, from banquettes to spacious stools and chairs in the bar area. The result is a bar that has a modern feel and is attractive to the young, but also offers a relaxed daytime atmosphere for people who simply want to have a drink or a light meal.

Figure 2. The Tun Ton bar offers a variety of seating areas and a sense of freedom.

Figure 3. Axon's design for Red Lemon Studios, a computer game company, features large glass surfaces and lively lighting.

Another of Axon's projects is the corporate headquarters of Red Lemon Studios, a computer game company. Although this project's secret is well kept since it's not a public space, it features the kind of expansive features Axon is known for, including large glass surfaces with lighting that amplifies the lively and exciting function of the space (Figure 3). The design includes public reception areas, design studio workstations, and flexible room layouts. The Red Lemon project won a Design Week Award. Another well-known Axon project is the Collage bar in Radisson's SAS hotel (Figure 4). The designers wanted to get away from what they considered the typically neutral feeling of most hotel bars. Instead, they created a place in which visitors feel relaxed and welcomed. To achieve that, the designers allowed the floor to sink to street level, thus encouraging the customer to develop a relationship with the world outside. This thought is also supported with booths on the bar's mezzanine, which is just above the head-height of the pedestrians. Axon-designed chairs in the bar feature lower backs to encourage socialization among customers. Relaxing in the aubergine-colored booths under pleated lampshades, customers can observe the street scene and enjoy plenty of light in an intimate and personal atmosphere.

Such projects underline an independent spirit and a willingness to take risks. Combined with much thought and attention to detail, they exemplify the type of work Axon has become known for.

Figure 4. For the Collage bar in Radisson's SAS hotel, Axon designers wanted to get away from what they considered the typically neutral feeling of most hotel bars. They tried instead to create a place in which visitors would feel relaxed and welcome. The windows allow customers to observe the street scene outside.

TO SUM UP . . .

My research on the Axon design consultancy illustrates many of the difficulties a creative organization has to struggle with to ensure its continuous development and growth. In this endeavor, the leadership role is critical within every part of the organization's life.

Leadership is the basis upon which the employees develop the trust and freedom to express themselves. At Axon, the founders lead by example and care for their staff, sustaining their collective and personal development.

In conclusion, Axon's culture is supported by a leadership based on four main principles: a vision that is sincerely held by the founders and encouraged in their employees; a belief in the results of collaborative work; a strong association between the working and the personal life of employees; and an acceptance of an independent attitude on the part of staff. These four principles underpin a culture that celebrates the creativity and the individuality of each member of staff as he or she carries out work that is fundamentally cooperative.

ACKNOWLEDGMENT

I would like to thank the photographer Keith Hunter for giving me permission to reproduce the images used in the article. I am also grateful to Ross Hunter and Emma Murphy for their help and support in my research.

Chapter 13

Serious Play: The Future of Prototyping and Prototyping the Future

By Michael Schrage[1]

Michael Schrage is a Research Associate at M.I.T. Media Lab
and a Merrill Lynch Forum Innovation Fellow

Serious Play *author Michael Schrage probes the nature of collaboration—from the Wright Brothers to Microsoft's beta partners—in this conversational article. Emphasizing "shared space" as fundamental to creative exchange, he shows how prototypes—increasingly easy and inexpensive to produce—become the basis for dialogue among a range of partners who can include colleagues, consultants, and customers. Collaboration is thus transformed into an editing process in which customers can insist on customized outcomes and suppliers can deliver products and services, with unique attributes that are highly valued.*

LOOKING BACK, I see a unifying theme to my work: I study design behavior. Not design thinking, not design knowledge, but design behavior. Certainly I'm interested in design, and I've always been fascinated by how people behave, but what really gets me is how people behave as they design.

Clearly, a lot of time and effort have been spent studying design methodologies, but I believe there has been a woeful under-investment in the behavioral side. People invest in the analytical at the expense of the behavioral. If my work succeeds in making designers usefully self-conscious about the way they're behaving—or the way their colleagues are behaving—as they design, then I think my work will have a shot at making an important contribution to the design agenda.

Bernd Schmitt and Alex Simonson have done a lot of thinking about designing experiences.[2] I find I look at that same coin from the opposite side. Their work makes it clear that successful designers do not design services or objects as such—they're really designing experiences for customers, clients, and users. What I'm interested in are the design experiences designers are trying to create for and create with design consumers. I think this is where ingenuity and creativity and opportunity really emerge.

Over seven years ago, I wrote a piece for the *Design Management Journal* that alluded to what I called design ethnography.[3] I spent a lot of time studying organizations in much the same way an anthropologist might study a remote tribe in the Andes or the Amazon—trying to describe design behaviors in the context of artifacts and prototypes. Eventually, instead of merely describing each little group, I began to study fundamental behaviors associated with design—the ethnological, the behavioral principles that one associates with designers. And these studies took me back to the area around which I wrote my first book, *Shared Minds*—collaboration. I've always been interested in collaboration and collaborative relationships—the kind of creative collaborations shared by Watson and Crick, Bracque and Picasso, Wilbur and Orville Wright. What makes these relationships different from other kinds of relationships?

COLLABORATION AND INNOVATION

Once upon a time, I was a reporter for the *Washington Post*. My beat was high technology and innovation. I ended up writing the innovation equivalent of the man-bites-dog story: Creative individual overcomes insuperable odds and achieves some sort of breakthrough innovation, goes public, makes fortune—and then goes chapter eleven about eighteen months later.

But when I went beyond the obvious clichés, I found the stories I was writing weren't quite true and weren't quite accurate. More often than not, I found that at the fundamental core of innovation was not a creative individual but creative relationships among creative individuals. If I looked for the best predictor of effective collaboration, I found not psychological profiles, but something else: shared space, the objects and artifacts people played with to transform their ideas from notions to innovations. The real key to getting inside collaboration was to look at the artifacts—the models and prototypes individuals used to collaborate—and to look at the way they interacted around those models and prototypes. You had, in effect, an ecology of collaboration built around these artifacts and the interactions around them.

This is incredibly important to us as designers. Why? Because our media and tools for modeling and prototyping are fundamentally changing. What's more, these changes are accelerating. Things we couldn't meaningfully model at all five years ago can now be prototyped or simulated quickly and cheaply. We are creating a new economics of interaction and a new economics of collaboration.

PROTOTYPING AND SHARED CREATION

Prototypes and prototyping have been obsessions of mine for a long time, beginning with my grounding in computer science and software design. I discovered that software people spend a lot of time discussing how to build software prototypes. I found this astonishing, because I knew there had been tremendous strides made in prototyping by industrial designers, but the software people didn't know about them—and vice versa. I viewed this as a real opportunity for research because I could see that prototyping tools for both industries were independently coming to resemble each other. This was an interesting convergence driven by technology, and I believed then—and believe even more now—this technology-driven convergence should enable new kinds of collaboration throughout the design community.

So what do I mean by collaboration? Collaboration is the process of shared creation—not just the coordination of activities in which you get to do this and I get to do that, and in two weeks we get together to match up the pieces only to find they don't fit—and so begins the iteration process. Collaboration means shared creation. It's probably the most important process and the most important relationship you have to manage if you want to innovate. It's where the real risks and rewards are found, and the key to it is that the value comes from the interaction. The value comes from people interacting with one another around a representation of their ideas. There is no meaningful collaboration without shared space.

Everybody knows of Watson and Crick and their discovery of the double helix. Do you know how many experiments they did to confirm the double helical structure of DNA? Zero. Watson and Crick built metal models based on the x-ray crystallography and organic chemistry data of other people. They didn't do a single experiment! Not one. Their models were their shared space. Their ability to collaborate around their models was the key to their Nobel Prize-winning discovery of the double helix.

Wilbur and Orville Wright were able to build their flying machine in 1903 not just because they were good mechanics or because they were brothers—but also because they were able to build wind tunnels and use them to test their prototypes of wings and wingtips. They used tools to create shared spaces for research on the propellers and the wings and on their flyer's steering capabilities.

Shared space is the essential medium for effective collaboration. If we really want to understand innovation and collaboration, we have to study and invest in and explore shared space. Shared space can be as basic as your classic sketch on a napkin—you happen to be in a restaurant with your partner or your team when you get an idea, and you're so excited you grab a napkin and begin to sketch something, and then another person says "Yeah, yeah, yeah, but what if you did this?" and begins to sketch on the napkin too. All of a sudden you're talking through the medium of the napkin—if the waiter were to come by and take that napkin away, along with your uneaten food, your conversation would go away. That napkin has become an integral part of the way you're communicating.

Blackboards and whiteboards can be media for shared space. Prototypes, of course—what with CAD, CAE, Internet, intranet, extranets, and the like, digital media are increasingly becoming the shared spaces that enable not just simple communication but also media-rich collaboration. This is a key point, because communication is not the same as collaboration. Let me explain the difference.

NOT JUST COMMUNICATION

The classic model of communication is the hypodermic needle—senders transmitting messages to receivers—and vice versa. Traditional information theorists argue that the key to better collaborating is better communicating. More communication equals more collaboration. In other words, it's a bandwidth problem. Theorists argue that all we've got to do is fatten up the pipe—expand the bandwidth so that there can be more transmission of more information per unit time. More is better. Lots more is better yet.

Forgive the digression, but this communications mindset really underscores why it's so much more important to understand design behavior than to understand design thinking. Survey after survey asks managers what they consider the biggest waste of their time. The answer? Meetings! But when you ask them what they want to do with the new media, their initial answer is video conferencing! Let's do video conferencing and recreate in virtual space the biggest waste of time in physical space! That's not even a joke. That's the cornerstone of a multi-billion-dollar industry.

But the issue here is not expanding the pipe, the bandwidth. The issue is creating a shared space that becomes a part of the ecology of communication. That's what matters most. If you don't have a shared space, you are not collaborating. Concerned about improving the quality of collaboration in your organization? The first question you need to ask is: "Where's the shared space?"

Mind you—I won't argue that communication isn't essential for collaboration, and that a shared space alone is not sufficient. If you walk into a dining room and find cutlery and plates but no food, that isn't a meal. It takes shared space to create shared understandings. But don't take my word for this. Look at your own experiences in regard to things that you've learned, things you've accomplished, and ask yourself: Was a shared space a marginal or an integral part of what took place? Was it a face-to-face conversation with someone or a couple of people or was it that face-to-face conversation around that model, that prototype, that sketch—something you were able to manipulate together? Shared space—and the definition of shared is every bit as important as the definition of space. That's important because the properties of the shared space shape the quality of collaboration. That's why I became so interested in the collaborative implications of digital media.

QUALITY OF SHARED SPACE

Take blackboards and whiteboards. I was an undergraduate engineering student, doing differential equations with a friend of mine on the night before the exam and—guess what?—we ran out of space on the blackboard. We had had to erase one of the answers we later needed to plug in, which was not funny at the time and is not much funnier now. We were up against the physical constraints of that technology.

Digital media transform those constraints and create genuine opportunities for people who are creative enough to exploit them. This is why I believe the fundamental collaborative design issue is the creation and management of shared spaces. The future of business innovation depends on the future of shared spaces. So the question is: What are the shared spaces that will matter even more tomorrow?

Let's define our terms: Innovation is the product of the way people interact around iterations of representations. In more accessible terms, innovation comes from the way people behave around versions of models (their innovation behaviors). The important questions become: Whom do we behave with? What constitutes a version? What constitutes a model? Should we use one kind of model or multiple models? These are the issues that frame an organization's ecology of innovation. These are the choices, decisions, and questions we as designers should be thinking about. To answer them, we need to become more self-aware in managing the innovation process.

As I argued earlier, using the idea of a napkin in a restaurant: It may begin as a communication, but once a shared space is discovered, whether it is a napkin or a model, it begins to drive the communication. It shapes us and then we shape it and then it shapes us. That's why it's an ecology. A feedback loop occurs, which I like to call BASS—Behavior Around Shared Space. If you want to understand what is going on in your organization, in your project—why you're succeeding, why you're failing—look at how your team behaves, or misbehaves, around the shared spaces it uses to innovate.

Now, here's another great design acronym: KISS (Keep It Simple, Stupid). However, it's very hard to keep things simple. You have to balance simplicity with your human skills, your interpersonal skills, when you're observing design behavior. I've found that organizations often have fundamentally different notions about what constitutes "appropriate simplicity." The shared space—whether a model, a prototype, or a simulation—can be a fabulous vehicle for testing and managing simplicity. Indeed, shared spaces are commonly used to mediate between the complexity of the initial design and the desired simplicity of the final product.

This job—this role—is custom-made for designers. What other discipline spends more time creating shared spaces than design? What other discipline uses models and prototypes as emulations to manage interactions? The market is coming to you. The trend is your friend.

The best designers always look for ways to leverage simplicity. The best design managers always look for ways to leverage behavior. But what is the core ingredient of leveraging behavior? Paying attention to the behavior around shared space. You use the shared space, you use the model, you use the prototype to gain insight and understanding into how people are going to behave. Whether the product is something you hope your clients and customers will want, whether it's something they'll need, whether they are your customers or an internal client, the question is the same: What is the shared space, and how can you use it? That's the knowledge, the understanding you, as designers, can own. That's the real opportunity.

HEARING OPPORTUNITY KNOCK

Let me give you a little-known example of opportunities missed and opportunities lost: NASA's Gemini missions into space. Remember back in the days of Walter Cronkite, when everybody paid attention to the U.S. space program? The ultimate goal even then was traveling to the moon and building space stations in orbit. One of the most important things in the Gemini program was studying how to work outside the space capsule. It was called EVA—extra-vehicular activity—space walks. I had the good fortune to interview Jim Lovell, whom you will probably best remember as the commander of the ill-fated Apollo 13 mission. But before Apollo, he was the commander of Gemini 12.

In an interview, Lovell told me that for Geminis 9, 10, and 11, attempts to work outside the spacecraft were utter failures. I didn't take his word for it; I talked to NASA historians as well, and they largely corroborated Lovell's story. The Gemini astronauts never succeeded in doing the things they wanted to do outside the spacecraft. In fact, one of them exerted himself so much his heart rate went up well past 200 beats per minute; he fogged his visor, and NASA was afraid he might suffer a stroke in space. It turns out that what NASA did to prepare the astronauts for space walks didn't work very well. So what is the obvious way to rehearse a space walk? The answer is pretty obvious: In water!

No pun intended, you don't have to be a rocket scientist to realize that you can create buoyancy and simulate weightlessness in water. But instead, NASA was obsessed with simulating real weightlessness in KC-135 "vomit comets." These were airplanes that did looping rolls to create periods of weightlessness lasting up to forty seconds. There was no water-tank training for the crews on Geminis 9, 10, and 11.

To be sure, it's not as if the folks at NASA didn't understand about water and neutral buoyancy—they just didn't think of it. In 1960s dollars, the total budget for Gemini was about $1.4 billion. In 1999 money, these three failed missions would have cost well over $1 billion—and these were the days when NASA's budget was not a big impediment. Moreover, this was a life-or-death matter. You screw up the space walk, you die. Not only do you die, but you die on national television.

It took three failed missions before NASA did any water simulation training. Lovell's crew got NASA to rent a swimming pool in a Baltimore boys' school, and the Gemini 12 mission went off, in terms of the EVA, without a hitch.

Clearly, money wasn't the issue here. Brains weren't the issue. Ability wasn't the issue. The issue was culture; it was mindset. The single biggest problem one observes in dealing with organizations and the management of BASS is cultural. It's not a resource constraint; it's a noggin constraint. In NASA's case, you had world-class engineers literally responsible for sending people to the moon not prepared to do quick and dirty simulation and prototyping. The problem isn't resources; it's the way people behave or misbehave.

Let's put it another way: If you care about managing uncertainty, opportunity, and risk, model and simulation management matters far, far more than information management. The issue of absorbing intranets and extranets is not an information management issue; it's a behavior management issue. And treating databases as if they were models or simulations is ridiculous. You need to look at the shared spaces, not the information. We shape our models and then they shape us. The feedback loop between what you choose and don't choose to prototype has an enormous effect on how you behave and how you design and what you show to the boss and what you show to key customers. We shape our models and they shape us, and this is at the critical intersection of what we should be managing.

Let's define what I mean by models. A model is a representation of a relevant reality. Some features are emphasized and exaggerated at the expense of others. People have different notions about what relevance means. This has a profound implication. What we choose not to model is often just as important as what we choose to model. Indeed, when I talk to sophisticated modelers at such places as the Rand Corp., they almost all say that when they audit a model or simulation, the first thing they look at isn't what the critical assumptions are. First, they look at what assumptions have been deliberately—or inadvertently—left out.

With this in mind, I'd like to offer three "prototyping parables" that illustrate what I believe are three key behaviors that are going to become far more important to the design community.

THE THREE RS

Traditionally, the three Rs stand for "reading, 'riting, and 'rithmetic." In the context of prototyping tomorrow, I'd like you to think of the three Rs as "rent-seeking, relationships, and reflection & review."

Rent-Seeking

Consider Microsoft's Windows 95, which was one of the company's most successful product launches. Microsoft sent out no fewer than 400,000 beta versions of Win95 to its best customers for debugging and suggestions for new features. As a general rule, Microsoft's beta customers are treated even better than its "real" customers because they're doing really important work for Microsoft. Moreover, Microsoft doesn't send beta versions to just anyone; it sends them to their best customers; to customers capable of testing and using the software and communicating what they've learned in a productive and constructive way. What Microsoft is doing is leveraging the best of its installed base. The company does this extraordinarily well. It's a core competence.

Just for kicks, let's throw out 100,000 of those beta versions. What if Microsoft got no value at all from fully a quarter of the CDs or disks it shipped out? Let's look at the costs associated with those remaining 300,000 betas scattered worldwide. For Win95, there were actual hardware upgrade costs. The software required faster processors and more memory. People had to be trained. Then there was the logging and tracking of bugs.

There are costs associated with crashes and data losses. If you look at what Giga, Meta, and Forrester researchers say, we're talking a cost of several thousand dollars for being a beta. Think of a cost somewhere between $2,000 and $4,000 as the loss that Microsoft's betas incur as they're helping out the world's biggest software developer.

Now do the math: For all intents and purposes, Microsoft's beta sites subsidized the development of Win95 to about the tune of roughly $1 billion. Microsoft's best customers spent more on the development of Win95 than Microsoft did itself. That's a helluva good business model! Hypothetical question: How much more competitive might your company be with a billion-dollar subsidy from your best customer? Would you settle for half-a-billion-dollar subsidy? This is a world-class example of using prototypes as a rent-seeking medium for both design and development.

Relationships

Most designers know the Boeing 777 was the first plane Boeing designed digitally. The company used Catia CAD/CAE software to manage the design. One big problem was that the different parts of the company— avionics, hydraulics, mechanical engineering, structures, and so forth—were competing to put their subsystems in the plane. But then Boeing programmed the software to detect "interferences" between systems being programmed and to send out e-mail to people in those divisions so that these conflicts could be worked out. Boeing discovered that some of its groups were deliberately generating interferences. Was this a form of rebellion by the Boeing engineers because they didn't like the software? No. They were generating the interference because they wanted to meet their counterparts in the other divisions. Boeing at that time was very much organized as silos. The new software was being used as a vehicle for preemptive negotiation and management— because no rational manager wants to initiate ongoing design relationships with a fight.

Reflection and Review

In software development, in which I've spent a lot of time, people do requirements analysis. They gather specs, and they end up with spec-driven prototypes. Unfortunately, more often than not, after they've spent a tremendous amount of time listening to their customers, they go off and build the product or the prototype, and then they show it to the customer and the customer says, "Well, you know, that's exactly what I asked for, but now that I've seen it, I realize it's not what I really want."

I'm not embarrassed to tell you I've made a comfortable living going into these spec-driven, client-centric organizations and telling them to stop after compiling the top twenty-five or thirty-five specs and immediately do a quick-and-dirty rapid prototype. Instead of having spec-driven prototypes, create prototype-driven specs. Use the Q&D prototype to elicit specs based on how clients interact with the prototype rather than some verbal wishlist that gets bandied about around a conference table. Lure your customer, your client, into codesigning the product with you.

And one nice side effect of this is that, as a general rule, although clients may be quick to throw out work you do, they're not so quick to throw out work they do.

Prototyping the Future

So what's the lesson here? You can collaboratively prototype in ways that make your best customers subsidize your innovation infrastructures. Are you doing this? New prototyping media—Catia, CAD, CAE, intranets—can create new interactions among people and create new value. Quick and dirty prototyping can transform the way in which people articulate and assess key requirements. Instead of spec-driven prototypes, you get prototype-driven specs. The point? Transforming the prototyping process transforms how we create value.

Marvin Bower, who for all intents and purposes was the real founder of McKinsey & Co.—a not-unsuccessful consulting firm—had an interesting definition of "corporate culture." He defined corporate culture as the way we do things around here. Changes in modeling media, changes in prototyping media, change the way we do things around here. Everything you do in terms of using technology to build better models faster, to build rapid prototyping, affects your corporate culture. You are inherently agents of cultural change. This means that if you give short shrift to the behavioral issues in favor of the technical, you hinder yourself. You're in the behavioral design business, not just the product or service design business.

So what are the best practices here? Clearly, we've changed the modeling media. More is better. It's better to have more models than fewer models, and the difference between five or six years ago and today is that in the past, you had a finite amount of time to generate a finite number of models. Now, with CAD and these other technologies, you can generate lots and lots and lots of them. You can do multiple iterations per unit of time. This means you now need to be more focused on diminishing returns.

If you are familiar with software spreadsheets, you may be familiar with the term backcasting. Spreadsheets are often used for forecasting. You begin with your assumptions and predict the future will based on these assumptions. Backcasting is when you run the numbers according to how you'd like them to be; you're backcasting to the original assumptions to see how you can get to the numbers you want.

Backcasting is coming to design. You're going to say: Here's what we want the product or service to look like; how shall we use our design tools? Now, instead of a scarcity of design tools, we have an abundance, which means diminishing returns. But when does the cost of iterating outstrip its benefits? I don't know, but clearly, as many prototypes as you're doing now, you're going to be doing ten times more in the next three years—probably in digital form. And if you doubt me—remember doing spreadsheet budgets by hand on paper? Do you ever want to go back and do that again?

Role Playing

Use your prototypes to create design relationships that differentiate—that's the Microsoft message. If you have commodity relationships, you're going to have commodity products. You have to listen—it's the BASS thing. What are the unique behaviors? What unique changes have occurred? How are you using technology to create relationships that differentiate, that give you unique insights into individual customers and market segments? Instead of testing the validity of a concept, how are you using your models to differentiate? Not your products and services—your models of your products and services. Role play, but very carefully.

Here's another true story. I was in Norway not long ago, observing a merger between the Norwegian telecommunications company and the Swedish telecommunications company. I discovered that the Norwegians and the Swedes really don't like each other a lot. They mock each other. This merger has caused a lot of debate. There have been many issues, and one thing I suggested to one of their management groups was role-playing—having the Norwegians play the role of the Swedes and the Swedes play the role of the Norwegians in a mock negotiation. Both sides burst out laughing. They weren't willing at all. And thus far, that merger hasn't happened. (Author's note: In fact, the merger has definitively been abandoned, with much bitterness on both sides.)

What is the problem with role playing? What happens increasingly, I've observed, is that when you ask manufacturing to play the role of sales and sales to play the role of manufacturing, they tend to do a magnificent job of acting out the worst aspects of each other's behavior. This is interesting because, you know, you can have multiple perspectives on prototypes and models in this way, but you may be the person having to manage those role plays. It may be that one of the most important things you will be doing is not just managing those interactions, but making sure you know when to hire the right facilitators for managing these interactions. Role playing is a tremendous way of creating cross-disciplinary, multidisciplinary awareness of the tradeoffs associated with design and implementation.

World-class athletes, world-class sports teams, record their practices. They use videotapes to improve themselves. Most designers have observed focus groups in which customers interact with a product or service. How many designers videotape and review their own design sessions? If you really plan to use your design people and processes to differentiate yourself, you have to record and review design discussions.

As the marginal cost of doing more designs per unit time declines, as auditing and reviewing our design processes become less expensive, we'll see some fundamental changes in design. We're moving away from mere authorship to editing. The more you spend your time generating versions and iterations of models and simulations, the farther you move from being the pure originator of ideas and contributions to being the selector, editor, and annotator of the contributions and ideas of others—like your key customers, your key clients, the other departments in your firm. The industrial designer of 2003 and 2004 will be as much an editor and selector of ideas as an originator or creator of ideas. The trend is to let people customize their own products and services, as in My Yahoo!

How do you design for customization? How do you give people the power to customize in the way they want to customize? The marginal cost of making modifications is dropping to zero. So you have more opportunities than you know what to do with in this regard. This is going to become a key design theme. How do you customize for customization? The marginal costs of computational modeling are collapsing; we're shifting from the calculus of scarcity to the calculus of abundance. The upshot of this is: the more choices you have, the more your values matter.

Your values, your organization's values, and your design values now matter more than ever because technology liberates choice instead of constraining it. But I believe a lot of organizations are going to have more internal conflicts than external conflicts because of this.

I also think tomorrow's design management challenge will be: How will we model and prototype the prototyping process? I think this will increasingly absorb designers' time. It's not enough to come up with better models, prototypes, and simulations; we have to come up with better environments, cultures, and processes to manage the very process by which we arrive at these things.

Endnotes

1. This article is distilled from a lecture the author gave at the 24th International Design Management Institute Conference, October 24–28, 1999.

2. See Bernd Schmitt and Alex Simonson, *Marketing Aesthetics: The Strategic Management of Brands, Identity, and Image* (New York: Free Press, 1997).

3. Michael Schrage, "The Culture(s) of Prototyping," *Design Management Journal*, vol. 4, no. 1, 1993.

INNOVATE

Innovation is the high-profile dimension of a business. It grabs the headlines. It makes reputations. Ideally, it drives sales and moves companies into profitable markets. What isn't so obvious is that behind these positive outcomes is a carefully executed combination of strategic and creative thinking, strong management, and hard work.

This section explores these attributes of innovation. It is rich with case studies. Stefano Marzano illustrates the innovation process at Philips Design with stories that includes a telephone and an MP3 player, of furniture that transforms space with a multimedia experience, and of CT scan rooms that can be programmed by patients to become an aquatic space or aerial environment. Raymond Turner discusses a clever new design for a knife block. Yvonne Weisbarth outlines the advantages of a cutting-edge Bosch air conditioning unit. Gianfranco Zaccai profiles an anesthesia delivery system developed especially for children. Philippe Picaud shows off Decathlon Design's award-winning swim fins. Peter Haythornthwaite tells of his work on a small, light foot-massage device that helps airline passengers on extended flights avoid blood clots. Dick Powell narrates the evolution of Calor's brand-defining Aquaspeed iron. Jessica Feldman and John Boult reveal innovations in how Eastman Chemical and Guinness relate to their markets and customers. Finally, Alison Rieple, Adrian Haberberg, and Jonathan Gander analyze how Sony and an auto supplier called Ricardo have been particularly successful at jump-starting innovation. If you like hands-on, you'll be well rewarded by reading these articles. You'll also learn about many options for approaching innovation and suggestions for using small companies as incubators for new ideas. Todd Cherkasky and Adrian Slobin explain how even organizations in crisis can reinvent themselves with a thoughtfully structured innovation framework.

There is much to learn in the pages that follow, but these may be the two most critical messages:

First and foremost, innovation is about meeting human needs. If there is one common theme throughout all seven chapters, it is that the pathways to the frontiers of design begin with an intimate understanding of people's desires and expectations. Sometimes an innovation is incremental. On other occasions, it is a new paradigm. In both circumstances and in all the case studies, success is human-centered. Technology or marketing is not enough, nor is simply asking individuals to articulate their needs. Certain revelations are only discovered with nuanced research. Whatever the methodology, it is always human desires and needs that bring us to the heart of innovation.

Businesses must be structured to sustain innovation. They must engage the right players—internal teams, consultants, other companies, researchers. They must nurture the right culture—an openness to new ideas and a vision that brings together the human, technological, and market perspectives. They must have an appropriate organization—including a venue for creative exchanges and a disciplined process for parsing and weighing innovation alternatives. They must have the right leadership—a commitment to invest energy and resources and a willingness to seek out creativity from both inside and outside the organization.

Chapter 14

People as a Source of Breakthrough Innovation

by Stefano Marzano, Chief Executive Officer
and Chief Creative Director, Philips Design

The product visions are startling—jackets with cell phones and MP3 players, multimedia furniture, a radiography department where patients design the scanning experience. With these and other examples, Stefano Marzano articulates Philips Design's human-centered techniques for exploring the frontiers of creativity—strategies that blend an in-depth understanding of markets, the firm's special competencies, and the interface with consumers.

TRADITIONALLY, RESEARCH AND development in manufacturing has focused on technological and other fundamental issues designed to answer questions of how benefits can be generated. The question of why one should seek to provide those particular benefits has been less often addressed, perhaps because of a general assumption that consumers would automatically value any breakthrough in technological power, whatever its form. But a breakthrough arguably becomes a breakthrough only when consumers place a high value on it. This suggests that it is to consumers we should look to find our breakthroughs. If we can identify what people see as new value, then we can focus our costly R&D efforts on providing precisely those benefits to the right people at the right time and in the right form.

DEFINING "NEW VALUE"

Consumers' perceptions of what constitutes new value are colored by their situation in time and space. It may be an improvement in material conditions, such as food, shelter, or some product that helps us in our daily lives, or it may be something immaterial, such as an emotional experience or an intelligent electronic environment. In seeking to create this new value, we need to keep an open mind. We have to be ready to look at things in new ways; to be more interested in asking the right questions than in giving quick answers; to make naïve inquiries and take others' naïve inquiries seriously; and to create mental pictures about the near future without self-censorship.

THREE-PRONGED APPROACH

At Philips, we apply this approach to three things: our market, ourselves, and our interactions with our consumers.

Our market. Our market is people. We therefore need to know what they want. But asking them directly rarely works because they often have no idea what they want until they see and experience it. That means we need to get information about them indirectly, particularly information about what they value. This is hardly ever a product; it is usually a benefit, within a given situation. Rather than focus on products as such, we need to look at the wider context in which people use them. By doing so, we may discover opportunities to apply our competences in ways that provide consumers with completely new benefits.

Ourselves. We also need to take a closer look at ourselves. Instead of thinking about companies in terms of business units, we need to think of them as a portfolio of competences and then consider how we can combine these competences in ways not limited by traditional business-unit boundaries. And we also have to consider whether, to give our market what it wants, we need new competences. If so, we may want to acquire such competences ourselves or partner with another company that has them. In the same way, we should look beyond the markets we have traditionally served and consider whether our competences can provide solutions to new markets.

The customer interface. Finally, we need to look at where and how we meet and deal with consumers—the customer interface. In physical terms, this means shops, our own premises, events, and the like; and in virtual terms, it means the Web, email, cell phones, and other new technologies.

VISION OF THE FUTURE

By combining all the insights we gain from looking at our market, ourselves, and the consumer interface, we can arrive at a general vision of the future. On that basis, we can then work out, for the next few years, what new types of benefits we should aim to provide, what new competences we need to do it, and how we should interact with our end users.

HIGH DESIGN STRATEGIC FUTURES

At Philips, we have developed a special process for implementing this general approach, which we call High Design Strategic Futures. This process has been behind some of our more striking products over the past decade.

We think of our method as scientific, at least in comparison with what is normally practiced in the design world. It has a strong multidisciplinary research component, and on the basis of that research, we formulate hypotheses about what consumers might value. We then filter these hypotheses, test them in experiments, and submit them to experts in various fields for critique. This enables us largely to avoid the subjectivity that typifies more traditional, intuitive approaches.

Three Core Competences

In implementing this scientific approach, we apply three core competences: understanding people, innovative integration, and design articulation.

Understanding people. We have developed considerable expertise in understanding people. We apply methodologies and insights from the social sciences to analyze current societies in terms of their key components and drivers, and we identify emerging trends and underlying movements, both short-term and long-term. All this gives us a good understanding of people around the world—how they live, what they cherish, what they think of technology, and so on. We are then able to generate hypotheses, directions, and strategies about what might constitute desirable future qualities of life for people in particular situations.

Innovative integration. To develop new solutions for products, systems, or services, a variety of people—engineers, marketers, strategists, and designers—need to come together to share and develop ideas. Given their different backgrounds, this is no easy task. Although they may all use the same words, they may understand them differently. Innovative integration skills allow us to help people understand each other so that they can work creatively together. Going beyond traditional design competences, they include sociological skills; an understanding of technological trends, media design, and business strategies, models, and processes; and psychology and ergonomics. Combining these with traditional design skills, plus special creative brainstorming techniques, we make the discussion tangible so that people can see exactly what is meant. And when shared mental images are made concrete, it is possible to talk about them in more detail, and to take ideas further faster.

Design articulation. Design articulation, a more typical design competence, comes into its own when a clear concept has been developed. It involves shaping that concept into a tangible, or at least a visible, solution. This may be anything from a product or service to packaging, from a book to a complex interactive interface, or from a fashionable electronic garment to sophisticated medical equipment.

The Process

Combining research findings. The first step in the High Design Strategic Futures process consists of research into social, cultural, and visual trends relevant to the particular target group. We map those findings against technological trends, combine them with research carried out by institutes and universities in various countries, and extrapolate trends into the future.

Avoiding historical bias. There is a natural tendency to base ideas about the future on what we know about the past. To avoid this bias, we do two things. First, we take it as axiomatic that a major driver in human development is the ambition to do everything, be everywhere, and know everything—with the minimum of effort. This ambition, reflected in the myths, folklores, and religions of widely separated cultures, can be seen as the continuous trigger for new technological developments. Over the ages, humans have created many external devices to amplify their powers. But, though useful, they have often been considered too bulky. People have therefore always tried to reduce the size of these devices, and today we even implant them in our bodies. Given these twin processes of "exteriorization" and "re-interiorization" and the human ambition that triggers them, we assume that products that take people one step closer toward that ambition are more likely to be perceived as providing value than those that do not.

Second, we take account not only of social trends that are well-established (and therefore also potentially moribund), but also of those that are emerging. Rather than take a static snapshot, we try to build up a dynamic picture of a situation, with all its tensions and interactions. Some trends are just emerging, others are well-established; some extend over a year or two, others over decades or centuries; some are growing, others are declining. The result is a dynamic synchrony.

Creating scenarios and visualizations. On the basis of all this input, we create scenarios of desirable, realistic future situations and experiences and define the roadmaps needed to take us there. These scenarios go beyond general or abstract descriptions. They specify what individuals might want to do in particular circumstances and how future products or services might help them. To make these scenarios more realistic, we develop personas, or fictional characters. We make them as authentic as possible, basing them on real lives and research data, using a structured methodology to bring them alive in all their nuances. By expressing sociological and trend information in this way rather than in report format, we make it easier for all members of the development team to understand and apply. New ideas developed with these realistic personas in mind are consequently more likely to be on target.

Filtering and validating. The scenarios are put to the test in a two-phase process. They are first submitted to a panel of international experts for filtering. The ideas that emerge as most promising are then given highly realistic visualizations—life-size objects you can almost touch, accompanied by video clips of real people using them in plausible future situations. In the second phase, these visualizations are shown to selected audiences or to the general public at exhibitions or media presentations. A good example of our long-term scenario development is Philips's ongoing Vision of the Future project, started in the mid '90s, the most recent part being La Casa Prossima Futura, which was exhibited in New York, Milan, Paris, Hamburg, Vienna, Tel Aviv, and Hong Kong.

This testing process goes beyond providing useful feedback on the suitability of our scenarios. It also plants in people's minds what Swedish neuroscientist David Ingvar has called "memories of the future." The work of Ingvar and American scientist William Calvin has shown that thinking about potential future developments opens your mind so that you are ready to see the signs relevant to those developments if and when they occur. The brain uses plans and ideas just like real memories and experiences to filter information and guide decisions. These memories of the future potentially lead to new aspirations and desires.

Finding partners. Exhibitions also encourage other potential partners, both within the company and outside, to join us. With the same purpose, we publish a quarterly magazine (*New Value* by *One Design*), exhibition-related Web sites, and books. Our most recent book, *The New Everyday: Views on Ambient Intelligence*, for instance, is designed to trigger thinking and to gain feedback about the increasing "intelligization" of the domestic environment as more and more networked digital devices are incorporated into walls, floors, ceilings, and furniture.

BREAKING DOWN BARRIERS

The High Design Strategic Futures process has already helped to break down traditional barriers and trigger innovative ideas, in collaborations with both Philips businesses and with outside partners.

Nebula

Nebula, for example, is a highly interactive projector that enables people to create their own personalized bedroom environment. It began as a project to extend the market for Philips beamers and projectors. Contained in an elegant vase at the foot of the bed, the projector beams images onto the ceiling. These images (which can also be games or messages) can be personalized and manipulated by the people in bed. You choose the content you want to appear by putting a "smart pebble" into a small container at the side of the bed.

To deliver the best solutions in today's complex world, it is often necessary to join forces with other parties in flexible configurations. In this way, over the past decade, we have worked together with companies in many different markets to develop products by using the method described earlier. The following are just a few examples of our collaborations to date.

Nebula is an interactive projector that enables people to create their own bedroom environment. It began as a project to extend the market for Philips beamers and projectors. Contained in an elegant vase at the foot of the bed, the projector beams images onto the ceiling.

Philips-Alessi

One of our first joint projects was the Philips-Alessi line of appliances, launched in 1994. This collaboration enabled Philips to establish itself as a design innovator, while Alessi learned how to expand into the field of electrical equipment. Both companies benefited from the new experience, and consumers benefited by getting the more colorful kitchens they wanted. The Philips-Alessi line basically set the trend for the rest of the decade.

Cool Skin

For Philishave Cool Skin, Philips partnered with Nivea to combine the speed and safety of dry shaving with the refreshing feeling of wet shaving.

ICD+

In clothing, Philips joined forces with Levi's to produce the first range of electronic jackets, ICD+. The jacket contained a phone and an MP3 player, plus a microphone and earphones built into the collar or hood. Everything was controlled via a soft-touch remote control pad hidden beneath a pocket flap.

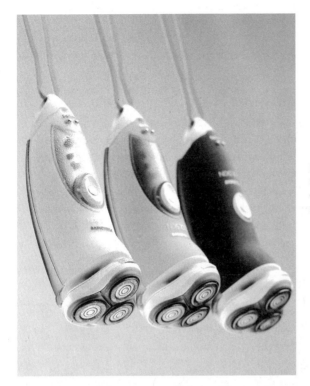

Philips partnered with Nivea to give customers Coolskin, the refreshing sensation of a wet shave.

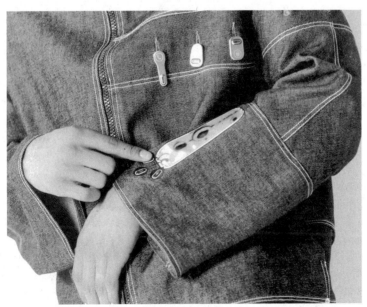

The Philips ICD+ jacket, a joint project with Levi's, contains a phone, an MP3 player, and a microphone and earphones built into the collar or hood. Everything is controlled via a soft-touch remote control pad hidden beneath a pocket flap.

PSA Nike

More recently, Philips has teamed up with Nike to produce PSA Nike, a range of portable audio sports accessories that enable people to enjoy high-quality audio while jogging and exercising.

Furniture

With Leolux, we developed a range of adjustable furniture with integrated video and audio equipment. Later, with FeliceRossi, we developed a range of multimedia furniture, including Domino, a fully wired, multifunctional multimedia couch whose modular design allows the creation of polyfunctional zones for relaxation and socializing. This collaboration also led to a reclining chair, complete with audio, projection video and screen, and computer. Most recently, with Cappellini, we have developed Paesaggi Fluidi (Flowing Landscapes), a range of multimedia sofas, sideboards, and shelving units that incorporate flat-screen home cinema technology and other top-of-the-line equipment.

Senseo

With coffee-producer Douwe Egberts, Philips has manufactured and marketed Senseo, a revolutionary new coffee-maker. This partnership not only gives our technology the seal of approval from a coffee expert, but it also opens up new sales channels, such as supermarkets.

CONSUMER INTERFACE

In addition to delivering innovative products, these partnerships enable Philips to meet consumers through new channels, where the focus is less on function and more on lifestyle, sensory or aesthetic experiences, and personal comfort—intangible values that are increasingly important to consumers. But we need to build long-lasting, intimate relationships with consumers that take us beyond the point of sale, in our own interest and in theirs. One way we do this is through products and services that develop and adapt to the user over time. In a project called Open Tools, we developed a number of devices that are relatively undefined to start with; users can specify which functionalities they want, when they want them. The tools also adapt themselves to their user's habits and needs. One such tool is the Open Desk, a device with a touch-sensitive display for manipulating digital media.

Experiences. Going a step further, in collaboration with Philips Medical Systems and the Lutheran General Hospital, in Chicago, we recently developed the Yacktman Children's CT Pavilion, in which patients can design their own scanning experience. In addition to a CT scanner, the CT Pavilion offers three main elements: projection, dynamic LED lighting, and RFID (radio frequency identification). Patients can choose from four themes, each geared for a different taste and age group: aquatic, space, fly-through, and a default lava-lamp-type ambience. RFID-encoded cards corresponding to the theme chosen by patients cause the lighting and wall/ceiling projection to change in the exam room as they enter. The ambient environment is more than just relaxing and entertaining. For instance, if the child is required to hold his or her breath during the procedure, a figure in the projection (for instance, a fish) can do the same, thereby offering encouragement and support while often eliminating the need for sedation and ensuring a smoother process. This is obviously better for the child, the parents, and the hospitals.

Digital branding. When people buy a single product, it is often the first element in a whole system, and they want to be sure it will be compatible with later purchases. Both consumers and companies therefore have a vested interest in maintaining a relationship beyond the moment of sale. The Web plays an important role here, helping consumers understand more about things that interest them, and helping us understand more about their needs. At Philips Design, we have been investigating a number of promising options in the field of digital branding. Possibilities include online concept testing, production on demand, registering customization requirements, codesign, and online communities.

People value communities especially because they enable like-minded people to come together. To understand more about how communities develop, both online and offline, we have been conducting some joint experimental research with universities in Scotland, France, and Italy. In this EU-sponsored project, called Living Memory, we have looked at the function of a community network developed in Edinburgh on the basis of a hybrid infrastructure of physical locations and a virtual network. This research will help us to develop a new type of consumer interface: a community within which consumers feel comfortable interacting with manufacturers and one another.

PEOPLE AS A SOURCE OF BREAKTHROUGH INNOVATION

Real breakthrough innovations depend not only on exploring the technological how, but more crucially the sociocultural and psychological why behind people's needs and aspirations. It is from the combination of these two that we can derive the what, the when, the where, and the who. I have described how we try to do this at Philips Design by developing explicit hypotheses of the future, based on a combination of research and liberated thinking, and then sharing them with consumers in realistic simulations. Of course, our method is continuously being refined and improved, and given the complexity of the material we are dealing with, this is a never-ending task. Nevertheless, I believe it is vital if we want to explore, in ever-more detail, the uncharted future landscapes of people's minds, which are ultimately the richest source of breakthrough innovation.

Suggested Reading

Aarts, Emile and Marzano, Stefano (eds.). *The New Everyday: Views on Ambient Intelligence* (Rotterdam: 010 Publishers, 2003).

Calvin, William H. "How to think what no one has ever thought before," in J. Brockman and K. Matson (eds.), *How Things Are: A Science Tool-Kit for the Mind* (William Morrow & Co., 1995).

Chapter 15

Insights on Innovation

by Raymond Turner, Yvonne Weisbarth, Kenji Ekuan, Gianfranco Zaccai, Philippe Picaud, and Peter Haythornthwaite

Six executives from around the globe share their thoughts on successful innovation. It is a rich set of lessons, with comments from Raymond Turner (independent consultant, United Kingdom), Yvonne Weisbarth (Bosch Siemens, Germany), Kenji Ekuan (GK Design Group, Japan), Gianfranco Zaccai (Design Continuum, United States), Philippe Picaud (Decathlon, France), and Peter Haythornthwaite (Creativelab Limited, New Zealand).

RAYMOND TURNER, RAYMOND TURNER ASSOCIATES

When thinking of innovation, it is all too easy to focus on advances in consumer technology—the iPod, robot lawn mowers, or even feather-light materials like Polartec—that we take completely for granted. However, there are less conspicuous forms of innovation that affect our everyday lives, yet rarely get acknowledged.

Examples of this include odorless paint; multimodal travel tickets; light, virtually unbreakable, plastics; knives that stay sharp; and cars that need servicing only every two years. Two particular favorites of mine in this category of unsung heroes of innovation are the simple but brilliant knife block designed by product designers Priestman Goode, and the flexible plastic holder for a six-pack of soda cans, which was first created by BIB Design.

The knife block consists of two identically shaped blocks of wood held together by magnets. The interface between the blocks is shaped in such a way that a series of narrow gaps are created, providing ideal spaces for storing sharp kitchen knives. The blocks keep the knives safe and secure but are easily separated for cleaning, something not possible with the conventional knife block—a real example of innovative thinking.

The six-pack holder, according to Nick Butler, who was chairman for BIB Design at the time, was conceived as a way of using waste material from the production of another, unrelated, product. And look how clever it is. A flat sheet of thin, flexible plastic, pierced with large holes, sized to go over the top of the drink cans and held in place by their rims. Once in position the six cans are easily carried, and the material cost is negligible, considering the plastic was going to be thrown away. Now, that's a simple innovation, if ever there was one!

These innovation heroes have at least two features in common.

Lateral innovative thinking produced this knife block—a design solution that seems to solve many problems associated with traditional knife holders.

The first is a response to simple human needs—cleaning, in the case of the knife block, and carrying, in the case of the six-pack holder. The second is that design is the source of each. Design is fundamental to the process of innovation, whether the focus is a new product or service, a built environment, a corporate proposition, or even a vision of the future. It is fundamental not because we like to think it is but because history shows that at the heart of all innovation is the rigorous challenge, lateral thinking, and practical approach of the designer.

There is much written about the process of innovation. In my experience, however, business as usual is not the way to stimulate innovative thinking. If the mindset does

Considering its weight, the plastic can holder supports a staggering level of load.

not change, neither will the solution! Creating an environment in which challenging the status quo is actively encouraged is at the heart of the innovation process. This process needs clear, firm leadership, and it is the design leader's responsibility to do just that—to make innovation part of the business's DNA. It is then the job of the design manager to help realize the innovative thinking. Designers can be the source of innovative thinking, but not the exclusive source—in fact, professionals from all parts of business can be innovative. After all, a good idea doesn't care who has it.

YVONNE WEISBARTH, BOSCH SIEMENS

Selling through innovation and design has become essential in today's fast-paced world. A good design evokes an emotional response in the client. An emotionally charged packaging of an innovation through design is critical to sustain success and to build a brand identity. Good design in combination with innovation adds value to a product, leading to an increase in sales.

One of the most challenging and innovative projects we've recently undertaken at Bosch Household Appliances was our new air-conditioning unit. The unit heats as well as cools. It also cleans, dehumidifies, and ionizes the air. Beyond that, its visual design and ease of operation are appealing. We improved the air inlet by moving it from back to front. For even more efficient distribution of air, the user can activate additional motor-driven air outlets on the sides of the unit. The air filter was also moved to the front of the housing and is consequently easier to remove and replace. A large LCD display leads the consumer easily thru the logic navigation menu, on which all functions, parameters, and messages are displayed. New safety features include an automatic shutoff if the water tank for dehumidifying is full or if there is a technical problem with the unit.

Innovation isn't the domain of a single department—it is a hands-on game played by everyone. The original idea may come from anywhere in the company, but the responsibility to turn it into a profitable product rests with marketing, engineering, and design. The innovations for our air-conditioning unit were brought to our designers by our technical team in Spain. From there, design developed a concept strategy for the product, exploring new opportunities and

This new air-conditioning unit, designed by Yvonne Weisbarth's team at Bosch Household Appliances, was one of the most challenging and innovative projects recently undertaken at Bosch Siemens. The marketing, design, and engineering departments all contributed to make this product a success.

checking closely to meet the needs of the technical team in Spain, as well as the wishes of the marketing department at company headquarters. Marketing and design worked on the user interface in close collaboration, improving what was there and adding to it.

Innovation for a new product is a process of give and take, with leadership and responsibilities rotating among the principals involved.

To nurture and support the processes of innovation, it is crucial to anticipate changes in consumer habits with research into trends and fashions at trade shows and fairs. Healthy competition, as well as brainstorming sessions with colleagues, can spawn a brilliant idea that leads to a new and innovative product.

KENJI EKUAN, GK DESIGN GROUP

Innovation is a word often accompanied by a fantasy. A fantasy tends to get bigger unless it is contained by knowledge of what is possible. This is something designers should keep in mind.

As designers, when we consider innovation, we first have to contemplate its significance. Since designing is, at the core, the art of matching a material thing to a human—namely, to humanize the material thing and to formulate it for use in a purposeful activity—it is necessary to clearly verify some points. What is the innovation for? In what way shall we humanize the material thing—and to what effect?

I like to view innovation from the perspective of the ethics and attitude of a designer. After all, designers are responsible for the influence on the human psyche of all kinds of built surroundings. We must therefore seriously consider the truth, good, and beauty of all the objects we build. It is decadent to give in to an easy and superficial approach of so-called function and convenience.

The chemistry created between built objects and humans has historically revolved around physical comfort and efficiency. However, if the definition of innovation is taken to extremes, the result can be negative and unanticipated social and cultural changes. Mobile phones, for instance, are a wonderful innovation, but they opened up whole new avenues of criminal activity that no one expected.

In Asia, Western civilization has been a vigorous import and has reached the mainstream. We are now seeing a potential trend criticizing its influence on local cultures. Although Asian cultures, which comprise more than half the world's population, have been sucking in and digesting foreign cultures for centuries, currently the result seems to be a trough filled with opaque water! It's hard to forecast what will happen when these cultures strike out on their own.

Continuing the metaphor, this trough seems to have great potential as a cultural whirlpool of Asian civilization. But it's impossible to imagine what types of innovations might arise as a result, and consequently many designers are watching with great interest. It behooves us all to be well aware of the Asian ethos and direction in which its cultures are heading.

If designers seek to affect the chemistry between humans and materials, they must learn to pay attention to cultural anthropology and the ecologies of civilizations. And these kinds of innovations will require input from many disciplines—philosophy, religion, and science, as well as art.

As designers aim to form good relationships between humans and materials through all the human senses, they must learn to imagine the future, hypothetical as it may be. This should be a basic capability for designers.

GIANFRANCO ZACCAI, DESIGN CONTINUUM

The world is littered with innovative ideas that fell short in some critical way—that never captured the imagination (and the wallets) of customers and users. It is also littered with mediocre and, at times, over-styled solutions that misunderstood consumer needs and failed to engage them.

Design is not always innovative, yet the best designs usually contain an element of technological and market innovation. As a result, trendy designs that are not appropriately innovative are quickly rejected. On the other hand, technical innovators, who often think of design as a cosmetic, nonessential element (at least during the early stages of the development process), often find their innovative ideas are best embraced when embodied by designs people can understand, use, and connect with emotionally. Often, a more successful embodiment comes from a "fast follower," which then reaps most of the rewards.

Design innovation and technological innovation represent two sides of the same coin and two sides of the brain—the rational and the emotional. When design and technological innovation complement and support each other, the result is a complete, engaging, and sustainable experience.

Perhaps my favorite example of this is the Pedi-Sedate anesthesia delivery system. The Pedi-Sedate system was the brainchild of Dr. Geoff Hart, a brilliant and highly sensitive physician who theorized that using nitrous oxide on children during medical procedures could greatly reduce their discomfort, since it is administered without injection. Hart also realized that there are strong psychological factors at work within the context of medical procedures and that the true goal should be an overall reduction in children's fear. Usually, for instance, the child is given a pre-sedative to calm him or her and then brought into a sterile field surrounded by strange equipment and

The Pedi-Sedate anesthesia delivery system is toy-like and allows the patient to play video games or listen to music as nitrous oxide is delivered.

medical staff wearing masks. There is little to distract them from the procedure itself. In contrast, the Pedi-Sedate headset is toy-like and allows the child to play video games or listen to music as the gas is administered. Continuum was contacted to explore this concept and to fully design and develop the system. The work was fueled in part by funding from the National Science Foundation.

Together our researchers, designers, and engineers focused on understanding the physiological, as well as the emotional, issues from several perspectives. The team considered scientific and regulatory issues, the needs of the healthcare professionals, the hospital infrastructure, the parents and, most important, the young patient. The result was a highly innovative product that integrates many new features inspired by emotional, as well as rational, considerations. Prototypes are now being used in extensive clinical testing in two North American hospitals.

The innovations achieved in this product are the result of interdisciplinary exploration of the user's total experience as seen from multiple perspectives. Its success also owes much to the creative application of multiple skills. In a sense, the medical profession has understood this need for some time. Healthcare really addresses psychological and aesthetic issues, as well as physiological issues, and thus internists, psychologists, and plastic surgeons are all potential contributors to the well-being of the individual. Design innovation requires complementary skills if it is to create solutions that are appropriately innovative at all levels and that connect, through all the senses, to both sides of the amazing human brain.

PHILIPPE PICAUD, DECATHLON DESIGN

Decathlon is a leading sporting goods manufacturer and distributor worldwide. The corporate design operation, or Decathlon Design, comprises eighty designers in the domains of fashion, product, and graphics; they create more than 4,000 models per year for the sixty-five sports proposed (ranging from bicycles to sport clothing, shoes, and so forth).

At Decathlon Design, we've recently introduced processes specifically to support innovation. This development comes from the creation of a project management structure, as well as the enhancement of the design function and culture. Innovative solutions come about only when they run in parallel with the standard creation process. At Decathlon, we like to use an active approach to innovation, one that communicates the distinctive capability of design. Designers propose a different vision of established models and vocabularies that is contrary to the common marketing approach, which only analyzes the current market situation.

One of the first products we developed in-house using the new approach was inspired by a brief to design a more comfortable fin for leisure diving. This was an opportunity to demonstrate the value of design in the creative process. Instead of giving the project directly to a single designer dedicated to the product range in question, the design manager in charge organized a workshop session with designers from a variety of disciplines and domains.

The FLP 500 swim fin was the first product Decathlon Design developed using a design process intended specifically to support innovation. An open window in the blade of the fin gives swimmers a more powerful kick with less effort. In 2004, the FLP 500 won design awards in France, Germany, and the US.

Our research and development department worked with us to identify solutions that would increase the fin's comfort without reducing its power. The project team, made up of the product manager, an ergonomist, designers, engineers, and users worked hand-in-hand throughout the creation process. The result was the creation of an opening in the fin's blade, allowing an ideal distribution of pressure. This makes it easier for the swimmer to stay near the water's surface. The foot pocket is flexible and thin where the foot is most sensitive and thicker in the section that produces the most power. The result is a very light and comfortable fin that allows a longer diving period without fatigue or muscular trauma. Our orders have increased by 80 percent since this product was brought to market.

Innovation is in the nature of design. Added to that is my conviction from the very beginnings of my career as a designer—that our job focuses on offering people a better quality of life.

Today's institutions realize the power of design in this domain. In 2002, the European Commission launched a project called Design for Future Needs (www.dfn.org) aimed at understanding the ingredients design has to employ to lever innovation and translating them for the benefit of other disciplines. Decathlon was one of the four European companies selected to take part, in recognition of our IMAGINEW process, which addresses either a domain or a user target to identify concepts for future development.

The process begins by sharing the specific knowledge of a multidisciplinary team: information about the use and usefulness of a particular type of product, its services, and how best to sell it. The next steps include brainstorming, clustering of themes, user scenarios, and finally concept definition. The results are evaluated by a ranking of criteria identified at the first "knowledge" session. After the selection, the concepts are translated into potential products or services; these are accompanied by an evaluation of resources and a business plan. They then enter the standard project road map for development.

The ultimate condition for innovation is the relevance of the solution for the user. At Decathlon, which owns its distribution network, we decided that the teams should be located within store locations to ensure greater intimacy with the consumer. Our brands are now moving to where their sports are practiced; for example, Quechua, our mountain sports brand, is now located near Mont Blanc in the French Alps. Our designers are therefore confronted with users and their real needs daily. Observation, evaluation, and feedback are immediate.

It is noticeable that design is a discipline that identifies innovative solutions or, if the innovation comes from a technical source, that translates and gives visibility to the technological breakthrough. Design itself carries a leadership role in innovation and is often supported by the passion of the designer. Summarized by four words, the conditions for innovation would be knowledge, process, resource, and passion.

PETER HAYTHORNTHWAITE, CREATIVELAB

In 2000, a young woman returning from the Sydney Olympics died on arrival at Heathrow Airport and greatly heightened the awareness of the danger of deep-vein thrombosis (DVT) or, as it has been called, economy-class syndrome. A DVT is a blood clot, usually developed in a leg, which can lead to complications if it breaks off and travels in the bloodstream to the lungs. The Heathrow tragedy launched a plethora of devices aimed at reducing the risk of DVT. Most of these solutions were based on inflatable pads or mechanical contraptions to simulate walking—some noisy, some bulky, and few well-conceived. Primarily, their aim was to offer some form of in-flight exercise, but none of them really addressed the issues that caused DVT.

The idea for Legflo sprang from research undertaken by three leading respiratory specialists from New Zealand who had been studying the risk and incidence of air travel-related DVT,[1] as well as the physiology behind the syndrome and possible preventive measures. According to a principle known as Virchow's Triad, the risk of DVT is increased by any of three factors: reduced blood flow, increased blood viscosity, and damaged or abnormal blood vessels. Focusing on the first factor and using simple and available components, the New Zealanders developed an approach that actively forced pooled blood in the foot to move to the leg and to cause the calf muscle (acting as a second heart) to contract. Early testing against products on the market showed they had a superior solution but that it fell short of being a marketable answer.

Creativelab was engaged to take the principle and design and develop a product that met airline criteria, demonstrated improved exercise benefits, gained full acceptance of medical experts, was low-cost, lightweight, and durable, and had a "life after

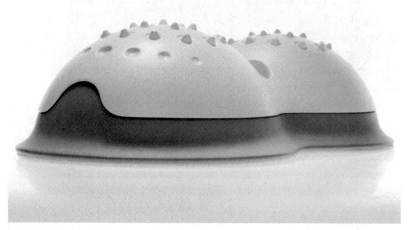

Legflo is designed to help alleviate deep-vein thrombosis (DVT), often called economy-class syndrome. The product was the result of a design and innovation collaboration between three highly respected respiratory medical researchers and Creativelab (Auckland, New Zealand).

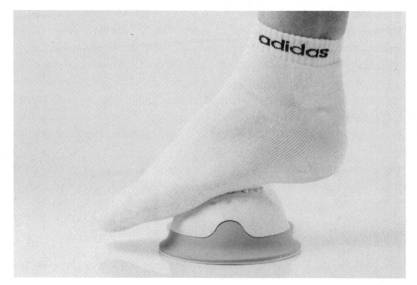

Legflo features a light but robust base and a co-molded flexible synthetic rubber skin that serves to massage and stimulate the underside of the foot. The action of pointing and lifting the toes while gently pressing the sole of the foot onto the rounded surface of the product forces the blood up into the calf muscle (which works like a second heart), thus maintaining good blood flow.

flight." The design process involved comprehensive testing of each solution via Doppler ultrasonography to measure venous blood flow. The resulting final design is a two-part, injection-molded product—a rigid shell and a flexible skin with nodules to massage the underside of the foot. Not only is the product of a minimal size and stackable, but comprehensive medical testing has shown that it offers a marked improvement over competing devices.

Innovation and design go hand in hand, in that the design process inevitably involves innovation. But not all innovation involves design. Innovation tends to focus on the development of a new means of, or a device for, achieving a particular purpose. And while innovation may create a workable solution, that solution may not be suitable for the market or capitalize on the opportunity. In this relationship, design's primary role is to interpret the intentions of innovation and to create a solution that addresses or forecasts human needs and ensures that the solution is fit for use and production.

Innovation grows from the ability to identify need or opportunity. It occurs through many means, from pure serendipity to rigorous research and testing. Innovation necessitates a balance between logical and illogical creativity. It demands the ability to ask the right questions and spot the right answers. Environments and conditions can fertilize, facilitate, and help implement innovation. But the most potent nurturers of innovation share a passionate belief in the mission and the ability to identify latent needs and opportunities. They tend to be in the right place at the right time, demanding and empowering leadership, encouragement, and processes that facilitate fermentation and don't shrink from urgent deadlines.

Innovation tends to be considered the province of the scientist, researcher, inventor, and engineer, and their approach, by necessity, is likely to be systematic. However, introducing a designer at the outset of the innovation process increases the likelihood of radical thought, of ensuring both a micro and macro perspective, of a focus on environmental issues, human needs, and user requirements, and of the generation of holistically considered, but marketable, solutions. Design is an innovative process, but equally important, it is the means of uniting solutions (and companies) with people's hearts and minds.

Legflo was realized through the vigorous efforts of medical science coupled with a systematic approach to innovation and the spontaneous and pragmatic innovation that occurs through the design process.

Endnote

1. The research undertaken by doctors Beasley, Holt, and Hughes is to date the largest, most comprehensive study into DVT risk and incidence worldwide.

Chapter 16

Innovation in Practice: The Calor Aquaspeed Iron

by Dick Powell, Director, Seymour Powell

*In this case study, Dick Powell translates innovation theory into reality.
The challenge was to bring new vision to an old problem—redesigning
a steam iron. Researchers mapped design, product, and social trends
and reconfirmed the corporate brand message's successful engagement
of customers. They distilled breakthrough opportunities, and then the
development team and the CEO made it happen with a design that is
now changing expectations and exceeding sales projections.*

THERE'S A LOT of baloney spoken in the name of innovation theory . . . and
some useful truths. After twenty years of designing consumer products, I can offer
these observations:

▲ Innovation requires a consummately well-articulated vision of what you are
trying to achieve—one that all parties, from the engineers to the eventual consumer, can believe in.

▲ Innovation requires at least one person who fully understands all the ramifications of that vision and is armed with the authority and means to make
it happen.

▲ Innovation requires experience, and the insight that comes with it, to balance
what's important and what isn't, at any one point in the process.

▲ Innovation is often not a big idea that changes everything but rather a series of smaller ideas that fit together in a unique way to create something new and better.

Oh—and two more:

▲ All people are creative, but some people are more creative than others.

▲ It's never as easy as you think.

The Calor Aquaspeed iron project reflected a number of these observations.

THE NATURE OF THE BEAST

Seymour Powell has designed a huge number of products, from trains and cars to digital watches and laptops. When people ask me, "What's the hardest product to design?" I say it has to be the steam iron. Why? Because the complexity of a steam iron's internal workings is wholly inseparable from its external form, which in turn is determined by its ergonomy on the one hand, and its functionality on the other. Factor in the need for ease of manufacture, low cost, and reasonable investment, not to mention on-shelf differentiation in a market in which products are more alike than different as a direct consequence of all this, and you can begin to understand why the word styling (and by that I mean external design) is a wholly inappropriate word. It's a huge design problem . . . and that's before you even contemplate being innovative.

Calor is a French company and brand that belongs, along with SEB, Tefal, Rowenta, Moulinex, Arno, and Krups, to the SEB Group. SEB stands for La Société Emboutissage de Boulogne, which originally started life as a metalworking company making pressure cookers. Having variously bought and acquired Calor and Tefal, SEB became the SEB Group, which continues to sell products under all three of these well-established brands in France, but sells the output of all three companies elsewhere under the name of Tefal (except in the US, where the brand name is the slightly amended and hyphenated T-Fal). As a group, they are one of the world's largest and most successful manufacturers of domestic products and appliances.

Seymour Powell's relationship with the companies of the group goes back to 1985, when we designed the world's first cordless kettle, the Freeline, for Tefal. In the ensuing nineteen years, we have worked with the Group to create a considerable number of innovative products, including deep-fat fryers, vacuum cleaners, beauty-care items, irons, kettles, and toasters.

Avantis

The redesign of Calor's Avantis steam iron was Seymour Powell's first linen-care project for the company. We had worked with Calor before, so we already knew that the firm well understood the importance of expressing its brand values and communicating functionality clearly and persuasively through the design of its products. We hoped to continue that tradition with the Avantis project.

Calor irons already had a unique differentiation point: Their soleplates, which in other irons are typically made of stainless steel or anodized aluminum, are enameled. This gives them a finish that makes them very durable and resistant to scratching and discoloration. Even more important, however, is the fact that printing two different colors of enamel—one as a base color and the second overprinted as a series of lines and details—allows the iron to float on the ridges created by the two-color surface, decreasing friction and increasing its glide and hence, the speed of ironing. Calor designers made the most of this by aiming for a streamlined, dynamic, "fast" look.

For Avantis, Seymour Powell modernized the fast look by removing its edginess and softening it. We created a highly streamlined, dynamic, contemporary iron with a new sole plate design that featured a point at the back of the iron to help part the fabric on the backward stroke (Figure 1).

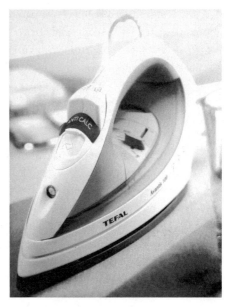

Figure 1. Avantis, Seymour Powell's first iron design for Calor, modernized the "fast" look.

Steam Generators

Seymour Powell then moved on to other categories of irons and linen-care products, including a complete rethink of the steam generator, a category that Calor had pretty much established. (For those who have not seen or used a steam generator, they improve and speed the ironing process because they produce much more steam.) Previous generators were basically boxes with irons plunked on top; the box acted like a glorified kettle. This design creates a fantastically effective ironing system, but there are drawbacks:

Figure 2. The Calor Pro-Express and Express generators (front and rear, respectively) won a DBA (Design Business Association) Design Effectiveness Award for Calor and Seymour Powell.

The iron is unstable, and using it is tiring, since the user has to lift the iron back up onto the steam-generator box at the end of each burst of usage.

To combat these problems, Seymour Powell reconfigured the generator's internal architecture to achieve an inclined iron "rest" at a significantly lower level (see Figure 2). This proved to be ergonomically better (less lifting and wrist rotation), and it also allowed the iron to be nestled into the "box" for greater stability and safety. The product, available in two variants called Calor Express and Calor Pro Express, was more integrated, both visually and in use, than its predecessors and the competition. It changed the whole game in the category, increasing sales and market share, and in 2002 won for the Seymour Powell/Calor team a DBA Design Effectiveness Award.

Avantis 2

After the design of further ranges of both high-end and low-end irons, the moment finally came, four years after its creation, to reconsider Avantis—the mid-range line. It was a moment to pause and reflect on where we were and where we were going. As a business, Calor is passionate about innovation. It spends time and money looking for ideas to give its products a competitive edge. The shelves in the company's R&D department testify to that. They groan under the weight of prototypes and mock-ups of every conceivable idea. It's not for lack of trying that very few make it; it's because it's so difficult to produce a new and unusual product but still sell it at a competitive cost (especially alongside Chinese products). As is so often true, the process of developing new products is analogous to pushing a big boulder over rocky terrain—much time is spent in studying which way looks the easiest and most promising, when what's really needed is a helicopter to take an overview and scope out the big picture and all the factors that might bear upon it—a strategic review.

Enter our research, branding, and strategy team (SPF—Seymour Powell Foresight), which had not been involved in previous Calor design projects. Bearing in mind that the core value of fast had been evolving without any real strategic purpose for close to 10 years, and that the competitive context had changed significantly over that time, the key brand question was—does fast still work as a core value? To map this context and answer that question, I briefed the Foresight team to look at a large number of relevant landscapes for the client, including:

- ▲ A timeline showing a visual history of recent developments in the Tefal/ Calor range.
- ▲ National market analyses of key irons mapped against price and visual sophistication.
- ▲ An analysis of the success or failure of brand language used by Tefal/Calor and its competitors.
- ▲ A presentation of the opinions of an independent, external panel of design experts.

▲ An analysis of the most pertinent general, social, and product trends.

▲ A strategic formulation of the way forward, based on this initial analytical and trend work.

SOME ANSWERS

The fundamental conclusion was that fast still worked as a basic identity for Calor/Tefal, communicating efficiency and contemporaneity. We believed very strongly as a result of our analysis that fast had established for the brand a relative degree of distinction in terms of brand language within a highly homogenized marketplace, where products are more similar than they are different. Pointing the way forward, we stated:

> ... We need a "beautiful" product which engages emotionally. Beauty is not a word designers are comfortable with, but a beautiful product needs to be harmonious, balanced, proportioned, and express a simplicity of use and purpose.

The strategic review also identified several potential strands for development that mirrored changing patterns of use among consumers (these must, for the moment, remain confidential, since they are still under development).

In parallel with SPF's research (and that's important—because serial idea generation is never as effective as doing it in parallel, in my view), the creative team began to generate concepts around specific ironing problems that might then be applied to Avantis 2. We hardly needed a focus group to tell us that number one on consumers' wish lists was a truly cordless iron. In fact, cordless irons do exist, but current technology leaves them quite compromised in performance, and for cost reasons alone they fell outside our brief. I mention them here only because they illustrate what's wrong with the kind of innovation theory predicated on consumer "insights," which too often allows for the complete dislocation of new ideas from the harsh realities of both science and commerce. Instead, what's truly needed is balance—balance between what you want to do and what you can do. Balance requires extensive knowledge of all the issues surrounding the problem, along with an instinctive feel for how their resolution might physically be realized—long before you can actually try to do so.

Many ideas were generated, some of which have gone into longer-term development at Calor and so can't be discussed here. But again, we didn't need a focus group to identify two immediate problem areas: filling an iron with water through a hole the size of a postage stamp, and stability—to combat the iron's annoying tendency to topple off the ironing board. The solutions too are blindingly obvious: as large a filling hole as possible, and a huge heel for stability. But how to achieve these without being ungainly, ugly, heavy, and unwieldy?

Usually, innovation lies neither in identifying a problem nor in proposing abstract solutions, but rather in embodying those ideas and solutions effectively. This, I think, is the designer's greatest strength—the ability to conceive a vision of the whole quickly and fluidly, without losing sight of the myriad factors that ultimately affect its resolution.

In contrast, my experience of working with talented creative engineers is that they are rarely at their best trying to resolve an abstract problem. But give them the same challenge armed with a credible and compelling vision, with which they can understand exactly what is needed and in what form, and they will examine an array of potential solutions methodically and analytically until they find one that works. Far too many companies rely on their R&D departments as their primary source for innovation. But what this achieves, while it's not always a bad thing, is the development of a new process or technique for which designers have to find a use and marketers a user. For Avantis 2, we were able to articulate a concept at the very beginning of the process, initially as a series of sketches from the creative workshop and quickly thereafter as foam models, which the company's development team, as well as its senior management and marketing, could immediately get behind. Yes, many of us could see serious problems with it, but everyone could also see that it was compelling—that if we could get it to market at a competitive price, it would be a winner. After that, it became a question of how the hell to make it work and to manufacture it.

FOLLOWING THE CONCEPT: THE AQUASPEED

The concept we put in place was for what we called an "open-back" iron, in which the heel is completely open and separated from the body—a large loop on which the iron could sit for enhanced stability, but without adding bulk and weight (Figure 3). Inside this loop, at the back of the iron, was a large trapdoor through which the reservoir might be filled more quickly and more conveniently. We suspected too that this new architec-

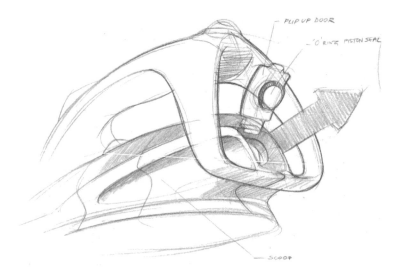

Figure 3. One of the earliest sketches for the "open-back" concept, which would make it possible to fill the iron with water via a trapdoor at the rear. Even at this very early stage, the whole idea of a light, open, airy structure at the heel (in order to reduce bulk) is considered in the context of allowing excess water to flow through and around the iron.

ture might prove a useful solution to new and more rigorous EU-inspired "drop tests"—the loop potentially helping to absorb shock—and this proved to be true.

As the development team got to work in detail, we put aside some of the known problems and forged ahead as rapidly as possible to a finished model (Figures 4-9). This was a change of process for us, as well as for the client. Previous to this project, we generally went through extensive development on each new product, absorbing considerable time and money establishing feasibility before that product could be researched with consumers . . . and then potentially be rejected. Better by far to gauge consumer interest in the broad concept as quickly as possible, which the model allowed us to do.

Figure 4. One of many early hand-made foam models that encapsulate the concept in three dimensions and allow more-detailed evaluation of the complex molding issues. The photo of the foam model has then been worked in Photoshop, coloring the tank blue and looking at alternative split-line positions.

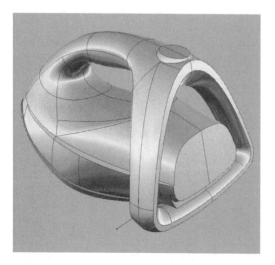

Figure 5. Defining the 3-D form using Alias, the preferred software for resolving complex forms. These early surfaces were used to machine more-accurate foam models to better reflect the technical probabilities and required volumes.

Figure 6. Finished photo-realistic rendering. Renderings and animations like this are a useful by-product of defining final surfaces in Alias. The primary purpose of final surfaces is to allow the rapid production of a finished model.

Figure 7. The finished model, machined from Alias data. This model was crucial on a number of levels—it encapsulates the whole team's best thinking at a particular moment (even though much remains unresolved); it was used in consumer research; it became the focus for subsequent development; and it allowed preselling both within the business and outside.

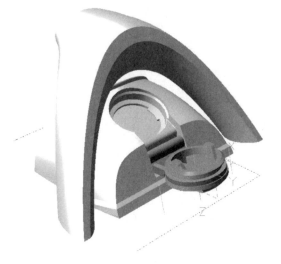

Figure 8. Detailed resolution of the trapdoor—many different solutions had to be explored. Details like this are often detached from the whole and studied piecemeal. Here, the designer is working in Pro-E looking at the implications of hinging low-down.

Figure 9. Getting closer to the final resolution—Calor's engineers are working on specific problems alongside Seymour Powell's designers. This is a screenshot from their Unigraphics CAD system.

The Calor team's problems (only some of which had been anticipated) were just beginning—and this project would no doubt have failed in a company with a lesser culture of innovation than that of Calor. Crucial to its success was the vision, decisiveness, and guiding hand of CEO Jean-Pierre Lefevre, who has an instinctive feel for his products and their market. In my time, I've seen many great ideas at other companies become diluted, changed beyond recognition, or abandoned completely in the face of demanding technical challenges. But this CEO ensures that his team does not lose focus on the important issues.

Figure 10. Aquaspeed—the finished product. Compare this with the finished model and (other than color) spot the differences: a "blink test" would say they are the same; a closer inspection would reveal some less obvious changes. Their similarity illustrates the close working relationship, respect, and understanding between Calor and Seymour Powell—which, for anyone buying design services, is something to look for when assessing technical competence.

Not surprisingly, most of the problems revolved around the innovation of filling the iron from the rear and had to do with sealing, air pockets, and venting, and with keeping water safely away from the electric components. Some of these problems required design changes from our side, particularly in optimizing the filling angle, but none required great compromise. It's a testament to the creativity of the development team that their work in finding solutions yielded new patents, which will make it difficult for Calor's competitors to catch up.

The new Avantis was eventually christened the Aquaspeed (Figure 10). It was launched last January, and since then sales have more than met expectations— not just because this is a better innovative product, but because its design effectively communicates its benefits—speedy, fuss-free filling and improved heel stability without weight. In short, this iron sells itself. Aquaspeed is a credit to every member of the Calor and Seymour Powell team—and to the company itself. The Calor culture understands that innovation is the best, perhaps the only, way to maintain a strong brand in the face of low-cost "me-too" OEM products from the Far East. Of course, as a manufacturer of consumer products, Calor understands the fundamental role of design as a creator of attractive products. But much more important, it values design at a strategic level and as a creative catalyst for innovation . . . and that's why Calor is my favorite client!

Chapter 17

Third-Generation Design Consultancies: Designing Culture for Innovation

by Jessica Feldman, MA, Design and Branding Strategy, Brunel University
and John Boult, Associate Professor, Design Strategy, Brunel University

Jessica Feldman and John Boult assert that within corporations, de-sign consultants can catalyze cultural change in ways that stimulate and support innovation. They carefully outline the circumstances, in-sights, relationships, and communications required for such a trans-formation and share stories of Guinness and the Eastman Chemical Company as models of this consultant-led metamorphosis.

HISTORICALLY, DESIGN CONSULTANCIES have been hired for their aesthetic savvy and, more recently, for their ability to understand consumers and their "unknown-as-yet" needs and to parlay those needs into better products and services. But now, with globalization and competition on the rise, the need for innovation has corporations aiming to change their organizational culture to make their businesses more conducive to innovation—and design consultancies are showing themselves to be the perfect part-ners for this journey.

Design consultancies are cited by many, including Tom Peters,[1] as being experts in innovation. Consultancies exhibit many characteristics in their work processes, as well as in their organizational design (for instance, the use of multidisciplinary teams and low hierarchical structures), that are known to be conducive to innovation. This is an opportunity for design consultancies to deepen the nature and level of their involve-ment with their clients. Design consultancies have moved on from contributing strictly

The Brewery design consultants worked with Eastman Chemical Company to develop these pebble-shaped samples of Tenite cellulosic. This innovation allows for improved demonstration of material qualities.

aesthetically to making proactive and strategic contributions. Consultancies that have the appropriate skill set and disposition—or are willing to develop it—will join a third generation: design consultancies as partners in cultural change.

A recent pilot study undertaken at Brunel University in the UK sought to explore the premise that design consultancies might act as catalysts to make corporate cultures more innovative. Four consultancies specializing in product design and branding were interviewed to investigate whether the use of a design consultancy can be a catalyst to developing an innovation culture and, furthermore, whether design consultancies are good innovation partners. To yield a more holistic understanding, a two-pronged empirical study was utilized wherein consultancy interviews were followed up with an interview of the client. Where a client interview was not possible, case study data were used.

Of the four consultancies studied, two emerged as successful in delivering change by virtue of their methodological and philosophical approaches and the buy-in of their clients. Consequently, the study also yielded insights on the complex relationship between those consultancies' solicited and unsolicited deliverables, as well as their clients' preparedness for and acceptance of those deliveries. Conclusions can be drawn about the circumstances and strategies for delivering cultural change.

UNDERSTANDING THE CULTURE CHANGE PROCESS

Before discussing how to change corporate cultures, it is first necessary to understand the elements of their composition. In his book, *The Corporate Culture Survival Guide*, theorist Edgar Schein lays out the basic structure of culture.[2] He argues that culture is made up of three layers—artifact, espoused values, and basic underlying assumptions—each increasingly deep and complex.

Artifacts are the more visible elements of culture: dress code, environment, and behavior, for example. However, the meaning of these artifacts can be misinterpreted if deeper layers of the culture are not understood.

Espoused values are the values the company claims to hold. But these can be changed to support changing objectives, and they are not always true to the company's core values.[3] An understanding of culture is not complete without understanding the third and final layer.

Basic underlying assumptions, or tacit assumptions, are the deeply held but mostly unconscious and invisible beliefs that inform the other two layers of culture. These assumptions have been reinforced and institutionalized over the course of a company's collective history.

Schein also writes that the most successful way to tackle culture change is by aiming to address business objectives. This suggests that change may be more readily achieved by retaining a design consultancy to develop a new product or service rather than by hiring a management consultancy to specifically address culture change. By modeling its own innovation behavior, a design consultancy can lead its clients—or the teams or individuals within them—to internalize the methodologies, mind frames, and cultural attributes of the consultancy itself. The process by which culture change comes about, the roles design consultancies can play in the process, and examples of success will be discussed below.

THE CULTURAL CHANGE PROCESS: TRANSFORMATIVE CHANGE

Culture change transpires through transformative change, which takes place over the course of three phases: motivation to change, learning, and internalization (see Figure 1). In simple terms, transformative change requires that old behaviors be unlearned, after which new concepts can be learned and internalized. However, in practice it's a complicated and time-consuming process. The following are descriptions of what is entailed in each of the three component phases of transformative change.

Phase 1: Motivation to Change

Creating motivation to change is a three-pronged process, beginning with disconfirmation and followed by the creation of survival anxiety tempered by psychological safety.

Disconfirmation can be defined as "intellectual preparedness for change." It is the realization of organization members that their current method of operation no longer works toward a desired end. For example, an organization that hopes to increase the use of cross-functional teamwork will have difficulty making this transition if their employees share a basic underlying assumption that runs counter to the objective—an unspoken animosity, say, or distrust of other departments.

Once disconfirmation exists, an impetus to action must be created. However, it is difficult to persuade individuals to change if the environment is unstable, or when they are unsure of the future. Therefore the creation of anxiety must be balanced with the creation of an environment of safety. New thinking can be difficult to conceptualize.

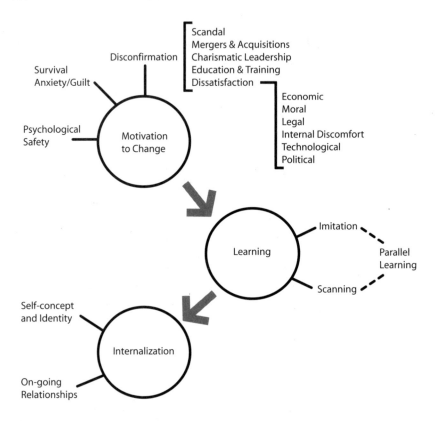

Figure 1. The three phases of the transformative change process: Motivation to change, Learning, and Internalization. An organization must pass through these phases in order to realize significant culture change. Adapted from Edgar Schein's *The Corporate Culture Survival Guide* (Jossey-Bass,1999).

One way to compensate is to see the thinking in practice before integrating it into the organization. This fits well with parallel learning, to be addressed in the next section.

Once members of the organization know change is necessary and feel responsible for changing (survival anxiety), as well as supported and safe in doing so (psychological safety), the process of learning can begin.

Phase 2: Learning

Larry Senn and John Childress, of the Senn-Delaney Leadership Consulting Group, in Long Beach, California, write that lectures and seminars will not satisfy the educational needs of the objective of culture change. To change both habits and culture requires "insightful, personal experience."[4] For his part, Schein suggests there are two educational frameworks that can meet this goal. One method is scanning and trial and error: continuously experimenting until a viable solution is found. The other method is imitation and identification: when emulation of and identification with role models is used to test solutions that have been successful in another application. Imitation and identification blend well with the idea of insightful and personal experience and suggest that a design consultancy can be a holistic role model for innovation behavior to catalyze culture change.

Senn and Childress note that employees tend to be consumer-focused. Design consultancies, in aiming to improve products, also focus on the user or consumer. Consultancy tools, such as customer journeys (stories of consumer contact with the brand, through touch-points both tangible and intangible) and user-centered research, help product developers to see their products and services through their customers' eyes and can help companies change attitudes and behaviors.

Team-based learning may also be conducive to this effort. Senn and Childress find that team-based learning accelerates the process of culture change by encouraging co-workers to reinforce new ideas and behaviors among themselves. Schein agrees that "cultural assumptions are embedded in groups" and that training teams together allows "new norms and new assumptions" to be built jointly.[5] Parallel learning can also aid in the group learning process.

Parallel learning can be used in both the imitation and the trial-and-error models. In either case, a department or a test group is separated from the remainder of the organization. Removing the team from central management frees them from cultural pressures and expectations and offers greater autonomy for experimentation with changes. Because those who are surrounded by a corporate culture are largely unaware of the ways in which it affects them, they are unable to clearly assess and evaluate it. However, outsiders who have no previous experience with that culture are unable to successfully navigate it in order to conduct a high-quality evaluation. As Schein describes it, a parallel system would include "key insiders who then work with consultants to decipher the culture and plan the change program."[6]

Phase 3: Internalization

Success in a parallel learning community is achieved by identifying new behaviors that are acceptable to, or adoptable throughout, the whole organization. If they are supported and reinforced, these can then be disseminated and, if supported and reinforced, will ultimately become a stable part of the new culture.

THE ROLE OF DESIGN IN CULTURE CHANGE

On the basis of this understanding of the process of transformative change, it can be hypothesized that designers can play a role in the process. Central to this hypothesis is the assumption that design consultancies can fulfill the "role model" position.

To begin testing this theory, we undertook a pilot study to qualitatively investigate the extent to which design consultancies are engaging in this activity. Interviews were conducted with consultancies and, when possible, their clients to better understand the impetus, nature, and outcome of their collaborations. By interviewing both client and consultancy, it was possible to achieve a more holistic understanding of the project scenario and outcomes. A direct attempt was made to understand attitudes toward the idea of design consultancy as partner in culture change. The research indicated that not all consultancies and not all clients believed in the efficacy or appropriateness of the involvement of design consultancies in culture change. Yet some cases, like the two that follow, offered concrete evidence that design consultancies are excellent culture-change partners.

Case study: Eastman Chemical Company and The Brewery

Eastman Chemical Company is one of the largest chemical manufacturers in North America, producing chemicals, fibers, and plastics used in thousands of everyday products. The Tennessee-based supplier engaged The Brewery, a London-based product and branding consultancy, for help with creating a new Web portal aimed at making information about its materials more readily available to designers and brand owners who might use them in their products. In addition, Eastman was looking for assistance in developing a more innovative culture. It should be noted that this collaboration was unique within the survey population, since Eastman was the only client to directly seek this sort of assistance.

With a structure carried over from the Eastman-Kodak organization, Eastman Chemical Company was heavily divisionalized. The company felt this structure hindered interdisciplinary communication and thus innovation. In an effort to improve its innovation behavior, get closer to the design industry, and ultimately increase its competitiveness, Eastman began a series of collaborations with design consultancies. Eastman Chemical already had a favorable opinion of design and hoped it might be able to lead it toward a more innovative culture. In fact, it was not just the collaboration with The Brewery but actually a series of events—all design driven—that catalyzed change for Eastman. Its first main design exposure was a sponsored project carried out in 2001 with the industrial design department at Auburn University. The success of that project led to another academic collaboration, this time in partnership with a major client. In 2002, these enlightening experiences led Eastman to seek out design consultancy IDEO for a fresh perspective on the uses of some of its materials. The Vision 2020 project with IDEO was a great success and encouraged Eastman to grow its design focus. By better understanding the ways designers were using its materials, and the challenges they were facing from a design perspective, Eastman gained an improved understanding of the market for its materials.

The collaboration with The Brewery therefore did not begin until 2003, when Eastman began looking for a partner to help develop an online interactive portal, hoping this resource would provide designers with the knowledge and inspiration that would encourage them to use Eastman's materials. Though the stated purpose of the collaboration was to reduce the gap between the materials and design worlds, Gaylon White, Eastman's manager for design industry programs, says the company's work with The Brewery was equally about culture change. Eastman wanted to expose its staff to the way designers think and thus help them develop a different viewpoint.

Case Study: Imagination and Guinness

The Guinness brewing company engaged Imagination, a London-based multidisciplinary design consultancy, to help Guinness develop a new customer brand experience center. Guinness's popular visitor attraction, The Hopstore, had outgrown its capacity, and the company was hoping to update, as well as to expand, that venue. After visiting the site, the Imagination team returned offering two proposals. The first was a proposal to meet the requirements of the original brief, an expansion of the Hopstore. The second proposal suggested, in lieu of the expansion, to adapt a vacant multistory facility into a brand experience center for customers, employees, and city residents. This new brand experience center was to be called the Storehouse. Guinness has a deep history of social benevolence—for its employees and for Dublin residents—but its abilities in that capacity had diminished over the years. Imagination wanted to capitalize on that history in the development of the new concept. Therefore, in addition to making the Storehouse a home for the brand, Imagination sought to create a home and an icon for the city's residents (Figures 2 and 3).

According to Ralph Ardill, Imagination's marketing and strategic planning director, a considerable element of the Guinness project was the design of the methodology used to achieve its goals. Integral to the viability and success of the project, he said, was creating synergy around ideas—putting together a network of people who had a vested interest in the idea, so that the idea would not rest with one person. In this way, ideas and their fruition became everyone's responsibility.

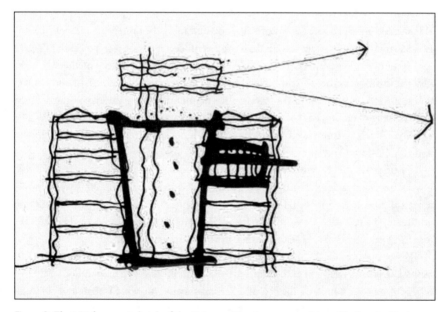

Figure 2. The initial concept sketch of the Guinness Storehouse, as envisioned by Imagination directors Ralph Ardill and Adrian Caddy. Imagination's proposal was a drastic expansion on the brief set out by Guinness.

Figure 3. The team envisioned that the building would be more than just a brand experience center—it would be a "global home" for Guinness. Imagination wanted the Storehouse to be an icon for the city of Dublin, one that would bring together a variety of people, including Guinness employees, tourists, and the citizens of Dublin.

INFLUENCE ON CHANGE

What made these cases successful? The collaborations of other consultancies in the Brunel study, though successful in their project outcomes, were less successful in catalyzing culture change. This is attributable, in part, to two factors: views on the role of the design consultancy that were more conservative on the part of both client and consultancy; and the clients' attitudes toward the client-consultancy interface—particularly the interface of employees so critical to parallel learning. These clients either saw little validity in such an interface, or made grand attempts to prevent one from forming. In contrast, Eastman and Guinness embraced parallel learning.

Eastman was very open to allowing its employees to be exposed to the design thinking and working style of The Brewery. Eastman was looking to The Brewery to model its innovation behavior to the Eastman team to promote new ways of thinking and addressing its business. At Guinness, the sheer ambition of the project galvanized the teams. These situations made the change in culture much more likely.

Figure 4 examines the process of disconfirmation, referred to earlier in this article, as it relates to the Eastman and Guinness collaborations and to collaborations with two other companies, which we'll call X and Y. Disconfirmation, which we define as "intellectual preparedness for change," was present to varying degrees in these four cases.

Eastman and Guinness were at opposite extremes on the scale of disconfirmation. Eastman had the higher degree of disconfirmation. Under extreme market pressure and cognizant of the need for change, the company sought out The Brewery to assist it in developing more innovative behavior. In contrast, Guinness was less predisposed to major change; it was looking to attack a contained business problem. The company knew a change was in order, but perhaps not as big a change as the one that took place.

In the cases of clients X and Y, neither they nor their chosen consultancies were convinced of the appropriateness of culture change or of the consultancy's ability to influence the client toward a change in culture. In the case of client X, for example, the managing director at the client company was averse to his employees working together with members of the design consultancy. He felt the role of culture change was internal to the organization and believed it was inappropriate for a design consultancy to be involved. As can be seen in Figure 4, the use of parallel learning by these clients was comparatively low, and this had an impact on the outcome. Though both X and Y were successful in achieving their business objectives, neither experienced significant culture change. True, neither X nor Y specifically looked to their consultancies for help in culture change, but neither did Guinness, which demonstrates that change is possible in the absence of a direct desire. The real difference is attributable to the use of parallel learning, which Guinness allowed, and the others did not.

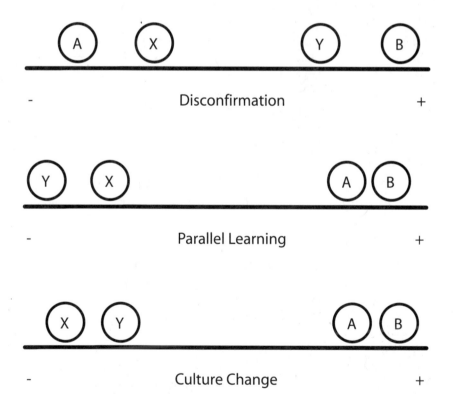

Figure 4. A comparison of disconfirmation and parallel learning relative to overall culture change among the clients.

CATALYZING CULTURE CHANGE

As Figure 1 makes clear, disconfirmation comes in many forms. For most clients studied in this research, disconfirmation was typically experienced in the form of dissatisfaction or threat—the impetus to retaining design consultancy services being a competitive threat that endangered market share or profitability. However, the case of Guinness demonstrates that a design consultancy can also play a role in creating disconfirmation.

At Guinness, there was no perceived need for a fundamental change. However, as previously mentioned, the project resulted in major changes to the way in which the company worked. Thus, it can be said that the Imagination consultancy led them into disconfirmation through education. By immersing themselves in Guinness's environment and conducting research for the project, Imagination uncovered a number of brand and culture issues, illuminated them, and addressed them in the holistic package that was the Storehouse.

The sheer ambition of the Storehouse project brought the teams of Guinness and Imagination so close together that the traditional idea of "client and consultancy" broke down and the relationship became truly collaborative. This inspired a great deal of change at Guinness: the use of multidisciplinary teams, the move of the branding and training functions into the Storehouse to increase proximity to customers, and new ways of communicating and evaluating ideas. Says Imagination's Ralph Ardill, "Our collaboration with Guinness on the Storehouse project was a transformational project in the fullest sense. Not only did it transform the way Guinness thinks about building brands, but it also transformed the thinking of all those involved in terms of what it takes to build the key client-agency relationships that enable such ideas to move from dreams to delivery. The project has changed the way Guinness thinks."

INDICATIONS FROM THE RESEARCH

The Brunel study suggests two potential scenarios for design consultancy involvement.

1. The client, after experiencing disconfirmation—whether simple dissatisfaction or something more disruptive—seeks out the assistance of a design consultancy.

2. Because education and learning are also forms of disconfirmation, working with a design consultancy, in terms of both project and exposure to the "design mind," can lead the client to disconfirmation.

Through parallel learning, design consultancies are able to model behaviors and methods that are conducive to innovation and use them to positively influence culture change.

RECOMMENDATIONS FOR CONSULTANCIES

The research demonstrated that the use of design tools such as user-centered research and multidisciplinary teams has a salient impact on clients and is effective in catalyzing culture change. To better capitalize on this opportunity, pre-existing strengths can be bolstered by the following efforts.

Expand Knowledge of Culture Theory

Many tools effective in catalyzing culture change are already in use within design consultancies; therefore, transition to this activity could be misperceived as easy. However, to really excel, design consultancies must also develop their knowledge of culture theory.

Consultancies should educate themselves about the nature of organizational culture and about change methodologies. Designers are idealistic and comfortable with change. However, it is important for them to recognize the significance of culture change and to understand its ramifications. A better understanding of culture theory will also help to identify opportunities for design influence, as well as parallels between the particular expertise of a consultancy and possible methodologies for culture change.

Though some examples covered in this research were successful, none were based on a deep understanding of culture. Culture is deep, tacit, and difficult to decipher. Social scientists, such as psychologists and anthropologists, are trained to understand culture more quickly and certainly. Adding them to design teams will enable a better understanding of the client culture and allow the consultancy to better tailor its offerings. Importantly, the advantages of incorporating social scientists in the consultancy team are not limited to benefiting culture-change work. Such professionals add a new dimension to many aspects of a consultancy's work. Their skills add to the competency base of the firm.

Preparedness to Promote New Areas of Success

Design consultancies should be prepared to promote and further develop their success in effecting cultural change. To date, publicity surrounding such achievements has been minimal. To grow both the competency and the practice within the industry, it is important that consultancies engaged in this activity discuss and promote their involvement, their success, and the repeated business it brings them. For Eastman and Guinness, their collaborations have resulted in longer-term partnerships. Indeed, these types of projects result in fundamental changes to an organization's culture and develop a strong rapport between consultant and client. For the consultancy, they are a way of solidifying relationships with clients and ensuring repeat business. Clients are less likely to seek the services of another firm when they have a bond with a capable consultancy that has a deep understanding of their culture and the way they work.[7]

RECOMMENDATIONS FOR CLIENTS

The trust and collaboration exemplified by Eastman and Guinness, and the doubt and resistance seen in the cases of X and Y companies, provide valuable insight and yield these suggestions for more-successful collaborations.

Consider Culture in Creating Alliances

The importance of a simpatico relationship between the cultures of the consultancy and the client is potentially overlooked. This should be considered before entering into a working arrangement. The potential for impact on the success of the project, as well as on the client's culture, is great. However, culture is not readily decipherable. As we have seen, what many perceive as culture is actually a collection of tangible manifestations of basic underlying assumptions—but to truly understand culture, the assumptions themselves must be understood. It is the compatibility of these core beliefs and assumptions within the cultures of both the client and consultancy that will affect collaboration outcomes, and must therefore be understood. This is in part why the collaborations of X and Y were not successful in catalyzing change. By not allowing them deeper involvement, X and Y prevented the consultancies from understanding the deeper aspects of their clients' cultures, and therefore from helping them to change.

Precedent for Viability

Some clients seem uncomfortable with the idea of involving design in culture change. Nevertheless, through success in applying design thinking to other areas—branding, service design, and corporate social responsibility, for example—consultancies are demonstrating the wider applicability of their skills. Mark Shickle, managing partner for The Brewery, notes that customers are becoming savvier about how design fits into the innovation process. But clients must also come to see how design can make their organizations a better place for innovative behavior. The successes we discussed suggest clients have less reason to be doubtful than they might think.

Embrace Parallel Learning

The willingness of Eastman and Guinness to allow their employees exposure to design consultancies, their methods, and their thinking netted them great rewards. Clients should follow the lead of these cases and avail themselves of parallel learning opportunities. Rather than fear the consequences, clients and consultancies should work together to channel creative energy into viable results.

ACKNOWLEDGMENTS

Sincere appreciation goes to Ralph Ardill and Chloe Couchman of Imagination, Mark Shickle of The Brewery, and Gaylon White of Eastman Chemical Company for their generous participation and interest in this research.

Endnotes

1. Peters, T., *Re-imagine!* (London: Dorling Kindersley, 2003).

2. Schein, E., *The Corporate Culture Survival Guide* (San Francisco: Jossey Bass, 1999).

3. Thornberry, J., *Living Culture* (London: Random House Business Books, 2000), p. 23.

4. Senn, L., Childress, J. (2001) *The Secrets of Reshaping Culture* [online] p. 6 Available from http://www.sdlcg.com/sdlsite/Articles/secrets_reshape.htm. 2001

5. Schein, p. 125.

6. Schein, p. 131.

7. See B. Nussbaum, "The Power of Design," in *BusinessWeek* (May 17, 2004), and Smart et al., "The English Patient," in the *Design Management Review* (Spring 2004, p. 46–52) for additional examples of consultancy collaborations yielding culture change resulting in longer-term partnerships.

Chapter 18

Hybrid Organizations as a Strategy for Supporting New Product Development

by **Alison Rieple,** Professor, University of Westminster
Adrian Haberberg, Senior Lecturer, University of Westminster
and Jonathan Gander, Senior Lecturer, University of Westminster

Alliances between large, well-established corporations and highly creative small companies or consultancies can be an effective method for promoting innovation. Alison Rieple, Adrian Haberberg, and Jon Gander cite examples and analyze circumstances, cultures, and the role of individuals they call "boundary-spanners."

IN MANY INDUSTRIES, such as computer hardware, aircraft, and car manufacturing, product innovation is a critical source of competitive advantage. Such industries have seen increasing numbers of alliances in recent years and a fragmentation of their organizational structures, so that they resemble networks or federations. In these types of structures, firms cut back to their core areas of expertise and obtain whatever additional resources they need from specialists. These developments appear to have come about as a result of the increasing awareness of the knowledge content of innovative products and recognition that management expertise, as well as organizational culture, is specialized and not easily transferred among different product and operational types.

Within this article, we focus on one aspect of this type of structure, in which one firm (normally a large, multi-product corporation) obtains critical product-development resources, such as design or technological know-how, from an independent firm (normally a smaller and more specialized design consultancy or a technology developer).

The two firms develop a fairly close relationship—perhaps only for the period of a specific assignment, but often over a longer period spanning several projects. These hybrid relationships are governed through informal means, such as unwritten agreements between key individuals, as much as through the more usual form of legal contracts.

The new-venture or new-product divisions that are found within many highly innovative companies (Procter & Gamble, Nokia, Lucent, and Sony come to mind; see the box at right) are another version of the hybrid structure.

RESOURCE ACQUISITION AND USE

There are three principal methods of acquiring the resources needed to achieve successful product innovations: develop them in-house; buy them on the open market; or develop them within strategic alliances or partnerships. Deciding which structural route to follow depends on a number of factors: the risk of opportunistic behavior, the irrevocable commitment of nontransferable resources (which may include ideas, knowledge, and other intangibles, as well as tangibles such as customized product components or materials), and the amenability of such resources to hierarchical control. However, there may also be a number of noneconomic influences on such decisions, including trust and affection, reputation, and perception about desirable outcomes.

Crucial to the success of a hybrid are "boundary-spanners." These are members of the partner organizations who are able to move freely within both, translating the requirements of each into language and behavior that is acceptable to, and understandable by, the other.

Trust between the senior managers who set up a hybrid in the first place, and the boundary-spanners who maintain the relationship subsequently, is a critical factor. Trust lowers cost and raises productivity. Cooperation increases under conditions of trust because with trust such costly barriers as formal contracts and detailed monitoring can be removed. The resulting less-formal specifications can also allow the parties to respond more rapidly to any changes in circumstances. Trust may initially arise in response to the manufactured image and reputation of a firm and perceptions of its reliability and competence. But it also can develop subsequently with frequency of contact, affection, and social similarity among the people who move between the organizations—the boundary-spanners, who are likely to increase in number as the relationship progresses.

Much previous work on the potential misappropriation of important product development resources has examined resources that are explicitly transferable or have a physical presence, such as copyrighted or patented designs or technologies, or product components that can be bought and sold openly. Less attention has been paid to intangible resources, such as creativity and design knowledge, and less still to resources that are relational and derived from the synergistic interactions between two or more people. With such resources, management styles, systems, and cultural issues are important structural considerations. In relationships between two very different organizational types, as is characteristic of hybrid structures, there is always the possibility of clashes among processes, cultures, and environment.

SONY'S INNOVATION STRUCTURE

Sony is one of the most innovative companies in the world. Many of its product design functions are carried out in its local markets, outside Japan, and in its established business divisions. However, these activities tend to focus on improvements to established product ranges. For more blue-sky developments, Sony has two types of hybrid product development divisions—hybrids because they are neither completely autonomous nor fully governed by the parent. They are mainly located in Japan and report directly to Sony's corporate headquarters. They focus on areas that are unrelated to current business areas or on strategic developments of business areas in which the company is already involved, such as display or storage technologies. The more blue-sky the activity, the less control there appears to be from corporate HQ. Sony's annual reports distinguish R&D units described as "headquarters research laboratories" from those called "independent research laboratories" with a separate legal structure. One of these, Sony Computer Science Laboratories, Inc., carries out fundamental research and research into user interfaces; the other, Sony-Kihara Research Center, Inc., researches three-dimensional computer graphics and image processing technologies that combine sensing, image processing, and parallel computing. Independent though it may be, the Research Center's relationship with Sony's head office is maintained through Nobutoshi Kihara, who was in charge of Sony's research almost from the beginning. Although he has been retired from Sony since 1988, he is president of the lab that bears his name.

Source: Sony's 2003 and 2004 annual reports (http://www.sony-krc. co.jp/en/index.htm and http://eetimes.com/special/special_issues/mill ennium/companies/sony.html), both accessed 26/1/05.

Entrepreneurial units often resemble those in a craft organization in which each product is comparatively unique and the development process is comparatively random and dependent on intuition and experimentation. Such units are often characterized by informal working practices. This environment is very different from that of the commissioning firm—typically a large organization characterized by clearly defined hierarchical roles and a preference for planning and rationality in decision making.

Sources of conflict also arise from the nature of some innovative products, such as furniture and fashion, the creation of which can be described as an "expression of difference." Thus the creative designer/artist's attempts to distinguish his or her work from others' can work against a large economically driven firm's desire to maximize the number of units sold. If, by expressing his or her uniqueness, the artist ends up appealing to minority tastes or fails to be familiar enough to be acceptable to decision makers within the commissioning firm, his or her ideas are rejected. And yet it is this innovative difference that commissioning firms hope to capture.

Such clashes hint at some problematic paradoxes that have to be reconciled, and hybrid organizational forms are a way of solving them. Hybrids protect the smaller firm from the stifling effects of the larger firm, while allowing its creative knowledge to be exploited. This happens through what is, in effect, a "semi-permeable membrane" in which certain features are blocked from movement while others are transferred. In this process, boundary-spanners have an important role in translating the requirements of the two organizational types to each other and protecting some key resources from the degrading influence of others.

THE INCOMPATIBILITY OF RESOURCES

As suggested earlier in the case of Sony, some hybrids develop within organizations. This is also the case for 3M and Xerox, which like Sony have three different types of structures—blue-sky, product development, and product improvement. Each type represents a continuum of incompatibility of resources and ownership/hierarchical control (see Figure 1).

Blue-sky units within a parent organization are likely to have the same problems of coordination and integration faced by inter-organizational hybrids. And they have similar benefits. They enable firms to enjoy economies of specialization, without the cultural clashes characteristic of integrated development. In fact, each partner has organization-specific resources the other lacks and needs. The larger or parent firm has the finances, marketing skills, and promotional reach to bring a product innovation to market. Experimentation and market forces over time make the larger firm an expert at managing its current customers and operations. For its part, the smaller firm offers creativity and a knowledge of trends that is critical to the process of new product development.

We contend that these two types of resources are complementary and vital to the successful development of innovative products, but are essentially incompatible. The smaller firm's resources are not easily managed in a hierarchy without destroying its

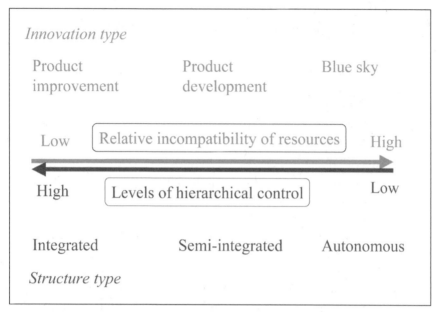

Figure 1. Different types of organizational innovation-development structures based on levels of control/independence needed.

creative value, and the possibility of the commissioning firm learning how to replicate them is forestalled by a number of culturally embedded factors.

First, new product development is generally unpredictable and depends on outcomes that cannot be planned in advance. Hierarchy works best when the factors to be controlled can be predicted in advance, usually on the basis of what has happened in the past.

Second, non-financial aims, such as the pursuit of a reputation for nonconformity, can be a major part of a small firm's raison d'être. This may be in conflict with the larger firm's focus on providing risk-free returns to shareholders. Its reward and control systems, and its employees' behaviors, will reflect these priorities.

Third, and linked to the previous point, are the creative tendencies of innovators. Such individuals typically have a need to challenge the status quo; their behavior is not particularly adaptive. They are driven by intrinsic rather than extrinsic motivators and do not welcome being controlled through bureaucratic means. In order to bring about frame-breaking change, they have to remain outside existing paradigms and resist corruption by established interests. This implies the need for a structural middle ground, where some protection can be offered to the creation of difference, while allowing necessary knowledge to be shared.

The culture of the partners in hybrid structures is thus an important issue, and bringing those cultures together represents a particularly potent form of risk. The more

INNOVATIVE TECHNOLOGY DEVELOPMENT IN THE MOTOR INDUSTRY

The motor industry depends on regular injections of innovation and high-quality design. It is also characterized by a small number of very large consumer-facing firms that typically contract out many of their design and product development functions to smaller specialist suppliers. These companies have often cut their innovation teeth doing technology development work for racing teams.

One of the best known and most respected technology suppliers is Ricardo, an independent British firm that has operations around the world and that works (often secretly) with many major European and US automobile manufacturers on long-term new product development projects. Recent examples include hybrid diesel/electric and advanced fuel cell engines, and the new Mini for BMW. More than fifty engineers who had been employed at Rover, the creator of the original Mini, were recruited into Ricardo to work on the Mini project after BMW acquired the British car manufacturer (although it subsequently sold it), allowing valuable knowledge to be transferred from one firm to the other. In fact, they are still working for Ricardo.

Some of Ricardo's clients are happy to remain relatively hands-off; others are much more specific in terms of outcomes and timescales. Many are long-term clients who have engaged the company to work on a number of initiatives.

Ricardo has considerable expertise in certain types of technology. The question is, why have none of its partners either attempted to develop this technology in-house or tried (as far as one knows) to acquire it? We would argue that resource immiscibility (that is, its nonmixability—think of oil and water) is at least partly the reason.

homogeneous a group is, the less risk it undertakes in terms of coordination, conflict, goal congruence, and information flow. But by definition, the ideal partners in a hybrid will subscribe to different paradigms and have different experiences, assumptions, and beliefs. They may even have different expectations of the relationship. Bringing two such cultures together in any sort of tight arrangement is apt to lead to conflict, misunderstandings, and a swift end to the interaction. Key staff from the smaller company might leave or be less effective as a result of discomfort from working in a more formal environment. Structures in such circumstances are therefore likely to be more effective when they are semi-permeable, allowing the selective adoption of practices, beliefs, or other organizational elements.

For example, one of the most common activities of a bureaucratic firm is to measure profits. Innovation units cannot easily do that, because their activities are unpredictable, and time-spans over which costs and income can be allocated are nonstandard. If these activities were to be imposed on the innovation unit, it would probably wither and die. So there has to be some way of stopping a parent company, for example, or an ally (probably a larger company) from imposing these practices on its partner. The membrane in this case may be physical (geographical distance or separate buildings), metaphorical (disparate cultures kept apart by little commonality between members), or contractual (legal definitions of who should do what). In each case, it is possible for some elements of various practices to be exchanged or shared—that is, to be semi-permeable—perhaps by stipulating some exceptions to normal practices within a contract or by the occasional meeting of people from the two groups.

Other ways of conceptualizing such semi-permeable structures include the idea of allowing "looseness" at one level of the organization—perhaps the project or the team—to coexist with stronger bonds at other levels, such as senior management. Another way might be to allow autonomy of local operations, such as the design process or product prototyping, to be coupled with strongly defined organizational objectives or project goals. These structures allow independence, yet mandate mutual influence. Figure 2, on the next page, identifies eight of these loosening/tightening mechanisms.

Setting up this type of permeable membrane as part of the hybrid structure offers many benefits. The innovators at the smaller firm need to be allowed to feel they are not selling out or risking losing their independence because they are offering their ideas to the larger firm for commercial gain. For its part, the larger firm has to allow its partner greater freedom and flexibility than it is used to and reduce its tendency to control and measure while simultaneously setting the sorts of output targets that please senior managers. Semi-permeable membranes preserve the idiosyncrasies of each partner and maintain their separate identities.

Such factors are particularly relevant to an understanding of the role of culturally specific tacit and explicit knowledge in the management of the hybrid. For example, process, social, and experiential knowledge are especially important in new product development, yet these often cannot be costed or valued so that they can be exchanged for resources the commissioning firm has—cash, for example, or knowledge of market developments.

Categories of Loosening and Coupling Mechanisms

Project-Strategy Connections

1. Widely held understandings about what the organization does: strategy, mandate for innovation, risk climate

2. Technological compatibility

3. Established markets

Project-Organization Connections

4. Funding

5. Senior management attention

6. Structural location

7. Standard operating procedures

8. Human resource deployments

Figure 2. Each of these is "a two-edged sword, bringing needed resources and legitimacy to the projects and, at the same time, exposing the activities of innovators to scrutiny, intervention, and possible sanctions." (From Trudy Heller, "Loosely Coupled Systems for Corporate Entrepreneurship: Imagining and Managing the Innovation Project/Host Organisation Interface," from *Entrepreneurship Theory and Practice*, vol. 24, no. 2 (1999), p. 25–31.)

Such semi-permeable arrangements have other benefits besides protecting key resources from degradation. They serve to buffer awareness of problems. If a prototype in a market test fails, for instance, the more risk-averse partner may unfairly perceive the smaller firm as incompetent. Such arrangements also allow boundary-spanners to mediate cultural or strategic misunderstandings.

There appears to be a straightforward relationship between the codification of knowledge and the costs of its transfer: The more an item of knowledge or experience can be codified, the more economically it can be transferred—and, paradoxically, the less valuable it is. In other words, tacit, implicit, and socially contextualized and embedded knowledge is more valuable, but it is also much harder to transfer and, in fact, is most easily transferred in a tightly coupled setting. But there is a dilemma here—

tight coupling will expose creative staff from the smaller firm to cultural or operational contamination. We argue that boundary-spanners have an important role in solving this problem.

THE ROLE OF BOUNDARY-SPANNERS

Boundary-spanners, or bridgers, as they are sometimes described, are people who move between both organizations, translating the norms of each into language and behavior that are acceptable to, and understandable by, the other. There is almost no research on the role that boundary-spanners have in hybrid organizational structures, and yet they are likely to be one of the most important factors in the success of those structures. After all, new product development is a social-, collaborative-, and interaction-intensive process involving experimentation and negotiation over the life cycle of the new product's evolving form, bringing together knowledge, expertise, and technologies from different sources into a whole. Learning involves the negotiated resolution of constraints and generates new knowledge, which may then be embedded in the design of new technologies, products, or processes. Thus boundary-spanners need to be skilled first of all in the nuances of creating a new product.

Individuals with little experience of working in a larger company are likely to be unsuitable as boundary-spanners. They may never have seen corporate overhead charges, annual plans, safety rules, or other corporate policy and personnel regulations. On the other hand, a representative from the commissioning firm who has never worked anywhere other than a major corporation is likely to have little tolerance or understanding of the chaotic creativity of small entrepreneurial units. The most effective boundary-spanners appear likely to be those who have worked in small entrepreneurial units, as well as larger, more bureaucratic firms, though this has yet to be researched.

Boundary-spanners, particularly in an international context, need to be able to understand and transcend the cultural and linguistic norms of the partners. They need to be able to talk intelligently about, for example, the psychological impact of a product's color, trends in new music, or the physiological risks of a new drug, and translate that understanding into the language of discounted cash flows, return on investment, and net present values. Boundary-spanners from the smaller, more creative unit must be able to convince their colleagues from the larger partner of the value (economic and strategic) of the project they are undertaking. They may need to report on the costs involved in the product development process, or to assess and forecast the time a particular initiative might take to reach positive profitability—using, perhaps, comparisons gleaned from research carried out in other firms. Similarly, boundary-spanners from the commissioning firm must be able to reassure the smaller partner that their intentions are hands-off and worthy of trust; at the same time, they must be able to clearly articulate the deliverables to which their firm will contribute—design briefs, performance specifications, and the like.

In addition to being "bilingual," boundary-spanners must remain mindful of the partners' respective cultures and manage potentially conflicting cultural forces—especially relevant nowadays because of the global nature of NPD networks. International hybrids may enable a commissioning firm to respond to local market needs. However, two groups separated by a wide cultural divide may find it hard to verify each other's credibility, a potentially important factor in the development and retention of trust and affection. Boundary-spanners may need to learn to behave in different ways in the two partner environments—to use a particular body language or wear particular clothes. Acceptance and trust is more likely to develop between people who are socially similar in terms of educational levels, appearance, and experience. Given the likely cultural distance between our prototypical creative firm and the larger commissioning firm, these may be important considerations in the choice of boundary-spanners.

The bridging role is important not only between organizations but also between the boundary-spanner and his or her own organization's power-holders. Boundary-spanners are often called upon to negotiate solutions when problems arise that are (inevitably) not covered by the original agreement. They are also needed to get past organizational road blocks in the partner organizations. Being trusted, influential, and credible are important factors here. Success is likely to be based on the same attributes needed by inter-organizational boundary-spanners, but in this case it also includes organization-specific factors, such as having a successful track record, relationships with powerful managers, unfulfilled reciprocal obligations, and access to important information.

A perfect example of successful boundary-spanners can be found in an article in *Design Management Journal* written by Tom Mulhern and Dave Lathrop, of Conifer Research and Steelcase, Inc., respectively. Their article, "Building and Tending Bridges: Rethinking How Consultants Support Change," which appeared in the Summer 2003 edition of the *Journal*, detailed the way in which design consultant Conifer Research used its methodological expertise in furniture and workspace design to improve Steelcase's product innovation and organizational performance. Although Mulhern and Lathrop had not worked together before, they had "worked around each other" and knew a lot of the same people. They were both part of an established network of relationships and reputation, and this is likely to have facilitated the development of trust between the two organizational boundary-spanners.

But Mulhern and Lathrop also epitomize the internal boundary-spanner role. Steelcase had previously gone out of its way to seek external perspectives from a "host of brilliant, innovative, but generally outside resources, with the outcome generally packaged as a 'deliverable.'" But in order to achieve the impact they sought, Mulhern and Lathrop recognized that their job would be to inspire insiders to take up the cause. They described this process as developing "experience bridges." To do this, they identified three key "insider" groups at Steelcase whose engagement would be critical, and they deliberately focused on involving them in the developing project. The bridges they established linked people, information, and process and thereby "dramatically accelerated" progress through the development of shared understanding.

In any hybrid, there is likely to be a range of individuals with roles that span boundaries. Some will be assigned to the relationship for as long as it lasts; others will be temporary. However, there is a dilemma here again in that frequency of contact between key players is important. It aids the formation of the types of attachments that minimize opportunistic behavior and facilitate sharing tacit knowledge.

Proprietary knowledge is often a source of considerable competitive advantage. As we have argued throughout this paper, bringing together different types of knowledge is the best way in which to achieve innovation. However, knowledge has the potential to be misused or leaked to a third party unless the boundary-spanners are trustworthy. When there are high levels of turnover in those who would be boundary-spanners, or when those who entered the relationship in the first place are not the same people who manage it subsequently, trust needs to be negotiated again and again. Tenure is very relevant. A high turnover of boundary-spanners means the discontinuity of specific relationships and a loss of what is, in effect, relationship-specific knowledge capital. Yet transferring people into the hybrid on a short-term basis is a potentially useful method for ensuring that ideas do not become stale or that the benefits of an outsider perspective, which the smaller unit brings, do not get lost through over-socialization and identification.

CONCLUSION

In this paper, we have discussed several factors that appear material to the success of hybrid organizational structures formed to develop new products. In these structures, larger firms generally seek services from smaller independent units, which develop close relationships with their partners—sometimes only for the duration of a specific project, but often over a longer period spanning several projects. We have highlighted some issues that are currently under-researched and that we believe deserve more attention—for example, the need to protect specialist resources from contamination and the role of boundary-spanners in dealing with this problem. We have also identified a number of circumstances in which it is necessary to bring together incompatible resources. By bringing these issues to the surface, we hope to improve understanding of some of the tensions hybrid managers are likely to encounter when smaller, more creative firms associate with larger, more bureaucratic organizations.

Note: An earlier version of this paper was presented at the 2002 British Academy of Management conference and appears in their proceedings.

Suggested Reading

Alvarez, Sharon A, and Barney, Jay B. "How entrepreneurial firms can benefit from alliances with large partners." *In The Academy of Management Executive*, vol. 15, no. 1 (Feb. 2001), 139–148.

Bruce, Margaret, and Morris, Barney. "In-house, outsourced, or a mixed approach to design." In Margaret Bruce and Birgit H. Jevnaker. *Management of Design Alliances: Sustaining Competitive Advantage* (Chichester: Wiley, 1998).

Heller, Trudy. "Loosely coupled systems for corporate entrepreneurship: Imagining and managing the innovation project/host organisation interface." In *Entrepreneurship Theory and Practice*, vol. 24, no. 2 (1999), 25–31.

Millar, Jane, Demaid, Adrian, and Quintas, Paul. "Trans-organisational innovation: A framework for research." *In Technology Analysis & Strategic Management*, vol. 9, no. 4 (December 1997), 399–418.

Chapter 19

Innovation in Organizations in Crisis

by Todd Cherkasky, Director of Business Consulting, Sapient
and Adrian Slobin, Director of Business Consulting, Sapient

There is no black-box mystery behind innovation in the corporate world, say Todd Cherkasky and Adrian Slobin. They define it as a disciplined process for generating, realizing, and evolving ideas that improve business and the customer experience. More importantly, they outline the capabilities and catalysts that facilitate the innovation process and, in a case study, demonstrate how these helped revive a company on the verge of collapse.

INNOVATION. RARELY DOES a term emerge from so wide a conceptual field. From creativity, invention, and experimentation to method, discipline, and execution, innovation resists definitive application. Theories abound. Those who believe that innovation emerges from creative geniuses who have a knack for tapping into cultural trends probably do not collaborate with advocates of TRIZ and other structured methodologies. Product design firms sell innovation workshops to generate innovative ideas. Conferences, conventions, blogs, newsletters, and magazines prescribe, assume, and debate various theories of innovation. They ask questions such as: What makes an idea innovative rather than simply a good idea? Is design the source of innovation? Does realizing "innovation intent" require "intersectional" thinking? Does discipline in innovation drive out creativity?[1]

While many of these questions tempt us to engage in long-running debates, we do not intend to argue for a theory of innovation. Instead, we aim to elaborate on a management precept common since Peter Drucker's 1985 article that characterized innovation as a discipline.[2] Following his suggestion that "innovation is work, rather than genius," we aim to describe how that work can be carried out.

First, we suggest that innovation as a discipline can be realized by engaging in repeatable, well-known practices that, while possibly unfamiliar to some organizations, are neither radical nor new. Second, we illustrate the utility of focusing on practices with an example of how innovation takes hold in organizations in crisis. Finally, we outline a framework of innovation that can be useful in catalyzing innovation for such organizations.

INNOVATION IN THE PRACTICAL CONTEXTS OF DESIGN AND STRATEGY

While we begin with a practical principle instead of a theoretical standpoint, some conceptual housekeeping is probably helpful, particularly to clarify which contexts and set of practices will be addressed. Instead of adjudicating which process is right or which companies "get" innovation, the following will instead identify practices that catalyze innovation. For the purposes of putting innovation "on the ground" in actual contexts where design and strategy play out, innovation will be defined here as simply finding new ways of creating value and bringing them to life.

Design has similarly enjoyed a broad range of definitions and usages, from the carefully explicated (for example, design as a discipline[3]) to the commonsensical (for example, design as goal-directed practice), from demarcating a set of domains ("the design community") to representing an omnipresent feature of our world ("design is everywhere"). For the purposes of this article, design will be viewed as commonsensical—a set of practices, or a portfolio of capabilities, that is intended to support the goal-directed activity of organizational actors invigorating business through innovation.

ORGANIZATIONS IN CRISIS

When considering the kinds of organizations in which innovation thrives, what may first come to mind is an image of a start-up with twenty-somethings whiteboarding excitedly in a loft office—fresh thoughts flying back and forth, possibilities endless. Underlying this image is a view of innovation as the outcome of an unconstrained flow of ideas. Lock the right creative people in a room, come back in a while—and innovation will have happened.

This image is deeply misleading. Innovation can come as readily—and more consistently—from a set of simple, structured practices. To illustrate this claim, consider an organization in many ways the antithesis of our free-thinking start-up above—namely, a real Fortune 50 company (for confidentiality, we will refer to it as Widgets, Inc.) that is:

1. Reluctant to embrace change

2. Financially unstable

3. Focused on cost-reduction (job cuts, reduction in IT spend, and so forth)

Let's examine each of these factors.

Having existed for more than fifty years, Widgets, Inc. has a strong corporate culture of "this is how we have always done things." As a result, innovative ideas or approaches face the twin pressures of inertia and fear of change. Innovations, if they occur, tend to involve incremental changes to existing solutions rather than wholesale shifts in approach. Moreover, for internal and market-related reasons, Widgets, Inc. faces the real possibility of bankruptcy—an event that would substantially disrupt the US economy and shake global markets. Corporate leadership recognizes the need to take a new direction, but the pressures and risks associated with innovation are severely amplified by the overall state of the business; in the starkest terms, people are unwilling to try new things for fear of sticking out and possibly losing their jobs as result. Moreover, the budgetary environment at Widgets, Inc. is focused not on investment in new ideas, but on squeezing costs out of its current people, processes, and systems.

The question, then, is this: How do you innovate within an organization in crisis? More specifically, how do you support innovation despite all the stultifying constraints of such an organization? If innovation can occur—and occur consistently—in such an organization, then it must not be the result simply of "creative minds in a creative environment."

THE PRACTICE OF INNOVATION

To get at the constituent components of a repeatable practice of innovation within our chosen context—that of organizations in crisis—we will share stories from our own work with such organizations. These stories will focus on two basic components that jointly make up a practice of innovation: capabilities and catalysts.

Think of capabilities simply as packaged expertise—services or offerings that may be sold to the marketplace or provided to an internal group. In the case of Widgets, Inc., the capabilities on offer fit broadly with the IT services industry. They include program management, user experience research and design, business application planning, and so on. Catalysts, on the other hand, are assets that increase the likelihood that an innovation will happen. These catalysts can be specific tools that are used to execute work (for example, a certain way of tracking and sharing new ideas), a culture that encourages certain types of thinking (for example, one that encourages risk-taking), or any resource that in itself will not lead to innovation, but in its absence will make innovation more difficult.

INNOVATION IN PRACTICE: ONE STORY

To illustrate the utility of thinking about the discipline of innovation in terms of capabilities and catalysts, we'll use an example of an organization precisely positioned not to be creative—like Widgets, Inc. The story starts with the following general business problem: How could Widgets, Inc. become easier to work with in the eyes of its B2B customers? This general problem led to a specific challenge: How could it reduce the numerous and divergent systems through which its customers were forced to transact with the company? Given Widgets's reluctance to embrace change, the urgency of its financial situation, and its bias against new ways of conducting business, the likelihood of this seemed remote. So, how could innovation occur?

Before we discuss the catalysts that created a viable space for innovation, let's briefly describe the specific capabilities in question, as well as the innovative solution itself. The capabilities in this example were what could broadly be termed user experience capabilities, traditionally associated with specialist design firms and rarely employed within companies like Widgets, Inc. The project used in-context ethnography to understand how Widgets, Inc.'s B2B customers carried out their daily work. It also employed visual methods to solicit user input rather than rely on dry, text-based documentation alone—for instance, we used paper prototyping (hand-drawn, low-fidelity design sketches) and high-fidelity prototyping (fully designed HTML pages) to illustrate user requirements. End users and project stakeholders alike iterated collaboratively on requirements by using these visual illustrations.

The result was a "workspace" that customers would use to conduct their daily activities: an integrated Web solution that created a seamless, process-based interface to the previously diverse set of systems and tools. Because it was designed from the start with users in mind, it required little to no training. Support calls went down. Customer enthusiasm increased dramatically. Buzz spread among competitors that Widgets had hit on something that could change the industry. The project also changed how Widgets, Inc. conducted systems development, replicating the value of the user experience process throughout the organization. The same project managers who had previously checked boxes to ensure that system architecture diagrams and test cases were complete were now monitoring whether in-context user research and analysis was properly conducted. An innovation had occurred within an organization in crisis.

REPEATABLE INNOVATION: THE CATALYSTS

As unsurprising as the above story may sound to someone trained in user-centered design—and this is part of our point—innovation occurred in our example in part because a specific capability was brought to light within the organization that unlocked new business value and changed the status quo in the industry and the organization alike. One key point is simply that innovation lay in this capability—as a specific practice, not simply as a great idea. Furthermore, it wasn't merely the capability that led to the innovation. Just as important were the general, repeatable catalysts that enabled the innovation to happen.

Drawing on innovation cases from more than fifteen years of consulting work, we have catalogued a number of catalysts—the enablers that increase the likelihood that an innovation will happen—into four categories: focus, culture, tools, and expertise. In our example above, these catalysts allowed the workspace innovation to take hold.

Let's review examples of each of these catalysts.

Focus

Keeping a complex organization aligned to critical, priority objectives requires focus. Creating an organization with focus is an ongoing activity, not a one-time effort. Indeed, focus comes as much from managing objectives as from the compelling nature of the objectives themselves. Regular engagement with the overall purpose of an initiative keeps it alive in the minds of stakeholders—making for real change and not another empty organizational promise. Similarly, having a change agent—someone who is willing to stake his or her career on achieving an initiative's objectives—as part of the project leadership helps a great deal in driving that focus. The key point is that innovation will be more likely to happen when the collective energy of an organization is focused on a consistent target. As obvious as this last point may sound, it stands somewhat in contrast to the divergent thinking of a "creative brainstorm" that, as discussed earlier, often underlies the image of innovation.

With the workspace project, focus was created, in part by assigning a relentless and energetic project sponsor to act as champion. A significant percentage of his time was dedicated to executing a detailed communication plan that anticipated potential sources of stakeholder resistance. To minimize the daily distractions Widgets, Inc. faced as an organization in crisis—from falling sales to labor troubles to outdated product lines—the project team conducted regular project walkthroughs and shared success stories with a broad range of stakeholders. These walkthroughs not only reminded the organization why the initiative was important, they also invited regular contributions from stakeholders—the idea being that it is easier to focus on something for which you feel a sense of ownership.

Finally, instilling focus opened the organization to trying the unfamiliar ("If we are really committed to meeting these objectives, we should be open to new ways of getting there"). This focus led to the willingness to give user-centered design a try.

Tools

A variety of simple, supporting tools help to catalyze innovation. Tools extend our ability to perform a task. They are communication planning templates, collaboration software, project "dashboards" that track and make visible status, team rooms with wall-to-floor whiteboards, and so on. One such tool that catalyzed innovation for Widgets, Inc. was a project showroom—a space where project objectives, insights, and ideas in progress are visually displayed. Such a showroom not only keeps stakeholders interested but also allows them the opportunity to comment and add to the work. In today's digital era, this nonvirtual form of a "wiki" has particular potency. Such a project showroom had never existed at Widgets, Inc.—and after it was installed, the effect was remarkable. One would find executives wandering through the room during lunch, pens in hand, commenting on the work they saw. The project champion regularly led tours through the space, showcasing his own association with the project, but also reinforcing that change could be exciting, not frightening, for an organization like Widgets, Inc.

Another, related tool is a conducive physical environment, one in which people are free to interact (not boxed into cubicles). An open workspace promotes organic collaboration and—like the project showroom—creates the possibility of building upon ideas rather than just dreaming up new ones. Widgets, Inc. is a "cube farm," like many such corporations, but the simple action of commandeering a large conference room for the duration of the project created a collaborative environment that broke down barriers based on roles, types of expertise, work styles, and divergent objectives.

Culture

Although this catalyst is the most complex of the four, one of the characteristics of an innovative culture is clear: It encourages risk within safety. Individuals must feel supported by the organization when they stray constructively from the normal way of doing things. In the case of Widgets, Inc., this catalyst was particularly important, given the precarious nature of employment at an organization in crisis. To combat the tendency to generate "safe" ideas, the project regularly recognized team members who were willing to try out new ideas or new methods of addressing old problems. The point is not that all such ideas are innovative (in our example, most were not), but rather that encouraging people to explore them without risk allowed for that one breakthrough idea not only to emerge, but also to be realized.

Another important aspect of an innovative culture is the encouragement of constructive feedback. As simple as this sounds in theory, the practice can be challenging to implement, especially in an organization in crisis. Mistakes must be openly recognized and addressed in formal and informal processes. A strong culture of feedback is also a precondition for the cultural dimension noted above—supporting risk within safety. Unless people understand that their efforts will be fairly and openly judged, they will be unlikely to venture too far beyond ingrained ways of doing business.

Expertise

Cross-pollination of expertise is, in our experience, a critical enabler for innovation. The two components here—expertise and the exposure of such expertise across traditional functions or disciplines—are equally important. In our example, the project was executed by a fully integrated team of designers, technologists, project managers, and subject-matter experts. In addition to the obvious benefit of having an informed team, fostering such cross-pollination can lead to refreshing insights. For example, having a visual designer provide feedback on a system architecture diagram may not, at first glance, seem to add much value—but in one case, a designer suggested rendering the architecture in such a way that it identified a major opportunity for system integration.

The examples from these four categories of catalysts illustrate that there are concrete enablers to innovation that any organization can initiate, even those least willing to change. These catalysts are not in any way sufficient for innovation to occur—it would be absurd to suggest, for example, that creating a project showroom will guarantee an innovative project. However, in our experience, having such catalysts in place increases the likelihood of innovation. Moreover, they are neither mysterious nor, in many cases, difficult to initiate—and they can bring out innovation in places where one least expects to find it.

TOWARD AN INNOVATION FRAMEWORK

We have described an organization in crisis that managed to overcome cultural, process, and technical constraints to transform its business. Innovation succeeded not because stalwart heroes mastered creativity exercises or because charismatic leaders facilitated ideation work sessions. Rather, the organization benefited from a discipline of innovation.

Discipline, in this sense, simply means establishing clear goals and systematically aligning organizational resources to meet those goals. It means, for example, getting managers in large, stodgy manufacturing organizations, who often cite the "not-invented-here" script, to introduce new capabilities such as ethnographic research into their system development process. The discipline we advocate involves not only knowing when to apply innovation capabilities such as ethnography but also investing in innovation catalysts that make those techniques part of the new way of doing business.[4] In other words, don't merely import capabilities known to be useful elsewhere. Choose change agents who are full of energy and willing to take risks. Repeatedly tell the success stories and recite the vision. Make people feel comfortable with the new capabilities until they are embedded in standard processes. In other words Institutionalize innovation.[5]

Building an innovation discipline within an organization is more likely to occur if people clearly define the type of innovation they intend and have readily available a catalog of practices known to enable this type of innovation.

Here, we provide a brief introduction to what such an innovation framework looks like (Figure 1). First, we need to recognize that there are many types of innovation. Innovation doesn't just create new products or services—it also unlocks hidden value in

Type of Transformation

	Offering (Product, Service)	Business Process / Operations (Internal How)	Technology (Artifacts, Tools Infrastructure)	Marketing	Business Model (External How)	Organization and Culture
Team						
Firm						
Market						
Industry						

(Scale of Transformation)

Figure 1. Innovation framework identifying types and scale of innovation.

existing ones, thereby reinvigorating a business without necessarily reinventing it. Secondly, innovation occurs at different levels of scale, from teams to an entire firm to a whole market (for instance, insurance) to an entire industry (for instance, financial services). This framework focuses otherwise unstructured and unbounded conversations and enables people to state the business problem clearly, identify unambiguous metrics for success, and draw upon practices applied previously to the same class of innovation (in terms of type and scale). In other words, as a knowledge management tool, each cell of the framework can be used to point to a library of capabilities, best practices, and metrics applied to a particular type/scale of innovation.

A REFINED DEFINITION OF INNOVATION

A more complete definition of innovation that aptly describes how some organizations in crisis have managed to innovate can now be suggested: Innovation is a disciplined process by which an idea is generated, realized, and evolved, resulting in significant business value and an improved customer experience. As depicted in our innovation framework, innovation happens at different levels of scale. It follows, then, that the measure of "significant business value" is commensurate to the scale of innovation.[6]

We have already discussed discipline as the foundation of successful innovation, especially within organizations in crisis. The final element of the definition is the innovation life cycle (Figure 2), comprising three distinct phases of innovation. Even though innovation has been discussed as a monolithic enterprise, it is actually a three-stage process. The first phase—generation—defines an idea worth realizing through ideation, research, analysis, synthesis, and evaluation. In the Widgets, Inc. example, the work-

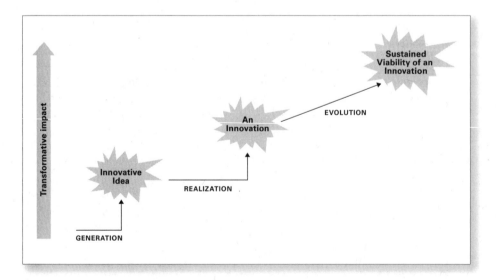

Figure 2. Innovation life cycle.

space idea was generated in the first phase. The second phase—realization—brings an innovative idea to life and realizes the intended value through planning, design, testing, iteration, measurement, and implementation. For Widgets, the realization phase resulted in a process-based workspace that made it easier for customers to do business with the company. In the third phase—evolution—the innovation is continuously improved until it can no longer deliver the intended value though reframing, optimizing, assessing, and extending. Widgets, Inc. evolved the workspace innovation by replicating it in other areas of the business.

This life cycle applies not only to our example at Widgets, Inc. but to all types of innovation. For example, consider the iPod as an exemplar of product innovation. In the generation phase, Apple defined an integrated system that supports an entirely new customer experience around sound. In the realization phase, they used their industrial design and user experience expertise to create an aesthetically pleasing artifact seamlessly supported by an intuitive music library. And they didn't stop there. They proceeded through the third phase of innovation to evolve their initial solution, adapting it to retain value against new competitors.

Like the innovation framework, the innovation life cycle clearly demarcates the type of problem addressed and enables application of the most relevant practices. For now, we have suggested the outlines of an innovation framework and drawn attention to the distinct phases of an innovation life cycle. At this point, we can only hint at the utility of employing this framework and situating practices with respect to an innovation life cycle. The key point we wish to leave you with is that the capabilities and catalysts that comprise the disciplined practice of innovation are like a toolkit—similar to a designer's portfolio. You need to select the proper tools for the situation. Selecting such tools can create substantial business value in successful organizations, as well as those in crisis.

Endnotes

1. Larry Keely of Doblin, Inc. presents widely on innovation intent. On intersectional thinking, see Franz Johannson, *The Medici Effect: Breakthrough Insights at the Intersection of Ideas, Concepts, and Cultures* (Boston: Harvard Business School Press, 2004).

2. Peter Drucker, "The discipline of innovation," *Harvard Business Review*. 1985.

3. Nigel Cross, "Design as a Discipline," The Inter-disciplinary Design Quandary Conference, February 13, 2002, De Montfort University. Also see R. Buchanan and V. Margolin, eds., *Discovering Design: Explorations in Design Studies* (Chicago: University of Chicago Press, 1995).

4. This type of discipline can complement other management disciplines, such as Peter Drucker's recommendation to methodically analyze seven areas of opportunity as a means of innovation (*op. cit.*).

5. As we've implied, the innovative capability need not be completely new. It simply needs to be new and valuable in the context in which it is applied. For example, a research methodology typically associated with creative firms can be innovative when it is newly applied to a traditional

About DMI

DMI, the Design Management Institute, is about having strategic conversations. We connect design to business, to culture, to customers—to the changing world. We bring together business people, designers, educators, researchers, and leaders from every design discipline, every industry, and every corner of the planet. The results are transformational. Over the decades, DMI has been the place where the world's most experienced, creative, and ambitious design leaders gather to share, distill, and amplify their knowledge.

DMI is a nonprofit (501c3) educational organization, with more than 1,500 members in forty-four countries. The Institute was founded at the Massachusetts College of Art and Design in Boston in 1975, and although it spent several formative years in London, it is presently based in downtown Boston. DMI has long-standing relationships with many of the world's leading country design councils, design schools, and business schools.

Our vision is to improve organizations worldwide through the effective integration and management of design and design principles for economic, social, and environmental benefit. Our mission is to be the international authority, resource, and advocate on design management, and our objectives are to:

▲ Assist design managers to become leaders in their profession.

▲ Sponsor, conduct, and promote research.

▲ Collect, organize, and make accessible a body of knowledge.

▲ Educate and foster interaction among design managers, organizational managers, public policy makers, and academics.

▲ Be a public advocate for the economic and cultural importance of design.

The heart of DMI is to connect design leaders to the inspiration, knowledge, and community they need to achieve their goals. Over the years, DMI has created the largest body of knowledge about design management in the world. The Institute has produced thirty-two case studies with Harvard Business School, published seventy-five issues of the *Design Management Review*, adding up to over 900 articles, produced over 100 conferences and 200 workshops and seminars. This book is an anthology of some of our best articles about corporate creativity. The DMI Web site is *www.dmi.org*.

Editors' Biographies

Thomas Lockwood, PhD, is the president and a board member of DMI. He is responsible for all aspects of the Institute, including research, education and editorial direction, as well as the production of DMI's events throughout the world. He has worked in the public and private sectors, and one of his most enjoyable projects was designing the racing skiwear worn by the US Nordic Ski Team in the Olympics. He holds a PhD and MBA in design management from the University of Westminster in London, and a BA in marketing and visual design from Eastern Michigan University. He is a visiting professor at the graduate school of the Pratt Institute in New York City, where he teaches in the areas of design strategy, methods, and operations. Lockwood is a design advisor to corporations and countries, and serves on numerous boards and advisory councils around the world.

Thomas Walton, PhD, is founding editor of the Design Management Institute's *Design Management Review* and serves on the staff of the US General Services Administration Office of Executive Communication. Previous to his current position, for twenty-five years he was a faculty member at The Catholic University of America's School of Architecture and Planning in Washington, DC, after which he joined GSA's Office of the Chief Architect. There he authored a series of monographs on contemporary federal buildings and was part of the team implementing the government's Design Excellence Program. Design as a strategic organizational resource has been an abiding theme in his work, one he examined in his book *Architecture and the Corporation* and one he addresses quarterly in the pages of the *Design Management Review.*

Authors' Biographies

Anne Archer has more than twenty years of experience in corporate and consumer packaged goods marketing. She has led numerous branding assignments in the capacity of Design Management Consultant for Fortune 500 companies such as Quaker Oats, Alberto-Culver, Kraft, and Unilever. Anne has developed and launched numerous new product initiatives and line extensions for the US and European markets. Anne holds a Bachelor's degree in design management from the University of Illinois, Springfield.

Mark Barngrover is a 1988 graduate of the University of Cincinnati with a degree in industrial design. In 1989, Mark joined Procter & Gamble as a Design Manager and worked in the food, fabric care, and personal care divisions on product and package design. In 1997, Mark moved to Japan to build a design group to support Asia. In 2002, Mark moved to Geneva to lead and develop design capabilities there before moving back to Cincinnati to lead design in global operations.

John Boult has considerable experience and reputation within the UK design industry, heading Productfirst, an award winning international design consultancy, and now championing design as a driver for excellence in innovation culture. John has also co-developed and trialed the Innovate Programme for the UK Design Council and has co-created assessment tools for Design Management Europe. He is an associate professor of design strategy at Brunel University.

Todd Cherkasky, PhD, leads the experience research and analytics group at Sapient. For fourteen years, he has managed and delivered strategy and user-centered research and design projects for Global 500 clients. Cherkasky was the conference chair for the Sixth Biennial Participator Design Conference. He received a PhD from Rensselaer Polytechnic Institute in the study of technology design and workplace change, a BS in computer engineering, and a BA in English literature from the University of Michigan.

Jessica Feldman is an Account Director for ePrize London, an interactive promotions company, and creates campaigns for top brands including Ford, Nectar, Nielsen, and P&G. Previously, she headed recruitment for Ford's North American design organization. Jessica received an MA with distinction in design and branding strategy from Brunel University (UK), where she researched how design consultancies can catalyze cultural change promoting innovation in client organizations. She also has a BA in organizational studies from the University of Michigan.

Jonathan Gander is a senior lecturer in strategic management at Kingston University Business School, London. He has experience as a consultant in fashion retail and has provided executive business training to multinational companies and government associations. His main area of research is in the organization of the cultural economy, particularly the popular music industry. He has published a number of papers on this topic in the *Journal of Organizational Behaviour* and the *Journal of Cultural Economics*.

Dr. Leonard J. Glick has extensive business, consulting, and teaching experience in employee and organizational effectiveness. His primary interests are in designing and running organizations that foster learning, commitment, and performance. He has pioneered creative, work-based methods to help managers develop employees from their work as they work. Since 1994, Dr. Glick has been a full-time faculty member in the College of Business Administration at Northeastern University, where he teaches organizational behavior, designing effective organizations, great companies, and strategic human resource management. He has taught managing creative staff for DMI since 2004.

Naomi Gornick is a design management consultant specializing in curriculum development for UK Design Colleges and training programs for in-house and consultant designers including teams in Nokia, Procter & Gamble, and Alloy product designers. She developed postgraduate programs at the Royal College of Art and Brunel University. Graduates are in senior management positions in international organizations. Naomi is Honorary Professor of the University of Dundee. Her research is published in *Design Management Review*, *Designjournalen* (Sweden), and *Innovation*. She is a Fellow of the Royal Society of Arts and the Chartered Society of Designers, and an international member of Industrial Designers Society of America (IDSA).

Adrian Haberberg is a senior lecturer in strategic management at the University of Westminster, London. His research interests center on the processes of strategy development, and he is co-author (with Alison Rieple) of *The Strategic Management of Organisations* (Prentice-Hall), the second edition of which is currently being written.

Nicholas Ind is a partner in the brand consulting firm, Equilibrium Consulting. He is the author of eight books including *The Corporate Image, Terence Conran—The Authorised Biography, The Corporate Brand, Living the Brand*, and *Inspiration*, which he co-authored with Cameron Watt. Nicholas is a former Director of the Design Business Association, a member of the advisory board of the *Corporate Reputation Review* and the editorial board of the *Journal of Brand Management*, and an Industrial Fellow at Kingston University.

Dimitris Lamproulis is in the final stage of completing his PhD in the management department of Aberdeen University. His research focuses on ways a corporate culture mobilizes the creation of knowledge within working environments. The findings of his research are presented in international conferences. He has been a teaching assistant at the University of Aberdeen and has consulted to a number of leading creative organizations. His research interests are in the areas of organizational culture, the creation of knowledge, and innovation.

Thomas Lockwood, PhD, is the President of DMI, the Design Management Institute. He is considered an international expert in the areas of innovation and design leadership, and the integration of design and business. Prior to working in the public sector he managed design and brand at Sun Microsystems and StorageTek and ran his own design firm for a number of years. He is a visiting professor at Pratt Institute in New York City and is researching the value of design for the triple bottom line. He holds a PhD and MBA in design management and a BA in marketing and visual design.

Stefano Marzano is CEO and Chief Creative Director of Philips Design, the international in-house design group at Philips responsible for all design work within the company. Stefano, one of *BusinessWeek*'s "Best Leaders of 2005" for innovation, is widely recognized for keeping Philips Design at the forefront of the design profession. He is a regular speaker at international design, business, and technology conferences, and has written or edited a number of books describing the work of Philips Design and the humanistic philosophy on which it is based.

Jeffrey Mauzy provides innovation consulting primarily in the areas of new technologies, new products, and strategy planning for Synectics, Inc., a consultancy specializing in business creativity and innovation. He has led the development of two business areas: Synectics training in individual creative thinking and an approach for speeding the research and development process. Currently, he is writing a book for the Harvard Business School Press, *Systemic Creativity in Corporations: An Approach to Sustainable Enterprise-wide Creativity and Innovation.* He is also chairman of Inventive Logic, Inc., a software company that develops and markets idea generation and creative problem-solving software.

Dick Powell, who formed Seymour Powell in 1984 with partner Richard Seymour, is one of Europe's best-known product designers. Proving through words ands deeds that design is about "making things better for people," the award-winning company has created many of the household objects that we now take completely for granted, such as the cordless kettle and the world's first genuinely pocket-size mobile phone. Dick and Richard's two television series, *Designs on Your . . .* and *Better by Design,* helped to "normalise" rather then "lionise" design and are now routinely used as course material in design and technology education in the UK and around the world.

Robert Rasmussen is a research and development specialist for the LEGO Company's LEGO PLAY for Business group and is principal for Robert Rasmussen and Associates, an independent LEGO SERIOUS PLAY consultancy. He is one of the main architects of LEGO SERIOUS PLAY, a concept and methodology that helps organizations solve complex business issues by maximizing the potential in people in order to achieve better results for their business. Robert Rasmussen, a native of Denmark, has a degree in psychology as well as a Master's degree in education. He has spent his career applying experiences and theories about play, learning, creativity, and teaching to product development for students and adults.

Alison Rieple, PhD, is Professor of Strategic Management at the University of Westminster in London, U.K. She has an MBA and a PhD from Cranfield School of Management. Her research is now focused on the management of design, innovation, and change, especially in the creative and cultural industries. She consults in the areas of design and innovation management, change management, and business planning for both public and private sector organizations in the UK and internationally. Her recent publications have included articles in journals such as the *Journal of Organizational Behavior, Design Management Review*, and the *Journal of Cultural Economics*.

Ron Sanchez, PhD, is Professor of Management in the Department of Innovation and Organizational Economics at Copenhagen Business School and a visiting professor in the Division of Engineering and Technology Management at the National University of Singapore. Dr. Sanchez has held faculty positions at Lund University, International Institute for Management Development (IMD), University of Western Australia, and University of Illinois. Dr. Sanchez also consults with leading global firms on strategy, design, and product development. He holds a PhD in Technology Strategy from MIT and has written numerous books and journal articles on strategic management, technology management, and knowledge management, including his forthcoming book *Modularity: Strategy, Organization, and Knowledge Management* (Oxford University Press).

Michael Schrage, a research fellow at the MIT Sloan School's Center for Digital Business and a Visiting Fellow at London's Imperial College, continues to explore the behavioral economics of innovation through the design media of models, prototypes, and simulations. He has published extensively on innovation and design themes in the *Harvard Business Review*, the *Sloan Management Review*, the *Financial Times, strategy+business, Technology Review*, and other publications. He both teaches executive education classes and runs workshops on innovation risk management issues at business schools and companies around the world. His clients have included Microsoft, Google, Siemens, PriceWaterhouseCoopers, Mars, SAS, Wells Fargo, NASDAQ, Fidelity, British Telecom, BP and other firms.

Adrian Slobin is a Director of Business Consulting at Sapient, and specializes in experience research and strategy. He has ten years of consulting experience working with Fortune 500 clients and has recently focused on process and IT solutions in higher education. Adrian has a BA with high honors in philosophy and psychology from Swarthmore College. He also has a graduate degree in ancient Greek and German philosophy from Northwestern University, where he was previously an adjunct professor.

Barbara Stefik, PhD, has a doctorate in transpersonal psychology. She is in private practice and helps people to overcome creative blocks.

Mark Stefik is an inventor at the Palo Alto Research Center, where he directs the Information Sciences and Technologies Laboratory. Mark received his PhD from Stanford University in 1980.

Raymond Turner is an independent design leadership and management consultant based in the UK and Ireland. He specializes in helping organizations improve performance by maximizing value from their design investments; delivering enhanced customer experience through design, communications and behavioral change; and developing design awareness in business leaders and managers.

Doris Walczyk has over eighteen years of domestic and international marketing experience working with Fortune 500 companies at the brand/product and corporate level. Doris received her Master's degree in integrated marketing communications from Northwestern University. After working in advertising, Doris went on to eastern Europe where she opened and managed the Young & Rubicam and BBDO advertising offices. Doris has taught for over five years at Dominican University and has worked as Director of Brand Strategy for Optima Group (a brand identity and design firm). Most recently, she works for Autodesk, Inc., as an Industry Marketing Manager.

Dr. Cameron Watt lectures widely on the subject of creativity, innovation, and branding. He also acts as a creativity and innovation diffusion consultant for organizations including IBM and Sainsbury's and advises the National Health Service on diffusing lean thinking and the use of human rights constructs to improve service provision. In addition, he develops and runs courses for SME businesses across the creative industries and has published widely including co-authoring *Inspiration: Capturing the Creative Potential of Your Organization*.

Yvonne Weisbarth is design manager for water treatment and personal care products at Bosch and Siemens Household Appliances GmbH, Munich, Germany. She wins numerous Red Dot, iF, and PlusX Design Awards for her products each year. In 1996, she received her Bachelor's degree in industrial design from Art Center College of Design, Pasadena, California.

Index

231

Books from Allworth Press

Allworth Press is an imprint of Allworth Communications, Inc. Selected titles are listed below.

Building Design Strategy
edited by Thomas Lockwood and Thomas Walton (6 × 9, 256 pages, paperback, $24.95)

AIGA Professional Practices in Graphic Design, Second Edition
edited by Tad Crawford (6 × 9, 320 pages, paperback, $29.95)

Green Graphic Design
by Brian Dougherty with Celery Design Collaborative (6 × 9, 212 pages, paperback, 100 b&w illustrations, $19.95)

How to Think Like a Great Graphic Designer
by Debbie Millman (6 × 9, 256 pages, paperback, $24.95)

Design Disasters: Great Designers, Fabulous Failures, and Lessons Learned
edited by Steven Heller (6 × 9, 240 pages, paperback, $24.95)

Creating the Perfect Design Brief: How to Manage Design for Strategic Advantage
by Peter L. Phillips (6 × 9, 224 pages, paperback, $19.95)

Designing Logos: The Process of Creating Logos That Endure
by Jack Gernsheimer (8½ × 10, 208 pages, paperback, $35.00)

The Graphic Designer's Guide to Better Business Writing
by Barbara Janoff and Ruth Cash-Smith (6 × 9, 256 pages, paperback, $19.95)

The Graphic Design Business Book
by Tad Crawford (6 × 9, 256 pages, paperback, $24.95)

Business and Legal Forms for Graphic Designers, Third Edition
by Tad Crawford and Eva Doman Bruck (8½ × 11, 208 pages, paperback, includes CD-ROM, $29.95)

The Graphic Designer's Guide to Pricing, Estimating, and Budgeting, Revised Edition
by Theo Stephan Williams (6¾ × 9⅞, 208 pages, paperback, $19.95)

The Graphic Designer's Guide to Clients: How to Make Clients Happy and Do Great Work
by Ellen Shapiro (6 × 9, 256 pages, paperback, $19.95)

Editing by Design: For Designers, Art Directors, and Editors
by Jan V. White (8½ × 11, 256 pages, paperback, $29.95)

How to Grow as a Graphic Designer
by Catharine Fishel (6 × 9, 256 pages, paperback, $19.95)

Design Management: Using Design to Build Brand Value and Corporate Innovation
by Brigitte Borja de Mozota (6 × 9, 256 pages, paperback, $24.95)